KING OF CLUBS

Eddie

and

Shirley

KING OF CLUBS
The Eddie Fewtrell Story

Eddie Fewtrell
and Shirley Thompson

BREWIN BOOKS

First published by
Brewin Books Ltd, 56 Alcester Road,
Studley, Warwickshire B80 7LG in 2007
www.brewinbooks.com

ISBN: 978-1-85858-406-5

A Cataloguing in Publication Record
for this title is available from the British Library.

Typeset in New Baskerville
Printed in Great Britain by
Cromwell Press.

CONTENTS

I dedicate this book to Marleen, who has been so helpful in making it. Also, for the love and pleasure that she has given me, over the past seventeen years, since we met. Hopefully, it will be something for her to remember me by, when I'm kicking up the daisies!

ACKNOWLEDGEMENTS

The authors are indebted to the following people, companies and organisations for their valuable contributions, various favours and support, which have been of great assistance in the publication of this book:

The Fewtrell Family:- Marleen Fewtrell (Eddie's wife); his daughters, Abigail and Rebecca; Eddie's son, Daniel. Eddie's brothers, Gordon, John and Roger, aka 'Bomber'; also Don Fewtrell (now deceased); Eddie's sister, Phyllis Wheeler and her husband Bill. Rebecca's husband, John Moon, and Daniel's wife, Leslie; John Fewtrell's wife, Carrie.

Mike Alexander; Stacey Barnfield; Patti Bell; Bev Bevan; Val Bevan; Chuck Botfield; Tony Brook; Alan and Alistair Brewin; Hartley Cain and his wife, Lynn; Jasper Carrott; Andy Cashmore; 'Big' Albert Chapman; Carl Chinn; Tony Christie and his son and manager Sean Fitzgerald; Kate Cook; Bryan Cooper; Pam and Keith Dawes; Ed Doolan; Seamus Dunleavy; Roy Edwards; Des Fitzpatrick; Raymond Froggatt; Steve Gibbons; Colin Goldsworthy; Ron Gray; Mary Green; Stephen Hands; Councillor Ken Hardeman; Kenny Hatton; Les Hemming; Martin Hone; Laurie Hornsby; Mike Horseman; Phil Inglis; Dave Ismay; Brendan Joyce; Dave Juste; Mike Lavender; Chris Lewthwaite; Kenny Lynch; Don Maclean; Bernard Manning; Stevie McCarthy; Ted and Ivy Morris; Norman 'Nobby' Nobbs; Gianni Paladini; Bob Price; Pam Price; Rita Radvanyi; Pam Robinson; Sue Sanders; Roger Shropshall; Frances Sinclair; Mark Smith; Jimmy Tarbuck; Phil Upton; Lucy Wallis; Colin Weatherall; Sheila Williams; Alan Wyant; Ashley Yeates; Brian Yeates.

Newspapers: Poppy Brady of the *Birmingham Mail*.
The Solihull Times (Editor Enda Mullen).

Please forgive any possible omissions. Every effort has been made to include all organisations and individuals involved in the book.

FOREWORD

Eddie Fewtrell – well a man like him is hard to find. I had to look in three massage parlours! In his youth he liked wine, women and song – thank god he can still sing.

When you thought of Birmingham night life in the 60s, 70s 80s and 90s, you thought of one man, Eddie Fewtrell, King of the Clubs and what a meeting place they were for show business folk.

Tom Jones, Humperdinck, Matt Monroe, Bassey and so many more would enjoy the company of a very generous man and host, Eddie Fewtrell, along with his brothers and his dear dad – what a man he was. He turned up one night at Eddie's club on a horse. Mr. Fewtrell Senior's thinking was that he couldn't be breathalysed!

If you asked Eddie to support a charity he was the first man in. Miss Wet T-shirt competitions, I enjoyed judging them and such nice prizes for the winner, two tickets to Marbella – one way. He didn't forget the senior citizens with Miss Wet Cardigan competitions, first prize, a new set of teeth.

He had great chat up lines to girls at the bar in his clipped Birmingham accent, "How do you like your eggs in the morning?" he asked. One young lady replied, "Unfertilised, now p**s off!"

Another Birmingham beauty: "Would you like a drink love?" he asked. She said, "I guess I'll have champagne." He said, "Guess again and have a beer!"

Once stopped by the police for drinking and driving he got out of the car and the policeman said "You're staggering" and he replied "You're good looking yourself, do you want to dance?"

That's Eddie. A loyal friend, a loyal supporter and great company and if I look old and haggard nowadays, nights out with Eddie Fewtrell have a lot to do with that.

Enjoy the book!

Jimmy Tarbuck

Never take no for an answer; I don't believe in the phrase: "Can't be done." Nothing is impossible – just go for it! And be nice to people, on the way up; because you might need them to be nice to you, on the way down.

Chapter One

A LOST CHILDHOOD

The story of Eddie Fewtrell, King of Clubs, cannot be told in isolation from the city of Birmingham, because it had a profound influence upon him, from the moment he drew breath. Birmingham made Eddie, and Eddie's life, undoubtedly, had a profound and enduring impact upon the city. The relationship was a symbiotic one – each having a significant effect upon, and drawing life and inspiration from, the other.

Thus Eddie's story, told by the two of us, will unfold against a Birmingham backdrop; the environment that shaped him, his close family and friends and the many and varied characters who inhabited his 20th Century world – and onwards into the 21st. Like a landscape artist, adding in careful stages the components of our painting: the background, the foreground and the fine details that create the total effect – whilst our eyes refocus, time and again on the central figure.

Kenny took everything out of the house, to sell. He'd go out every day of the week, as if he was going to work, but would always come back when my mother was in bed and my father was out. I'd be there, at the age of seven – minding Johnny, who was three years younger than me; cleaning the house. Kenny was about twenty-five at that time – the oldest of the ten children; even older than my two sisters. He was a picture maniac... in the Pictures all the while. He'd come back at ten o'clock at night, to our house in Mansfield Road Aston, after the cinema had closed. The only thing he would make for himself was porridge, or bread and milk: that's all he used to live on. He'd make a terrible mess of the house; he wouldn't do any washing up and you'd have to clean the place up afterwards. So as a young kid, I'd get the place 'spick-and-span', and my older brother would come in and mess it all up again. Then off he'd go to bed, and start ranting and raving. Friday would come and all of a sudden my mother would be waiting for him to bring the money home, but he'd have been lying about it, and nothing would turn up.

I was born in 1932, in Mansfield Road, Six Ways Aston: the sixth of ten children, born to Agnes and George Fewtrell. On my father's side, the name 'Fewtrell' may have a French Canadian connection, although it can also be found in historical English archives, perhaps even dating back to the Norman invasion – the French connection again!

My brother 'Bomber' later discovered that my mother, Agnes Louisa Cartmale, was from an Irish family. The oldest child in our family was Kenny, followed by Phyllis, Violet, Frankie, Donald, myself, Johnny, Gordon, Chrissie and Roger, the youngest. According to my sister Phyllis, when they lived in Winson Green, Birmingham, my parents went on holiday, by boat to Montreal, Canada, with Kenny, Violet and herself, to see my father's parents – another George and his wife, who were living there. Frankie was born while they were there; the rest of us were born in Birmingham.

I hardly ever went to school, from the time I was seven; I was permanently looking after my mother. When I was about five, I had a little bit of early schooling, at Albert Road School, but then I was evacuated to Gloucester. Although I went to school there for about two years, generally-speaking I taught myself to spell, write and add up.

My sister, Phyllis, started work at the age of fifteen; so at the age of six, I first began to look after my younger brothers. Phyllis had looked after us from when we were born, until she went to work. She recalls: "Even when Eddie was a little boy, there was something about him that you couldn't help liking; he'd always got that charming side to his nature."

Nobody seemed to have any money; you'd talk about a farthings-worth of bacon bits and two-shillings-worth of coal. You couldn't afford outside toilets or bedclothes. We had absolutely nothing and had to have Daily Mail Boots and jerseys...big hobnail boots and no socks. My younger brother, John, was born in 1935.

Phyllis explains: "My brothers, Eddie, Frank and Donald were evacuated to Gloucester. John was evacuated to Aberdare, in Wales in 1939 too, when he was four. We lived at 97 Mansfield Road, Aston. I was around sixteen. Needless to say, it wasn't a very happy time. I worked, doing ammunition, at Rippingills in Aston Road, during the day, but it was bombed at night."

I was seven, in 1939, when the four of us were evacuated. Three of us set out upon the coach to Gloucester, which seemed like a million miles away. When we got to Gloucester, we were put in a little country community hall, where there were loads of children, of our age group. We just sat there; we were there from about two o'clock and had pop and tea and sandwiches. Then at about four o'clock different people came in and they were walking round, and choosing the children. I was pretty lucky really, because I was separated from the two brothers because nobody would take three children; so I was put to be on my own. I was there for about two hours, until a couple who I later knew as Mr. and Mrs. Underwood, asked me if I'd like to come with them. So I said goodbye to my two brothers, and off I went to Stonehouse, which is in Eastern Gloucestershire, near to Stroud. I stayed in this little country cottage and went to school there, and started to learn country life.

It was a small, two-bedroom cottage, with strawberries and raspberries in the garden. They grew all kinds of vegetables. A milkman used to come round with a horse and a two-wheeled cart, with churns of milk on. He'd bring milk and eggs, every day. He ladled the creamy milk out into a jug. The homemade butter always tasted really special: I never had any at home, as it was wartime. I can still taste it now! Actually, everything tasted marvellous to me. Mrs. Underwood baked fresh bread, every day.

You went inside the cottage and there was a tiny little kitchen and a tiny little living room; that's where you were. The mother and father slept in one bedroom; their son, Cyril, slept in the other. There was another tiny little bedroom where I slept. I had to have a bath every night and go to bed at seven or eight o'clock at night. It was a total change – so luxurious compared to what I'd been used to. I used to call Mrs. Underwood 'Auntie' and her husband was 'Uncle'. I was too young to bother about names! It all seemed a bit strange at first.

I started to go into school. All the kids there were looking at me as if I'd just landed from Mars! Although the pupils in my class were of a similar age, there was only a small number of them; the whole school held about fifty people – if that.

I had to go to church, three times on a Sunday: morning, afternoon and night. In the night I had to take turns with another evacuee, a friend of mine, Ronnie Wilding, at pumping the organ. We had to stand behind it. It was hard work and this one time I said to Conkey, "Go on – it's your turn!" He said: "No, I'm not going to." He was a bit stubborn. We saw the weight coming down. The congregation were singing "Holy, holy holy." All of a sudden the organ started to screech and collapse, because we'd stopped pumping, so we started to pump like mad, to get it back to normal! We got told off about that when we got home. But it was a bit much really – having to go so often. We'd go in the week too, sometimes.

I went haymaking, with shire horses and a cart. I was there for about two years. I learned later that my two brothers had gone to a right rough place. I saw them, just the once, coming down the road, driving cattle with a stick. Frank and Don were living in squalor at a really rough farmhouse and had to work really hard, whereas I was living in this much cleaner place.

Eventually I was chosen to sing in the choir, and I had to sing a solo at the Thanksgiving Service, where they brought all the cattle and sheep to be blessed. This way of life went on for about eighteen months, before I decided to put on my roller skates and head for home. As I was doing so, I met Mick the milkman. I said: "Which way's Birmingham?" So he said: "That way. Where are you going then Edward?" I said: "I'm going home." He put me up on his horse and took me back to the cottage, so I got into trouble for that and my roller skates were confiscated. I got a bit homesick and fed up, although I was fed better and had nicer clothes to wear. It was a thousand times better than what I'd been used to. I was told I'd got to wash my hands all the while, clean my teeth; have a bath before I went to bed. With hindsight, living in such an improved environment made me determined to improve my situation... and find a means of getting somewhere in life.

"Gordon was born on 13 June 1940, so he remained at home with my parents," recalls Phyllis. "Johnny came back, speaking Welsh. I couldn't understand a word he said! I visited all my brothers, during the war. I went to see Edward at Gloucester. Frankie and Donald were at a farm. Johnny was in Wales. Eddie was in a really beautiful place. He's always been lucky really! It was just a visit to say hello to Eddie, and make sure that he was getting on alright. He was in the house when I arrived. He *seemed* happy enough. He had his own bedroom. When I went to the farm, to see Donald and Frankie it was a totally different story. It was terrible. Very upset I was – when I saw them! They were saying effing this and that. I said: 'Stop swearing!' but they were talking about the cows – they were heifers, weren't they?!"

I settled down again for a few months. Then one day, Phyllis and my mother and father turned up. They said: "Come on – get your clothes, we're going home." I was quite happy about that, because I'd missed all the people, although I was still sad to leave the lady who'd looked after me, because she was very nice – very kind. Mum asked me if I'd been treated well and I said: "Yes, very well." So I got in the car and off we went. We went to the farm and picked up Donald and Frank. They were scruffy and filthy. They just jumped in the car and said: "Thank God for that!" They came just as they were. They'd been treated just like slaves. They'd hardly had anything to eat at all.

John recalls: "When I came back from Aberdare, I remember the old man picking me up from Snow Hill Station. He drove a brown, Warwick Hire taxi and he'd got a gas bag on the top."

So there we all were...safely back home – but at a different address. Having seen how the Underwood family lived made me hungry to make some money, so that I could make life more pleasant. Up until I was evacuated I had nothing to contrast it with. I just accepted life as it was. From that point onwards, even when I was looking after the kids, I'd be doing things up and selling them in my spare time. I'd always be looking for something to sell...

Chapter Two

ALBERT ROAD

Eddie returned to Birmingham when he was nine. His parents had by this time moved from Mansfield Road, to 144 Albert Road, Aston. He began helping his mother again – looking after the youngsters – John and Gordon. Musical Director Mike Alexander also spent his childhood in Six Ways Aston, although he was ten years Eddie's junior, and his upbringing was very different; so did Ozzy Osbourne, Councillor Ken Hardeman and Hartley Cain, Raymond Froggatt's lead guitarist, all of whom are in our book! Mike was at Elton John's wedding in 2005: "That's where I met Ozzy – and we reminded ourselves about Aston and the Elbow Room, and Barbarella's."

Agnes had two more children: Chrissie in early 1943 and Roger on 25 March 1944. She wasn't well, for much of the time, so Eddie was looking after her and his four younger brothers as well. Don and Frank started work at the Great Western Railway.

There's a photograph taken by Alan Wyant, of me looking about eighteen, with Gordon, Chrissie and Bomber, all as young boys; Gordon has kindly provided us with a copy, for the book. You'll meet Alan Wyant, in Chapter Four.

At 144 Albert Road we had an Anderson Shelter in the garden, which slept about six people. I don't know how we all managed to get in there, but it was always cold and horrible. So at the beginning we went in it, but later on, we tried to avoid it if we could.

Inside the house we had what you would call a Morrison Table Shelter. It was a big shelter with big steel sides and a steel top: like a table, made out of steel. There was wire all round the edges. You slept in there, when it looked like being a long night.

The procedure was this: We'd be standing on the top of the stairs, leading to the cellar, so that if anything happened, we could just run straight down, into the cellar, which was supposed to be the safest place. My mother was down the cellar and she was starting to have the baby, as the air raid started. A massive bomb dropped. Just as the bomb landed there was a *massive* noise – I think it was a doodlebug. I'd never heard a sound like it before – in all the time we were there. All of a sudden, there was a cry of the baby being born... and that was Roger. He was Roger Alan Fewtrell, so my mother said: "I think I'll name him 'Bomber'." So we called him 'Bomber', from that time onwards, because his initials are RAF; also, because he'd been born when the bomb dropped. The next day, we found out that the *Lozells Picture House* had been destroyed; I always remember that, because they found the manager's head behind a chimney pot, some streets away from the cinema! I think it was during the fourteen or seventeen-hour air raid that Birmingham had. John adds: "Bomber is eight years younger than me, so he must have been born somewhere around 1944.

"A day or two after the *Lozells Picture House* was bombed," John continues, "we went to the site, looking for shrapnel – *Gone With the Wind* and Laurel & Hardy were on at the time. The Germans had bombed this wholesale grocer's called Kay's, which was on the corner of Wheeler Street and Lozells Road. The grocer's had white walls with black lettering on it, which said 'Kay's Ways Pays'.

John recalls spending seventeen hours in the Anderson Shelter in the back garden. "Our dad was on Fire Watch; everybody had to take a turn. There was an Ack-ack gun somewhere around – some distance away from our garden, but it used to go (imitates the sound it made). Eddie reckons it was in Kingstanding, protecting the factories, such as the BSA. The American army barracks were there too.

"I can remember the searchlights and the balloons and everything. I swallowed a nail. You can ask my sister Phyllis about this. We were in this shelter for seventeen hours, with the bombing going on around us. They took me to the General Hospital. I was trying to smoke the nail – mimicking the older ones I suppose – smoking cigarettes! It came through me, in the finish. I wasn't very old. I think Phyllis took me to the hospital."

My sister, Phyllis, explains: "We all went down into the Anderson Shelter. My dad used to get a chair, put it over his head, and say: 'I don't care what part of my body they get, as long as me head's alright!' John swallowed a two-inch nail, while he was in the shelter. I had to take him up to the General Hospital. When I got him there, they asked us to go down into the cellars, in case of air raids. When they x-rayed it they said how lucky he had been, because it had gone all the way down – and just missed his lungs! Donald stuck a button up his nose, on another occasion; you know, these little ankle-strap shoes… they used to have like a little button? So I had to take him to hospital too!"

According to John, "I can remember from around 1945-47 the *Swan* pub, on the corner of Victoria Road and Whitehead Road, Aston. There was a friend of mine and Edward's called Conkey Wilding. We used to have a den next door in what I think was a bombed building. We used to meet there and smoke cigarettes, from the pub next door, the *Swan*. There was also another fella called 'Macca'. His real name was Georgie MacIntosh. He was with us and he used to stop at the house. We put him up in a rabbit hutch. We used to hide him, because I don't think he had a mother and father; he lived with somebody and he palled up with us. We used to hide him and feed him."

Conkey Wilding was Ron Wilding; a very thin, scrawny kid. He was the son of the couple who ran the public house called the *Swan*. He brought me cigarettes from the pub, and everything else. I gave them to my mother, who used to sell them to my father. Macca looked like a Chinese guy. You know Joey Brown – with that great big laugh and a wide open mouth? He was just like that. He was a kid who'd been adopted from birth, because he had no parents; he was a lovely lad – and one of our people, as John says. He used to stop at our house.

John remembers: "Our day out, our entertainment, was picking up shrapnel after the air raids and seeing who could find the biggest piece. We'd put bets on it. Sometimes it was me, Donald, Edward and Frankie, but Donald and Frankie were in a different age group to us; they were older than us; so mainly it would be Edward and me who played together, with our own friends. Our mom, Agnes, was shot at, coming down Whitehead Road, by a German plane; dad had to duck into an entry – that was towards the end of the war in 1944 or 45. That was walking down to our house at 144 Albert Road. We used to call our address 'one gross'!"

Our house at Albert Road had nine rooms: six bedrooms and three down. It was a massive big house – very cold. There was a bath, but the plumbing never worked. We used bedrooms all over the place. All of us lot were in one bedroom, in the attic, because we hadn't got beds in the others. It was a villa, with three floors: a ground floor, a first floor and an attic. On the first floor there were three rooms; there was a big room up in the attic, where all the boys in our family slept.

As you walked in the front door of the house; there was coloured glass on the inside door. On the left was a big sitting room. The next room was a middle room; then straight the way through, there was a kitchen area. It was a little room, with a black-leaded fireplace. Your cooking was done on the coal fire, with ovens each side of it. Phyllis recently reminded me that there was also a gas stove. There was another little room, with an old crock sink; it was a washing room, with a boiler. As you came out of that room, the cellar door was right opposite. You walked out of the back door, into the garden, with the shelter on the right, dug into the ground. The garden was about twenty yards long, with rough ground and weeds; just somewhere to play and put the shelter. I put a shed in there and there was a toilet and a coal hole.

Going up the stairs, there was one room straight ahead of you. Next to that was the bathroom that didn't work. There was no running water and no toilet – just a big old-fashioned bath, but no boilers or anything. Then there'd be another big room, with mother and father in it. Another room where the girls used to be, or where Kenny would stop, when he was there. All the lads were up at the top, in the attic.

The house was rented, from the Corporation, and my father just paid the rent, but you never got anything done. There was no dole, or Social Security like there is today. If my father had got no money then we had no food, it was as simple as that!

Phyllis recalls: "The Albert Road house was just an ordinary Front House with a hallway. There were only three bedrooms. It had an outdoor toilet that we had to share and a brew-house – with a washing tub, an old wringer, and a 'dolly' that you used for getting the clothes clean. You'd get up at six o'clock; light a fire under the tub; get it going before it would boil."

By this time I would be about nine or ten years old. If we had any money, my mother would send me to the butcher's with two bob – two shillings. I'd get some bits of steak or stewing beef – Clewer's the Butchers was on the corner of Six Ways, Aston. Then round to the grocery shop, to buy some potatoes, carrots and onions. I'd come back, get a big pot and put in all the meat and vegetables, after I'd peeled them; add the water and Oxos. I'd put it on to boil, then as it was boiling, we'd start skimming all the rubbish off the top, then let it simmer away. My mother and my sister Phyllis told me what to do, so that's the way I did it.

Mother would go upstairs and leave me to it. Or she'd be lying on the downstairs settee. She couldn't get her breath, so I'd go to the chemist, to get her Dodo tablets, which were to help ease her asthma. I also used to fetch her snuff, which seemed to be good for her chest; she'd take a pinch of it. Phyllis confirms: "I taught him how to cook, you know? Eddie's a very good cook." Her husband, my brother-in-law, Billy Wheeler, adds: "All of the brothers are; even Donald used to cook his own cakes."

I taught Hazel, my first wife, how to cook; she couldn't cook because she'd never had to. Marleen could cook, but I taught her the English way of cooking. I was always good at cooking roast dinners, because you learn and you progress. Once I had my clubs, any time I didn't know how to cook a particular meal, I'd ring up my chef, Ricky Rickaby, at my club and ask him! There were more times in the early days, however, when we had hardly any money. You'd only have a piece of bread and lard or jam; you'd just have to get by.

We'd play mainly in the street, seeing the American guys go past. We'd run up and say: "Have you got any gum chum?" We'd have the Americans round all the while, chasing my sister Violet. She was very pretty. She'd come home late, at about twelve o'clock, with cases of oranges and some chewing gum and cigarettes; nylon stockings and various other things that they'd given her. Violet was three years younger than Phyllis. Phyllis is nine years older than me. When I came back from being evacuated, Phyllis was married, to Albert Garrington, but Violet was still single. Violet married Billy McDonald soon afterwards, when I was still a youngster. I don't have much memory of either of them living in our family home, although Violet would have been at work during the daytime, while I was looking after my younger brothers. I was diabolically annoyed, because I found out that it was only me who was helping with all the kids. There was no help from Frank or Donald – they would not do it. When they went to school, they would be out every night, going swimming and enjoying themselves. Later, when they were at work, they wouldn't help me because they were bringing money in. Phyllis recalls: "Violet's husband, Billy McDonald wouldn't allow her to help Eddie or myself look after the children. He wouldn't even let her out the house. She had a terrible time."

Kenny was the oldest son, but funnily enough, he didn't look anything like a Fewtrell! He was very dark and a lot taller than the rest of us – about five foot ten. He was a strange guy – he never worked – so he had absolutely no money at all. He'd have his dinner money – maybe sixpence or a shilling – to go to work.

Kenny always used to get a job with a uniform: usually the doorman at a Picture House or something like that; working in a hospital or as a fireman, or railway worker – because he loved uniforms. He had different jobs – you could never pin him down. He used to go off, saying that he was working, with dinner money off my mother. She was the only one who would look after him; my father had no time for him at all, because he used to take my father's clothes and new shoes out of the house and sell them. He didn't seem 'a full shilling'… you know? He was kind of backward.

Kenny would go missing, for about three or four months, and you'd get a phone call to say that he was in hospital, and would we go? When we went, we found that he'd just got himself in hospital, so that he could get sympathy and bathed. There was nothing wrong with him; that was the way he used to get bathed; they used to tell us how absolutely filthy and lousy he was.

When he came back to the house, he looked like an absolute tramp; he'd go up to bed. Mom would come down and say: "Where's he gone?" She'd drag him out of bed, because she knew that he was absolutely lousy and he'd infect the bed. The next thing you knew, she'd have all his clothes off him and burn them; then she'd get the tin bath out, in front of the fire, and we'd be scrubbing him. That's how we went on, for years and years, sometimes without hearing from him for a long time. Then all of a sudden he'd turn up again. He lived in all sorts of places.

Despite such hardships, my mother hardly drank at all, although occasionally, when she could afford it, she'd go to the *Swan*… which wasn't very often, in the early days. She'd have a half of draught beer. It was mainly for the company – she'd sit there with the other women. At breakfast time I'd be making porridge, or do toast with lard on; making bottles with Cow & Gate Red Powder, for the babies; full cream, half cream; then there'd be a blue one as well. When the kids used to cry, we'd put a bit of syrup or sugar on their dummy. Sometimes when they had stomach ache, we'd just give them a touch of Indian Brandy; bicarbonate of soda, to get the wind up – put them over your shoulder and pat their back!

I'd change nappies. In those days, you had to wash all the nappies – you wouldn't have disposable ones. Then I'd have to fetch coal; if you saw somebody with bananas and you'd got money, you could get that. If you were very lucky you'd be able to get a halfpenny-worth of sweets now and again – but we never had any! A halfpenny and a penny were a lot of money, in those days. Mother would give me the money out of her purse, to go shopping; she'd get what she could off my father. I did all of that right up until the age of fourteen, when I had to go to work.

My father, George, with the greatest of respect, would all of a sudden come home with a lot of money. He'd come home drunk and fish all of this money out of his pockets; there'd be *loads* of it – something like £400 to £500, in *those* days – he'd done deals and this-that-and-the-other. One time, he brought home a great big turkey, in the car. It was near Christmas time. Being a taxi driver, he'd driven a farmer out into the country and he'd paid him with a live turkey! He left it in the kitchen, tied to a chair; gone to sleep again, because he was absolutely drunk.

Mother woke him up in the middle of the night, saying, "There's somebody downstairs!" George came down, with a great big piece of wood. The turkey jumped up at him and my father hit it straight on the head and killed it! He used to come home with live pigs too. He'd take a farmer home, who was drunk; don't forget, these were the war years and it was difficult to get meat. So my father would have to bring the live pig home; the farmer couldn't kill it, otherwise he'd be in trouble – by giving it him un-slaughtered, he'd be in the clear.

George used to kill these live animals; I saw him chop a chicken's head off, and it ran round the yard with no head! He could skin chickens and rabbits. I came home the one day, when we were absolutely hungry and my father had killed my pet rabbit! It was horrible – I never forgot it. I was telling Marleen about it, the other day.

We always had plenty of milk and cod liver oil for the babies, because we got an allowance off the government. You had free milk at school and you got coupons for food for the kids too, if you were that poor. Then if you asked, you got your Daily Mail Boots and jerseys. You'd wear old silk stockings, cut off, because you had no socks. It was really bad. That's the way you went on.

When I'd got nothing to do, me, Conkey Wilding and Macca, possibly Johnny, I can't remember, used to go out 'horse mucking': that's following horses; there were quite a few around in those days, then shovel the muck up and sell it to people for sixpence or a shilling a bucket, for gardens. We'd get a few bob that way. We'd collect empty pop bottles and jam jars and get the money back. People might pay us to clean their cars or their windows, so we became very resourceful, thinking up these ideas for making money. I built a shed in the back garden, collected people's old bikes and did them up to sell. I'd scrape them all off, with a wire brush and sandpaper, then paint them. That led to renovating old cars too, as you'll see in the next chapter. The old bikes would cost me about three shillings; when I'd restored them I'd display them outside the shed and sell them for about thirty bob.

John recalls: "There was an old lady who lived next door to us at number 142. She was a big woman. She used to make us a bread pudding, because we were always hungry. The other side of us was a woman whose husband was an army officer – I think he was a major. There was Conkey Wilding and this Macca, Johnny Evans, who had a house further up Albert Road – the road where we were living at that time. Johnny had this orchard and we all used to go scrumping. We were that hungry you know. We all used to sleep upstairs in the attic; there were no proper bedclothes or anything like that: it was all army greatcoats and rag coats. So we all used to sleep together, to keep warm; we used to wee over each other... it was terrible!

"When everybody had gone to bed, we used to creep out, through the skylight, down... and just go scrumping – in this Johnny Evans' orchard. When we came back; especially on a November night, it was cold, so we could hear people walking past... with the ice and whatnot," continues John. "We used to crunch these apples – it always used to annoy me – people crunching in bed. This particular night we went scrumping and we were up this tree, acting as lookout, in case anybody came; and our Frankie fell down the tree. This bloke had got pigs; you see? In the war you could breed your own pigs and other livestock... you know, do your own thing? That's what it was all about. Anyway, Frankie fell down from the tree, into this pigsty and broke his toe."

Another evening, when we went scrumping, the light came on and I scampered down the tree. Just as I got to the fence, about to climb over it, a great big old Alsatian bit a lump out of my behind. An ambulance arrived, took me to hospital, and they had to put stitches in my backside. It taught me a lesson, never to do anything like that again. The funniest thing was that it went to bite Donald, but I was on the end and it took a piece out of me!

John recalls: "When I was at Albert Road School, which was down the road from our house, we took our 'Goies' – our home-made go-karts. There was a little shop called Lawrence's on the corner. You know how buildings had black-out sheets over them? Well, the door of the shop was on the corner. Me and Edward used to go in, so the bell would go. Then one of us would hide behind the blackout curtain. The bell would go again, as though we'd gone out; then the people used to go back into the living room. Then we'd pinch sweets and toffees, because they were all on rations… and bottles of Robinson's Blackcurrant Cordial, which had a picture of a golliwog on the front… do you remember?"

You'd be hungry all the while – to tell you the truth! You'd be so desperate; you'd have to nick something out of the shop to get food. While one of you hid behind the curtain, the other would be talking to the shopkeeper. The talker would then return about ten minutes later, as if he'd forgotten something, then the two of you would come out of the shop again, with all of the stuff you'd stolen. As John says, that was Lawrence's, in Albert Road, Aston. I remember it ever so well. But in all fairness, the shopkeepers realised how struggling and hungry we were; a lot of the time they would give us credit, for a couple of loaves, or something like that. Mr. Lawrence's 1932 Austin would be parked on the pavement, right outside the shop window. Albert Road School was directly opposite, on the other corner.

"Also, one time we went down to Aston Commercial School – me and Eddie in our 'Go-er'. Big Mac and Johnny Evans were with us. We went into the Science Lab. Don't forget, we were very young: he was somewhere between ten and twelve; I was three years younger," explains John. "So we went into the Lab, opened this door, I'll never forget it, and there was a skeleton that shook and jangled, because it had a hook through its head. It frightened the life out of us and we all ran out!

"We finished up in the kitchen of this school, where we came across these apple rings, so we took them home. Don't forget, we had to do all of the cooking for ourselves. They were in little barrels. In those days they used to dry all the fruit; there weren't any freezers or anything. They used to make apple pies with these rings for the students. So we had a couple of these barrels away," John continues. "When we got home, we opened them up and found the apple rings. We didn't know what was inside; we thought they were just barrels of booze.

"Going back to this warehouse, Macca, Edward, Johnny and me got our Goies, went into the warehouse and found these boxes, which we thought was salmon. They turned out to be sardines, but we took them home, thinking: 'Oh – we've got something to eat!' When we found out that they were sardines, we put them all along the back wall, at Albert Road. If they had been in tomato sauce we'd have eaten them, but they weren't – they were in oil. So we didn't like them. We put them on the wall, for the cats. We took a lot of them up to Aston Park, which was at the top of Victoria Road, and threw them in this great big water tank that they kept up there for putting out fires."

At first, we hid them in the attic – in the loft. When everybody had gone out, we used to get the tins of sardines out. As John says, we got sick of eating them in oil. Even today, I still buy sardines in tomato sauce and put them on toast. I say to Marleen: "I'll never forget when we were starving – and these were like a real luxury to us."

Also, down in that school there were great big stocks of coal. So we used to fill our Go-karts; we'd sit with big lumps of coal, the biggest ones you could carry, then pull it along. As it bumped over the flagstones, slack would come out and there'd be a trail of slack, all the way up to our entry – just like an aeroplane leaves a smoke-trail, where it's been. So I'd get this broom and go down and sweep the whole street!

When I could find some spare time, from looking after the kids, the first major project that I had was making skittle-boards. My father cut the plywood out of tea chests. We made a board around it, painted and lacquered them and made skittle-boards out of them. We used to sell them for 12/6d – twelve shillings and sixpence. I made them and assembled them with my father, then had the skittles turned by somebody – and the balls. I'd work all through the night, making them and screwing them together – getting them ready for my father to sell, the next day.

I used a saw to make the base; father had the corners 'turned', by a machine. Then we glued and screwed everything together. I was always good at woodwork and things like that. That's one of the things I learned in Gloucester – in Woodwork Class. I've got all of the machinery now. I built most of my place here – at the *Singing Stud* – and I built most of my own clubs too. I also built most of out stables here. I've got every machine that money can buy now. We're about to open a new night club, so I shall go down there and do the woodwork. I enjoy it – the fact that people are going to charge you a fortune to do it – but I can do it myself!

My early days down the markets, followed by conscription into the army would make separate chapters in themselves, but they will have to wait until another time!

Chapter Three

WOULD YOU
BUY THIS CAR?

Eddie leaves the army after two years, six months before Alan Wyant, and moves back with his old crowd. Alan frequents the Tower Ballroom, but Eddie is more likely to go to the Casino, opposite Lewis's. However, Alan and Eddie remain good friends and their paths sometimes cross, at the Casino, or with the in-crowd, down in the basement at the Kardomah. Johnny Summers is often there, together with Don Giles and Larry Farrington. Although Eddie has returned to the new family address, 33 Milverton Road, Erdington, his mother, Agnes dies soon afterwards, in 1953, when Eddie is just twenty-one and John has just been conscripted.

Eddie resumes market trading with Frankie: 'dodgy' sales deals. Eddie becomes a Midland Red bus driver – which he doesn't enjoy. His 'good days' are when he can make a reasonable living from being self-employed. Their father, George Fewtrell, master salesman 'Tutti-frutti' continues, as ever, to do deals.

Don marries Ivy and moves to Coventry; Eddie marries Hazel. Frankie and Eddie open a Washwood Heath car business, F & E Motors, and start a hire purchase company. Pat Roach helps them with the occasional deal.

I decided that I would try to make money by continuing to working for myself. As my father was a heavy drinker, I wanted to 'turn the tables' – I was determined to make money out of booze. Even at eighteen, when I was on leave from the army, and stayed at my parents' house, we'd go into the *Casino* in Birmingham, which convinced me still further to eventually sell drinks, when I saw for myself, at first-hand, what profits could be made.

I came out of the army after serving two years and went back to live with my mother and father. My brother Frank had already been discharged, because he was ill, so he lived at home too. Due to a road-widening scheme, the council had taken the Whitehead Road properties off us, without paying compensation; that's why the family had moved to Milverton Road. Frank and I decided to continue working down the Bull Ring, for the time being, selling nylons and so forth; we'd work down there, six days a week. We'd have good days and bad days. Frank began to get better, although he was still very weak.

John recalls: "When we moved into Milverton Road Erdington, George still wasn't allowed to drive, so he brought a live turkey home once, on the tram! I don't know how they stood for him doing that – he was drunk and he was talking to a live turkey. But you could bring anything home on a tram!"

At certain times of the year sales weren't good, so Frank and I decided to apply for jobs as a bus drivers on the *Midland Red*. I went on a six-week course, to pass a test for driving buses. The *Midland Red* garage was in Broad Street and we went out every day, for about four hours, driving buses, stopping on hills – on different types of buses: single-deckers, double-deckers, wide ones; old ones, new ones – we had to drive everything. After six weeks I passed the test and became a driver.

I drove buses for quite some time, but I didn't like it. It was forty minutes to Walsall and forty minutes back – but it was like a race track! You had to just keep going all the time.

I did that for about six months, then went back down the market, because things were getting a bit better. But they were that short of drivers, the inspectors used to come down and say: "Would you take this bus to Worcester?" or to Walsall. So I used to put my cap on, leave my brother, Frank, with a few cases of stockings, or whatever we were selling, and off I'd go to do an hour or two of driving, then come back – it was just extra money – depending upon how short they were of drivers. That went on for quite some time.

Then I bought a Standard 14 – a fairly new car, and started going around the shops with a little guy who was deaf in one ear. I'd do what my father used to do. I'd pull up at a shop, go in and sell anything to them – stockings, handbags, socks – things like that. Then we started selling things like fires. I got a guy to copy these fires; the coal part would be made of plastic – where the colour came out.

Roy Edwards, of Great Barr, knew me when we were both teenagers. Roy recalls: "In those days we'd see each other at all the meeting places in town.

That's when I first met Eddie. We'd meet at places like the Kardomah, or as we knew it 'KD'. Also, the *Casino Dance Hall*, Corporation Street; Lewis's Department Store, Bull Street, in the record department; the *Tower Ballroom*, and so on. Our big night was at the *Odeon*, New Street, when everybody dressed to kill. You wouldn't see anybody there who hadn't got their best suit on. They'd be clean-shaven, with their hair just so. And the great thing about those days was that you never saw any trouble." Roy also enclosed photos of Ted Taylor, a very good friend of his, who features later in Chapter Five. Sadly, Ted died two or three years ago.

At the *Odeon*, on a Sunday afternoon, you'd have all your DA haircuts – 'Duck's Arse', for the uninitiated! You'd see everybody there. That's where I had to go to find that Raymond Russell, one day. My brother Frank only weighed about seven stone at the time, but Ray was threatening to give him a good hiding. We'd been at a party at Pat Manning's the night before. Flo Frost was there. I'd got the Standard 14HP that I mentioned earlier – it cost me £350 – HEV 50. I arrived in the new car and Frankie was still recovering from his regular army service in Hong Kong, where he'd been very ill, so I was looking after him.

Everybody was a bit drunk at the party. Raymond Russell was there, with a girl called Vilma, who I used to go out with. Every time he saw me, he'd start setting about her, for being with me, but at that time I had a lot of girls, because I never settled down with anybody. So Frankie and I left to avoid further trouble, but Flo ran out to ask for a lift. She lived at Chain Walk, just off Lozells, on the right; by Madam Amy's – where I learnt to do the Quickstep. Raymond Russell ran out, just as Flo was getting in the car and told her to get out again, but I advised her to stay put.

Ray then asked Frank to get out of the car, so that he could fight him, but as Frank was so weak, I offered to, instead. It finished up with me arranging to meet Raymond at the *Odeon*, the following day. We met there at three o'clock, Sunday afternoon. I said: "I've come to sort you out." He was laughing. I said: "Put your hands up." He did, and I knocked him spark out. I said: "Goodbye – I always keep my promises!" and I walked out.

There was a guy called Harry the Spiv, who said that he'd got a houseful of sparklers. They'd been damaged in a fire – some worked and some didn't, so I could buy the lot for £15. The rooms of his house were full to the ceiling with boxes of sparklers; a gross in each box! There were thousands of them, so I hired the assistance of a guy called Pat Manning, a local lad. Pat, Frankie and myself spent all day, loading the car up with these boxes of sparklers, then took them back to Erdington, where we lived. They filled our rooms up, which made my father very happy, because he was always pleased when we'd got something to sell – when we had deals going on.

Me and Pat Manning went around selling them. This was just two or three months before 5 November – Guy Fawkes Night. Then all of a sudden, I just went into a Newsagent's/Tobacconist's shop, where the shop-owner had been a former policeman. I lit some sparklers to show him, but he said: "I know what you're doing. The others in the box won't work, will they?" So I beat a hasty retreat!

My father had nothing to do at the time, so he offered to come out and sell them with me. He was a master salesman – he sold fifty boxes at a time: we were on a fifty/fifty arrangement. We would go out, take three or four hundred pounds, then call it a day. This went on for a couple of months and then, of course, November 5th had gone and we had to wait for another year. But we'd sold hundreds and hundreds of boxes of them.

We carried on selling stuff in the Bull Ring for a while, but one day we went into a warehouse in Leicester, a big place where they had stockings, shirts, socks and so on. I'd formed a Limited Company by then. They had lots of socks and nylons that they couldn't sell. I ordered a hundred dozen socks of mostly grey, black and brown. I gave them my card and they said they'd deliver to this little Newsagent's shop that I'd bought in Whitehead Street, Aston.

I started getting up and doing papers – helping my mother. Just after he'd come out of the army, Don started courting this girl named Ivy, who turned out to be a gypsy. Her parents were supposed to be very rich. The next thing you know, Donald got married to Ivy and moved to Coventry. He then started to work on building concrete blocks. He didn't seem to want to know about the name Fewtrell, because my father owed various people money.

So they got married and bought a house and we didn't see them for some time.

On 9 March 1953 I had my twenty-first birthday party. We had a party at Milverton Road. Agnes had a few drinks and enjoyed herself, but she was ill the next day. She never survived from that, as she went into hospital and died of pneumonia. I was with her when she died. She made me promise faithfully that I would look after the kids. When she died my father George went totally to pieces and became an absolute drunk. He couldn't do anything, so from that day onwards I looked after them again. When they were old enough, they worked for me in the clubs... I looked after them until they got married.

Apparently, my mother's family were very Irish. My brother, Roger, returned from Ireland quite recently. He discovered a place near Dublin, called Cartmale, which is my mother's maiden name. My father has cousins in Montreal, Canada, and his parents used to live there.

John was conscripted into the army in 1953. He recalls: "Milverton Road was always an unhappy address for me because my mom died there. I went in the army on the Thursday; my mom died the following Tuesday, so I came back in a matter of days. I'd got no suit to wear, except for my plain army suit, which wasn't tailored and had no decorations on it; it was just as it came out of the warehouse. The only suit I had before that was Frankie's and I sent that back home.

"There was a fella at the funeral who'd just come back from Egypt and he'd got this beautiful suit on," John continues. "So I'd just gone into the army, my mom had died and I'll never forget walking up the back way to Milverton Road. They all came up and said how wonderful I looked; my hair had been cut really short – and my mom was lying in the front room – in the coffin. So 33 has always been an unlucky number to me, and Milverton Road sticks in my mind as an unlucky house."

Phyllis explains: "I looked after the boys here, at 10 Yerbury Grove, near the Ridgeway. Eddie lived here after our mother died, until he got married... and Johnny lived here too, although I'd got my own family by then."

Their brother, Gordon, remembers: "I was thirteen when my mother died. It was on 6th October 1953. I remember being in the kitchen, watching a programme about the Coronation of the Queen on a small television set. We were in the house in Milverton Road – then suddenly, everyone disappeared, leaving myself and my two younger brothers, Chrissie and Bomber, on our own. I tried to dress and feed them, as best I could. This went on for about three or four weeks. The teacher came to see us and brought us some oranges. Then Jack Rowan came to rescue all three of us, in his car."

Bomber elaborates: "We stayed with Jack Rowan for the first night, in Calshot Road, Great Barr. Chrissie went to live with Jack and Edie Poynton, in Saint Saviour's Road, Saltley. I went to live with Bernard Hunt and Florrie Hart, at 59, Great Hampton Row. Florrie was the Broadhursts' aunt. Gordon was very supportive of us, considering the circumstances."

"I stayed with Jack Rowan for a while, working as a thirteen-year-old, on roofs and laying concrete floors," continues Gordon. After that I went to live with the Hawkins family, then we swapped around and I went to live with the Poyntons. Jack Poynton repaired dentures. He had a factory in the back of his house, where he also used to make shooting sticks. I helped him with that, on the weekends."

Bernard Hunt was my father's friend and business associate. He was also associated with the Broadhursts – that's how I first came to meet them.

When John came out of the army in 1955 he became a butcher again for a while.

"Then Eddie got a job with B.R.S. so he got me one too, either in Nechells or Saltley, I'm not sure which, because I had only been getting £8 a week, as a butcher," recalls John. "That was still in the 1950s. He also drove a Midland Red bus, on the Great Barr route before that. I used to drive a parcels van and delivered to all the wholesale warehouses in Birmingham, like Warren and Mason and Gilberts, at the time, when they were wholesale warehouses, in Bourton Road, Sparkhill. So I had this little job, delivering things like peanut butter to them. Edward drove a big Seddon Diesel lorry, with a big tarpaulin top over it."

I first met Hazel in 1955, when she was eighteen. She was a *very* beautiful girl. I met her in the *Stork Hotel*, which was opposite Grey's department store and next to what we called the *Casino*, in town – a Mecca place. The manager was a chap called Albert Archer. I knew him quite well. We used to go in there and pay seven pence, upstairs. We'd watch the dancing, from the balcony. I was in the *Stork Hotel* – downstairs – and Hazel was there, with another girl. She looked at me and said: "You've got lovely teeth," which I had! I bought her a drink and this-that-and-the-other; so that's where I first met her.

I took her home; she lived at 42, Brantley Road, Witton. I started going out with her. At that time, I was living with my sister, Phyllis, in Yerbury Grove, just up the road, which wasn't too far to go. I had a big old American car at the time. I used to use more oil that petrol! It was called the Chrysler Airflow. By the time I started going out with Hazel I was selling stuff down the Bull Ring Market: stockings and all kinds of things.

Phyllis explains: "Eddie came to live with us for a while, before he married Hazel. They had a Registry Office wedding, in Broad Street, Birmingham, on 20th June, 1956. We came back here for the Reception. All of his brothers came back here too. It was mainly the family, although there may have been one or two close friends. Alan Wyant took the wedding photographs. Hazel was lovely.... she was my favourite. She was very attractive – Elizabeth Taylor – I used to call her: dark hair. She had a lovely personality, with no 'airs and graces' – she was just herself," concludes Phyllis.

We had a very rough start, when Hazel and I got married. We were supposed to stay the night at Hazel's house, but she fell out with her father, over a woman who was living with him. Her father threw her out and, sadly, never came to our wedding. We'd planned to stay at his house on our wedding night, before leaving for our honeymoon, the following day. But now we had nowhere to spend our wedding night and we were broke, we couldn't even afford a taxi!

We ended up walking into town and found a hotel, just off Corporation Street. We arrived in the foyer, after midnight. There was a guy there, mopping the floor. I explained that we'd just got married, but that we had no money. Luckily, he was very sympathetic, but as he turned his back to find a room key for us, Hazel was sick, all over his nice clean floor. Not wanting to upset him, I quickly mopped it up, before he could see what had happened! He allowed us to use a double room for the night, but warned us that we had to leave by six am the following morning, before the day staff came in. So we 'did a bunk' early the next morning, then hitch-hiked back to Phyllis's, to collect a Morris Eight. Luckily, I'd already paid for the hire of the car and for our caravan, so off we set, after a dreadful start.

We needed some food on our honeymoon, but I was waiting for some tax rebate money, about £50 – £60, to be sent through to me. The lady at the grocery store by where we were staying let me have some food on account. She said: "That's alright love. Good luck to you." She was a very nice lady. So I took it back to the caravan and cooked it. I've always been a good cook.

I had to be really, because Hazel couldn't cook – I'd brought up my three younger brothers, hadn't I? As Johnny was only slightly younger than me, he would often help with the chores too.

So then we could get started on our honeymoon. Hazel couldn't believe how I'd had the guts to walk into the shop and ask for food, without having the money to pay for it… she reckoned that I could talk my way out of a paper bag! Well, my money came through; I think it was about £60, which was a lot of money in those days. So I paid the woman off, leaving us about £10. We stayed there for about a week.

When we came back we'd got nowhere to live. So I spoke to my brother, Don and we lodged with him, at Poultney Road, Radford, Coventry. The next thing you know, we were living in Coventry for a while. Donald was working nights, at the *Dunlop*, or somewhere like that, and he agreed to let me have one bedroom. But I couldn't use the kitchen during the day. You can describe it as 'the worst existence that I can remember!' He charged me £2 a week, for the facilities we were getting. His mortgage repayment was only £6 a month, so I was paying for his house!

Then I got a job at Poole Meadow, which is a big Bus Station, working for a bus company there, called Godiva Coaches. Driving coaches was a piece of cake, because when I'd been in the army, I'd driven tanks, and various kinds of cars. I did the job for about two years. One excursion I did was a fishing trip. It was an old-fashioned charabanc that I was driving. I got on the old Maudslay bus, which was the factory one, to take people to work, who lived in Malvern, and then I'd wait for them and take them back. I suddenly had a phone call while I was there, to say that Hazel had gone to hospital to have the baby. I brought my passengers back, and then I went to the hospital. But she was in there for three days. When the baby was born he had to go into a special ward, because he had Spina Bifida, which is a break in the spine, brought about because Hazel hadn't been eating the proper food. Sadly, Hazel's father had been very abusive to her, right from the start of her pregnancy. Anyway, the baby died six weeks later. I can see it now. He was buried in a little white coffin, in a Coventry churchyard. Hazel was an absolute and total wreck!

So after that experience, the first thing I wanted to do was to get as much money together as I could. Hazel got a job in Coventry for about six months too. We got all the money together then I went back to Birmingham and saw her father. He said all was forgiven, so we went back to live with him for a bit. The woman who had been living with him moved out; Hazel went to work.

I started buying old cars, doing them up, and selling them. They were all Morris Series Es – I'd buy about six or seven. Once I'd sold one, I'd buy the next one. I also worked down the market, selling stockings. Then I finished up getting a car place in Washwood Heath, at the front of a butcher's shop. There was a passageway up the side with room for about twenty cars. So I went into business with our Frankie. We called it *F & E Motors*, because Frankie, was my partner. I'd mend the cars, rub them down and spray them. Then I'd mark them up and we'd put them on the front, for sale.

We started to go to car sales; down by where the racetrack used to be, at Bromford Bridge. I decided to finance them, through a company that I set up, called *Fewtrell Finance*. In order to arrange this, I went to a finance company. They gave me the forms and agreed to be my finance company. I gave them the deposits and put between fifteen to twenty cars on finance from myself. When I sold them I paid them off, so that was another way of borrowing money. We carried on like that for quite some time and became very successful. I finished up with six or seven places. At one stage, I think we had around a hundred cars. Although we had our own finance company, we found that times were hard, motor workers were on short time, so quite a few of the cars came back.

Our Frankie often went to a club in the afternoon called the *El Sombrero*. It was a coffee bar, with a tiny club at the top called the *Key Club*. I complained to him: "You keep going to Don's club. I'm doing all the work. You'd better stay here and help me." However, I decided to close the car place on one particular day; it was on the Alum Rock Road, Washwood Heath, at the very beginning, in the shopping area.

We went up to Don Carless's club, near where *The Dome* is. There was a girl behind the bar, who was Don Carless's girlfriend. She was serving, half naked! I said to Frankie: "I can understand what you kept coming up here for, now!" It was obvious that what was going on at the club was illegal. So I said: "How do they get away with it?" Frankie said: "I don't know – but they don't get touched!" Mark Smith worked there from when he was fifteen. He'll be telling you more about the naked girl… in the next chapter!

Ronnie Frost, a good friend of mine, owned a bar at the top of Snow Hill, called *The Jungle*. He phoned me up, because he'd got some trouble, relating to a car that he'd bought. Flo Frost worked there - we mentioned her earlier in the chapter. I'd known her for years. When I got up there, with my brothers, Frostie was there with two or three guys. They'd been there about an hour, but nothing was resolved – they were just laughing and hanging about. I said: "Come on Ronnie – let's get this sorted. I can't sit here all day. I'm busy!" Ronnie said: "Well, I think it's alright now." I said: "Well, ask them." This fella turned round and said: "What's the matter with you Wack?" He was from Manchester. I said: "There's nothing the matter with me at all. Have you come to sort him out, or not?" Because that's the way I was. I wasn't scared of anybody! The fella said; "Well, what has it got to do with you?" I said: "He's a friend of mine and we have come to make sure that nothing happens to him."

They said that they wanted Ronnie to return the car. I explained that he hadn't got it – he'd sold it. He said: "Well, can you deal with a shooter?" I said: "Yes, I've got one in my pocket" – which I had – a Lambretta. I'd got it for dealing with people like the Kray twins, and Joe the Greek. Then I punched the geyser, knocked him spark out, and took the gun off him. I shot the gun in the air – and everybody ran out! The only people left standing there were me, Frostie and our Frankie…everybody else had gone!

About five minutes later, who should come in but Wilf Floyd, a cop car bloke, a friend of mine, who was later to become a regular customer at the *Bermuda Club*. I sorted it out with Wilf, Frostie thanked me and I said: "Lock the place up."

Phyllis recalls: "I had dad living with me here, at Yerbury Close too, after mom died. He was a charmer. He was – how can I put it? You couldn't help but like him. He'd come home with his one eye closed. That's when I knew he'd had a lot to drink! He used to call me his little peacock; it was his nickname for me. He always used to call me that when he was drunk! I used to get on very well with him."

Bill remembers: "George was a brilliant salesman – without a doubt! He used to go out and buy and sell all sorts of things. He was a rogue. He used to go out; enjoy a drink; come home of a night time. Sometimes George would have no money at all, but other times he'd come back with a huge wad of notes…and you never knew where he had the money from! He had a helluva lot of money off Edward. When the lads went out of a night-time, they used to put a pound note around the outside of a wad of newspaper, to make it look as if they'd got more money. And they'd only got two halfpennies for a penny! This was before they *had* come into the money.

"I met George when I first met Phyllis – about 1950," continues Bill. "Johnny Fewtrell was Best Man at our wedding. He was Best Man at Eddie and Hazel's wedding too. Edward gave Phyllis away – at our wedding." "I've got a photo of Eddie, taken that day," adds Phyllis. "If you saw it, you'd think it was Daniel!"

Chapter Four

BERMUDA TRIANGLE – (EDDIE, FRANK AND KURT)

In the late 1950s there are few clubs in Birmingham other than working men's clubs. Following a fatal stabbing at the Victory Café in Navigation Street, in 1957, Eddie buys the premises and converts it into the Bermuda Club, arguably one of the first nightclubs of any real significance in Birmingham. Alan Manning is the licensee. After returning from Jersey, Bomber lives in a flat above the club; Alan Manning and Cynthia have one of the other rooms.

Eddie, Frank, Kurt and Alan, visit Monte Carlo, return with equipment and open a casino at the club, entered via a secret trap-door in the loft! The highly lucrative Gaming Room holds sixty people. Hazel wins a car from a rich Persian. Police raids: 'Ticker Jeff'; Lord Dane Thynne – (no police raids whilst he was on premises). The Krays pay Eddie a visit. According to Bomber, Eddie eventually sold the club in 1961, when it became the Capri Club.

By this time I fancied owning my own club. I heard about a place called the *Victory Café*, which was a coffee bar. All the young kids used to go in coffee bars, but at this time a young lad had actually been stabbed to death in the *Victory Café*. It was a one-off, because at that time you'd never hear of anyone in Birmingham being stabbed or killed – not like today! Anyway the lad died and I went along a couple of months later, because the place was for lease; it was ruined as a coffee bar, after the stabbing. So I bought it for about £2,000. I took the lease and did it all out. A friend of mine, Don Giles' father was a builder. I was a bit of a builder myself – we did it between us. It was called the *Bermuda Club*. All of the walls were plastered and made in bubbles called 'Freshtext'. We built a small dance-floor, and put in one Gents toilet and two Ladies toilets.

Mark Smith was award-winning cocktail bar manager at the *Albany Hotel* and later the licensee of the Navigation Inn, at Wootton Wawen, near Stratford-upon-Avon, for many years. He was a young lad of fifteen at this time, working at the *Key Club*, in the Horsefair, which was at the back of the *El Sombrero* right by the new club that I was about to open. We are grateful to Mark for taking time to help us with the book, when he came over recently from Tenerife, where he now lives.

Mark recalls: "I helped with the bottling up and the glasses; besides various other things, such as serving coffees. That was around 1958. I was born in 1943, so I was only about fifteen at the time. I met all of Eddie's family. Eddie used to come into the *Key Club* with his father and his three brothers – Frank, Roger – otherwise known as 'Bomber', and Chris. Roger and Chris were quite young at that time. I also met Eddie's father once or twice: not very often. They used to arrive about nine or ten o'clock at night, then stay on until about midnight or so."

Another of my brothers, Gordon, was also in there a lot too; usually with Philip Thomas, who was the brother of Vera Fewtrell, Frankie's wife.

"They were all very lively personalities," continues Mark. "You could see even then that they would do well, because they had the personality and the knowledge. The five brothers were full of confidence. We used to play all the Peggy Lee songs, on the big LPs. I don't remember it, but my brother reckons that Christine Keeler and another girl, (we can't remember if it was Mandy Rice-Davies or not) were always sitting at the bar there every night, before they went to London.

"There were some nice girls about too. There was a girl named Carol, who became quite well known later. I can't remember her surname, but I saw a picture of her in the paper, at a later point. I think she may have been the girlfriend of Don Carless or Rodney Hearne. She went on to do some modelling or something like that."

Her name was Carol Mayner. You may remember from a previous chapter, that my brother Frank used to go to the *Key Club*; Carol was the one who served him – topless! Years later, Don Carless got severely burned in a fire at his flat and sadly, died two years afterwards. Rodney Hearne, his business partner, lived in Spain for several years, but he eventually returned to the UK, where he sadly died too, some time after Don Carless.

Mark continues: "When I first started at the *El Sombrero* I was doing the coffees: two or three hundred a night – they were Espresso Coffees. We served them in glass cups with saucers to match. There was a downstairs room, where they had all the Espresso machines – I could do about six at once, with all the frothy milk! They were about a shilling a time. I was very young and naïve: in those days when you were fifteen, you really *were* fifteen! Not like nowadays. At weekends, there were long queues of people, waiting to come in.

"Then they opened a club up some stairs at the back, called the *Key Club*. It was only very small: probably twice the size of this room. It was just one big room. There was a bar as you went in, on the right. You'd only have about twenty customers at any one time. My main job was to stand at the door and let people in. They were mainly 'Townies' – a lot of car dealers. Edward was a car dealer in those days – he built up a series of car pitches across Birmingham.

"It was a locked door at the *Key Club*, because you had to be careful who you were letting in. Unfortunately, I let the police in and it was raided. I felt terrible but they never held it against me. Don didn't tell me off, because he said if they were going to raid us, they would have done it eventually – even without my help. They would have smashed the door down, if I hadn't let them in. The club was owned by Don Carless and Malcolm Hearne. Malcolm later ran a pub in Harborne, for many years.

"I went into the RAF. Between the ages of eighteen and twenty I quite often came home on leave, and they let me into Eddie's *Bermuda* night club. I went and said hello to people I used to know, from the old *El Sombrero* and the *Key Club*. If it was Chris Fewtrell on the door, who worked for Eddie a lot, he would let me in and I'd have a chat," Mark concludes.

I had a guy called Geoffrey Allen, who was an accountant. He was also an MP, but he left Birmingham, to live in Alicante. I rang him on the phone and said: "Can you get yourself over here and sort me out a way of getting a two o'clock licence, for the *Bermuda Club*?" So Geoffrey worked out what I'd got to do for this new club I was planning. He explained that I should form a committee of non-members, and get a Music Licence. We went to court and got all the licences. The only trouble was that we'd got to close at ten o'clock.

Don Giles' father was a builder. Don himself was a big, fat local lad; he had plenty of 'bounce' on him, but was not what you'd call a villain or a fighter. He thought he was a villain, but he was more like a little jelly baby really! I got his father to come down, to build bars and toilets and so forth, in the new club.

The *Bermuda Club* became the first nightclub in Birmingham. We opened it in 1958, having worked on it for some months previously. It had an absolutely solid door at the entrance, with a grille in it, so that you could talk through it to the prospective customers, outside. We had a system of flashing lights and a bell, to warn staff and customers, if a raid was about to take place. Leading from that main door was a passageway, which was only wide enough for two people to come down. A few yards down the passageway there was a second door, to act as another buffer, if we had unwanted visitors.

We added low lights and we put some juke boxes in there. We put in feed-in meters, all around the club, which took two shilling pieces – the equivalent of ten pence today. Everywhere around the club, people were choosing tunes; consequently, the music was playing all the time. That was before DJs came on the scene, so the boxes were continually taking money. Of course, they'd be dancing and playing all their favourite tunes. All you'd have to do was just keep all of the records on the box – it was a *Wurlitzer*. We'd open in the morning, at about ten o'clock and we'd also get all the afternoon trade, which consisted of businessmen – commercial travellers, bookmakers, crooks – all kinds. You never saw such a mixture in your life!

Frank and I were usually at the front door, with a third guy on the second door. So I was responsible for checking who came in. If by any chance we got done, they couldn't get through the next door, because the lights would all be flashing, then the drinks would be thrown on the floor. The rule was that customers had to be caught with a drink in their hand, not simply a glass. The thing was that everyone was instructed to throw the glass behind the bar… at that point a record would automatically come on – *Onward Christian Soldiers*. However, most of the time, the majority of our clients were either police, businessmen, bookkeepers, crooks, burglars – you name it – they were there! There was a fella there called 'Ticker Jeff' – he had that many watches on him, you could hear him ticking!

The *Bermuda Club* was my sister Phyllis' favourite club. "They were all 'Townies' in there… all 'wide boys'. We used to have a lovely time in there," recalls her husband, Billy Wheeler.

Ted Morris grew up in Towyn, North Wales. As a member of the Royal Army Medical Corps he saw action during the war in France and Belgium, including Dunkirk. He was later imprisoned in a German prisoner-of-war camp, for six months. When the war ended he joined the police force, on 21 April 1946, at Nechells. He became a sergeant at Selly Oak, was promoted to Inspector, then moved to Steelhouse Lane in 1960, shortly before I sold the *Bermuda Club*.

Ted recalls: "The *Bermuda Club*, in Navigation Street, was situated on a site close to what is now the NCP car park. I used to patrol the area. There was a police pillar on the corner of Navigation Street. Eddie would come out of his club and have a chat with me. The subject of our conversation was usually "How am I doing?" I used to say, "There's no complaints, but there's nothing I can do about it. You're illegal, so you'll be done!" He wanted to know when he was likely to be raided, but even I didn't know that. It was under such tight security. We did it on the Sunday, which is most unusual!

"Around Christmas 1960 Eddie said: 'Is your boot open?' I thought: 'My word – he's keen on security here!' I said: 'Yes, I should think it's open.' As I got home, I could feel a clink. I opened the boot and there was a crate of booze in there: whisky, Scotch; you mention it – it was in there. I showed it to the wife, Ivy. She said: 'You can't afford this, take it back.' I said: 'Well, I've had it given me. It's a bit embarrassing!' Anyhow, it was disposed of, very gratefully. However, at no time did Eddie Fewtrell ask me to go beyond my duty … and I never did. I didn't mind having the odd drink with anybody, but no way would I compromise myself.

"There was a Sunday Parade at Steelhouse Lane," continues Ted. "Chief Inspector Brannigan asked us all to '… hang back the Watch.' We used to parade about twenty men. On this occasion he said, 'You don't parade. We're staying here and we're going to raid a club.' That was the first I knew about it. The idea was we went down there. I went with big John Seddon; he was an ordinary constable – a smashing bloke. He was over six foot. He'd got a policewoman with him. They were to knock on the front door, with their macks on, and ask for admission. Their uniforms were underneath their macks. If they were refused, I was to break down the side door. There were probably about twenty of us altogether. I hit the side door with my shoulder. The following week I went on holiday. My shoulder was aching. At first I wondered why, but then I realised that it must have been when I broke the door down. When I landed on the floor, after breaking the door down, there was a big pair of police boots in front of me! Big John had come in through the front door; he'd actually gained access.

"We went down into the main lounge and everybody was there, with their drinks in front of them. Half of them knew me, from my exploits. They kept saying: 'Are you going to have a drink with us Ted?' I said: 'Is that your drink in front of you sir? – thank you.'"

As it turned out, I went to court following that raid and was simply fined £10. When the police came, the first person they'd get was me. Often they'd give me a good beating, because a couple or so of the police, (not all of them), at that time, used unnecessary force; they were usually the big ones. This one big policeman got me and gave me a right bashing and threw me in the Black Maria outside! They'd be saying: "Where's The Chairman? Where's the Secretary?" I'd call out: "I'm in here!" They didn't realise that they'd thrown me – the Secretary – into the van! They'd think that I was just the doorman. Then they'd take me back inside and say: "Mr. Fewtrell, please get this club in order." Inspectors Law and Donaldson were two high-ranking guys. They'd see the state of me and say: 'How did you get like that?' I'd say: 'That big guy did it to me.' Then they'd take him to one side and more or less give him a 'telling-off' – by way of an apology. They'd ask me to go round the club with them, because they needed my help. They didn't want a riot on their hands – which could easily have broken out, under those circumstances. During these types of raids, I'd be beaten up every time. I was raided about six or seven times.

So I went round the club with them. The lights were still off to begin with so it was pitch-black. There were two bookmaker brothers there, the Nixon brothers, who were twins – Stanley and Mick. All of a sudden you'd hear one of their wives say: "Oh officer – take your hands off me!" It was funny really, because we'd put some lights on, then everyone we came to would be asked: "What were you drinking?"... "I wasn't drinking."

We'd be there from ten o'clock in the morning, all day 'til 6pm when we'd close for an hour or two, if we could. I'd go back home for an hour then back to open again at 7pm. We'd only close for an hour if we could get rid of the people in there. Sometimes we couldn't so we just kept going. There was my brother, Frank, myself; Frank was my partner. We also had a fella called Alan Manning. He was to be the licensee and the manager. Another guy, called Barry Bartlett, used to sleep there, do all the bars, the cleaning and everything else.

We carried on like this for quite some time, until I decided that we would have a Casino upstairs. I had a friend called Kurt Pressburger, a big Jewish guy – *very* large. A real character he was – he really used to make me laugh! He was a tailor, who made suits for all of the people in the town. I understand that Kurt is also featured in *Auf Wiedersehen Pat* – the third book in the Pat Roach Trilogy, written by Pat Roach and my co-writer, Shirley Thompson.

So Frank stayed to look after the club, while me, Kurt and Alan Manning went to France – to the Casino there. We stayed in a hotel there and went to a nightclub that evening. Kurt would normally never drink, but when he *did* have one he used to go absolutely barmy! We sat there with a bottle of champagne in the middle of the table and six glasses on a tray. The girls kept coming up and saying: "Can I help you?" And we'd say: "Not just yet thank you." So we'd order two or three beers and the girls said: "Would you like to sit with us?" Kurt said: "Yes – sit down there!" The next thing you know, Kurt's saying: "What would you like to drink?" He'd had a few drinks himself by this time.

The girls said: "Yes, we'd like some champagne." That was the key of course. I said: "Kurt, you'd better find out how much the champagne is." He said: "Ah – it will be the same as in England!" I said: "Well, you'd better find out!" Anyway, the champagne cost £60, which was an absolute fortune in those days. So we opened it. Then they'd bring another one and another one. Kurt was talking absolute rubbish by this time and we were getting nowhere, so we asked for the bill, which came to about £350 – and he went absolutely ballistic! You could see that we could be in real trouble in this club, so I said: "Kurt, pay the bill." Anyway, he paid the bill, by credit card, but he never stopped going mad about it. He came into the hotel and all the shoes were outside the rooms. So like a big schoolboy, he got hold of everyone's shoes, from outside their rooms and threw them down the lift-shaft!

When we got to the room, there was one big bed and one settee. I got on the settee and Alan and Kurt go in this big bed. As Kurt got in, because he was so big, he bounced Alan Manning straight out of the bed, and onto the floor… and the bed broke! The next night we went back to the Casino and started watching how they ran it. There was a croupier there from Manchester and I said: "Would you teach us how to play this game?" It was *Roulette* and *Chemin de fer*. That's all we wanted to know because we already knew how to play *Brag*, *Pontoon* and games like that. We watched them night after night, for about three nights, and they taught us too, in their less-busy moments. They also told us where we could get the cloths and the wheels from. So we purchased a big Roulette Wheel, and cloths, 'shoes', cards and everything that we needed, and brought them back with us to Birmingham.

We then got somebody to make us a table. I think it was Don Giles' father. We also had a large Roulette table and a Card Table. I did out the upstairs floor of the *Bermuda Club* and put a little bar in there. It was a lovely room, with a cloakroom to one side and a tiny bar. So we now had a Gaming Room that would hold between fifty to sixty people. It was very quiet and cosy. We had background music playing, on a very low volume. The only trouble was, everybody tried to get up there, just to drink – which we didn't want.

We made Alan Manning the croupier. Originally, on the first night, we said that he could keep his tips, but we took thousands of pounds in there. Every time there was a £100 bet, we'd take 100 shillings. So it made us the equivalent of £5. We put that down the hole. Then every time the person won a thousand pounds, or whatever the amount happened to be, he would give a £20 or £30 tip to Alan Manning. During the course of the night he could make as much as £1000 in tips – so we changed that arrangement immediately – on the first night!

There was also all this money going into the box, down the slot, in the middle of the table; it was *unbelievable* – the amount that was going into it. Kurt was into a percentage of the Table, because he was getting all the big Jewish players to come there and take them away from the Roulette Wheel in the *Jewish Club* They'd all got big shops in the town – the big *Henry's* store and places like that.

There was another guy who used to come there – the wealthy motor dealer, Jack Evans, who owned all of the big motor places, like *Bristol Street Motors*. All those kinds of guys were playing. They would play for thousands. I'd have to be there, to keep plenty of money available, for cashing cheques, to keep money on the table. You could take cheques off people like Jack Evans, but in most cases we preferred to use cash, so that people couldn't stop the cheque the next day, making you thousands out. So it had to be on a strictly cash basis, with the exception of one or two people. We would play there for possibly two of three days and nights, until eventually, all the money would finish up going down the table. I always remembered where the money was. Of course, we had to keep changing the croupier: sometimes I'd take over the job for a bit. My brother Frank was a croupier as well. That's the way we went on. The Gaming became more profitable than the club, and I had to be up there all the time. Consequently, I never had any time, because I was working seven days and nights – sometimes 24 hours a day! The club was going on downstairs as well – Frank was running that. The Casino took us over completely.

Me and Frank would go to a place called *Saint James's*, which was a bar in the city centre, in New Street. Downstairs was called *Saint Jimmy's* and there used to be a nice restaurant and bar. It was a place to be seen. We'd go down there at night – take girls for meals there – in our bachelor days.

One night, Hazel won a Sunbeam Alpine car, because a lot of the students in there were wealthy Persians, who had absolute fortunes. They would gamble and if they had a car, they would sell it to me, with the key and titles. My wife was there, because she used to love playing cards, especially *Chemin de Fer*. She won thousands, she was obsessed with that particular game, always wanting to play – and me too. I played all the time because I used to take the Bank. A lot of people used to pass on the Bank, but I used to take it and go for it!

That went on for ages and ages, until eventually we got raided and all the police would come in and smash the door down. You'd get some nice policemen too. You'd have to walk round with them, and they'd ask the customers what they'd been drinking. But all of the customers were instructed to throw their drinks behind the bar, if we were raided. We'd sound an alarm if we were being raided. The police had about three strong doors to get through. Most of the time they couldn't get through the first door; it was in a very narrow passageway, so they'd usually be wedged and blocked.

The bells would be going off. When they finally got in they'd say: "What were you drinking?" They'd say: "I wasn't drinking anything." The police would say: "Well, why are you here then?" The customers would say: "We enjoy singing hymns!" One of my customers was the headmaster of a City of Birmingham College. The police asked what he was drinking. He said: "That's awfully nice of you. I'll have a large whisky!" He was the only one who had a drink in his hand so they nicked him! When they asked for names it was always Mr. Bloggs or Smith – or something like that.

There was one character who I used to call 'Ticker Jeff', because he sold contraband watches. When he stood by you, you could hear all of these watches going 'tick-tock, tick-tock.' It was like having a great big alarm clock next to you! When the police asked him what he'd been drinking he'd take the mickey, because it was so ridiculous. The lights would go out and Jeff would have all the girls going: "Oh officer, don't touch me there, you naughty man!" People used to be absolutely annoyed, if they missed a raid!

This happened two or three times. I'd go to court, as Club Secretary. It was funny really. I'd stand there and some of the magistrates would be customers, who used to come in the club. So they'd say: "You'll be fined £10 Mr. Fewtrell. Don't do it again!"

Harry Faber would ask me: "How did you know you'd be fined £10?" I'd say: "Because he was in the club last night. Most of the people here were!"

At one time there was a Lord Dane Thynne, who was actually planning one of the first armoured cars. He said to me: "You'll never get raided while I'm here, because the Chief Constable knows that I'm here and he assures me that he knows all about it and nothing will come of it." Strange as it may seem, nothing *did* come of that particular raid when he was in the club, because the authorities didn't want his name in the papers! They told me that they weren't going to proceed with the case.

Eventually, I decided that I'd had enough with the police. Just before that, somebody said to me, at the club one night: "Are you Eddie Fewtrell?" I said: "Yes." He said: "Do you own this nightclub?" I said: "Yes, I do." He said: "I want to introduce you to some very important people." I said: "Well, just a minute," because I was serving behind the bar, running for change for the Casino, and generally very busy. He said: "Come here – now!" I said: "Just a minute, I've got to do the door now, because I'm short-staffed." He said: "Well, these people won't be kept waiting." So I went to the door, and said: "I'm very sorry about that, but I'm very busy at the moment." They said: "These are two very important people from London – they're brothers. I suppose you've heard of them?" I said: "No, what's their name?" He said: "The Kray Brothers." But I *hadn't* heard of them. He introduced me to the two Krays. They said: "Who looks after you down here?" I said: "How do you mean. Who looks after me?" They said: "If there's any trouble." I said: "Well, I've got seven brothers and loads of friends, so I don't need anyone to look after me." The guy said to me: "Here, do you know who you're talking to?" I said: "I don't give a s**t. I don't need no-one to look after me!" At that I walked away.

So I was carrying on being busy, but about two or three nights later, I had five people come in. One of them was from the Meat Market; another was a doorman at the *Castaways*. Unfortunately, I'm not in a position to name them. You could see that they were trouble: they were looking at me and they kept saying: "You need some protection."

Anyway, about a week went by; meanwhile I was getting phone calls all the time. So I went to see this top policeman. I knew loads of policemen. I got on well with them actually. I explained what had happened and they said: "Yeah, we know all about it."

This top policeman confirmed that the Krays were using these fellas down the Meat Market, to put pressure on people. He warned me that the villains we were dealing with now had a long history of GBH. They were total maniacs – one of them had cut someone's head off – and that I would have to be very careful. It didn't worry me too much because I was twenty-six and quite fit. The only one of my brothers who wasn't fit was Frank. I made a statement to the police and asked them what to do now. They said: "Protect yourself. Now that you've explained it to us, don't worry about injuring them. Protect yourself as much as possible."

I went back home. My wife Hazel was very worried about it, because I was getting threatening phone calls. So I changed all of the phone numbers, and made them ex-directory – no one had my new phone numbers.

When I was in the club one night I looked around and they were all there. There was a guy called 'Taffy'. He said: "Don't be silly guys," in my defence, without realising the seriousness of the situation. They started to attack me, so I just backed off. I didn't know what to do for a minute, because it was all happening very quickly, but luckily I was sober. So I was backing off and the four of them were coming at me with coshes and all sorts of weapons. Taffy was a nice lad and he said: "Now just a minute," but they turned on him and slashed his throat! I jumped on a table, picked up a pint pot, and as the one came at me, I hit him on the top of the head, as hard as I could. Anyway, he went down and his head was split open. He dropped to the floor. Then the other three came at me and I did the same with them. I hit the four of them on the head and they all dropped like flies.

Then two of them ran out, which left two remaining, and the other guy – on the floor. Within minutes, the police were there – they must have been watching. An ambulance arrived and a policeman was there – a very nice guy and a good friend of mine. He later died of gangrene of the legs. He was only an ordinary police driver, but a nicer guy you couldn't wish to meet. He finished up marrying one of my barmaids.

Anyway, this policeman got the ambulance there and they took two of my assailants to hospital. Then the policeman came back and said: "Do you see all the excrement on the floor? That's because he was nearly dead – you almost killed him. But don't worry about it. We've collected all of their tools. They were coming to kill you. So you got out of that really well – well done!" But this Welsh guy who'd just said: "Pack it in mate," was in a very bad way. He had so many stitches in his neck. He was *very* lucky to survive. They were all massive men.

I don't know why but none of us was charged – not even my attackers. I saw this high-ranking policeman again about it and he said: "You did well." Anyway, it was all over the town. The villains were saying that all of the Fewtrells attacked them, but the truth was that it was just me, totally on my own, against the four of them. Alan Manning suggested that he should go, because perhaps they wouldn't attack me, if I was on my own. So nobody helped me, except this Welsh fella, who was just a customer – and it nearly cost him his life!

So that was the start of a problem that the police thought was associated with the Krays. I've never told this to anybody before, although it got around that I'd fought the Kray's henchmen in the club. After that I decided to move out of the *Bermuda Club*, it wasn't big enough, and to move away from the centre of town. We were too close to all the pubs at that time, so we were getting all of the drunken nuisances.

My brother, John remembers: "My father was in the *Bermuda Club*. I was in the Gents with him and he said to me: 'Where's our Gordon?' I said: 'I don't know – but I know where Johnny is.' He said: 'Where is he?' I said: 'I'm here – you silly old bugger!' He turned round and said: 'Well give us a score then' – which was twenty quid. He did the same with Eddie, but I think he asked him for fifty.

"When he opened a Casino at the *Bermuda*, he hired a carpenter to custom-make a unique roulette table with two wheels; there was a hole in the middle – we used to stand in the middle – it was massive! He had it in the *Cedar* after, you know? – because I used to manage that," explains John.

Gordon remembers: "Little Kenny Baker used to be in the *Bermuda* too. How on earth he used to hold his glass of beer I'll never know! He got so drunk, that at the end of the evening I used to help him find his mini; it had blocks on the pedals. I'd pick him up, put him under my arm, and walk up and down the street, until we found it. In those days, driving whilst drunk wasn't too much of an issue," explains Gordon.

There was another customer who was the Headmaster of the *Bluecoat School* in Edgbaston. He was a bit of a drunk. The policeman asked him what he'd been drinking. He said: "Oh – that's alright – I'll have a large brandy please!" They'd laugh at that, then we'd go round the whole club, and everyone would deny having a drink.

Eventually, they'd take all the money out of the till, and out of the gaming machines. So we learnt that from now on, we'd keep no money in the tills and the machines would need to be emptied every five minutes. So there'd hardly be any money for them to take. They took all the booze and said that I should wait to hear from them.

This Chief officer said: "The law is the law. You have to obey it, so I can't help you. That's the way things are." Next door to me was a bookmaker. I got talking to the guy and asked how come he didn't get raided? He said: "Well, you've got to pay, haven't you?" So I said: "Who do you pay?" He said: "You pay the Guv'nor."

About four months after that I got a message that I was going to be raided that night, at five past two, so I was able to hide all of the cash. There were undercover police there in the bar when you got raided, so they witnessed the fact that the barmaid had been serving drinks before the raid; there was no point therefore in denying it, because they'd be testifying against you in court. I could recognise them, because there'd always be four of them together, in two couples: two policemen and two policewomen in total – but it was rather obvious! You were expecting them… and what their people failed to realise was that I knew all of my customers personally – that's why I let them in. So when a different group came, it was obvious what was happening! You'd say: "Good evening officers!" They'd reply: "Oh hello!" Then all of a sudden we were being raided, at five minutes past two, the lights would flash, crash, bang wallop! There'd only be a little bit of money in the till, hardly any booze or customers in, because we'd say: "No, not tonight lads," to everyone that we knew.

The one night, we were waiting for the raid and I said to one of my guys: "You'll find the Black Maria parked out by the warehouse" – because they'd always park it in the same place, at the back of *El Sombrero*, which Mark Smith was talking about earlier in the chapter. When we found it, the engine was running, so we put matchsticks in the tyres, let them down, then drove off. I came back, opened the club again and started drinking. So we were all having a good time, and about an hour later they came. They told me that apparently, they'd had a puncture – otherwise they'd have been there earlier, so we'd got away with an hour's extra trading you see?

We only did that once. I only got raided three more times after that – and then it stopped. It couldn't have stopped automatically, before that; otherwise it would have been too obvious! It took a year to put all of the people in place. All in all I was raided about six times. Harry Faber said: "You can't keep going on like this. You've been to court seven times, in twelve months." I said: "I think you're right. It's time to leave."

Chapter Five

TOM JONES AND THE CEDAR SET

In his lifetime, Eddie has staged many cabarets, but take your seats now ladies and gentlemen, for the most extensive cabaret ever seen! So put on your dinner jackets and your designer dresses; settle back and enjoy a truly unique show, with Eddie as MC. You'll need some stamina though, because it lasts over fifty years!

Well over sixty people, including additional family members, friends, colleagues and performers, are about to join members of Eddie's family, to entertain you, until our story is done. A wide range of comedians, some of whom became good friends, will take centre stage in Chapter Ten.

You'll discover how Eddie converted a tumbledown factory on Constitution Hill, into his first substantial nightclub, the Cedar Club: fitted out with cedar wood – hence the name.

Bomber confirms that it opened in late 1962. Eddie begins to supplement his income as a rather doubtful driving instructor, while Hazel works in an insurance office. The Cedar, the first of its kind in Birmingham, develops into an intimate and highly successful club.

Former barmaids Frances Sinclair and Patti Bell remember what it was like to work there. Val Bevan adds her memories to theirs, in the next chapter, together with her husband, Bev. Tom Jones and the Squires play there regularly; the Walker Brothers, Lulu, Stevie Wonder, The Move… the list is endless. We've gathered enough material to write an entire book about the Cedar Club alone, but we must be content with just a selection, in this chapter and the next, because there are so many other things to tell you!

I wanted a more up-market image and more space, so in 1961 I sold the *Bermuda Club* to a motor dealer, for £4,000, which was a lot of money in those days. Although half of the money went to my brother, Frank, as we were partners, he decided not to invest his £2,000 in the new club, because his wife, Vera, didn't want him to. So I gave him the money, even though I needed it, to build the *Cedar Club*. Frank said he was sorry, but I was left to go it alone and try to find the money.

I looked around for a place, which I eventually called *Club Cedar*. It was in Constitution Hill. When I first looked at it, it was the biggest tumbledown factory that you ever saw, but I told the Jewish guy who owned it, "I'll have it!" He was so pleased to get it off his hands. We did a deal and I took on the remainder of the lease, which was about forty-odd years.

I contacted my accountant, Geoffrey Allen once again, saying: "Look Geoffrey, I've got the offer of a new place. There's a new law that just came out, in 1960, whereby if I put music on for dancing I can have a special licence, up to two o'clock in the morning. Look it up and find a way round it." About three weeks later he said: "I've got it." He was the first one to analyse the legal part of the 'Two o'clock Licence', otherwise known as an Entertainment Licence. Geoffrey was a very clever man. He got me all the documents and we went to a solicitor. I used a firm called *Edge & Ellison*. Nobody understood about the licensing laws at that stage. I was the only one who understood them, because my man designed them – he found a loophole.

We went to court and I was granted the first Two o'clock Licence in Birmingham, by the Licensing Committee. It meant that we could work after 10pm on a Special Hours Certificate, provided that we had live dancing, live groups, a DJ and a restaurant. We also had to charge on the door. The entertainment part was the band. Some police officers tried to rule, over the years, that a band wasn't entertainment; they even took me to court on this issue, but I went in front of a High Court Judge and won the case. It made a tremendous difference because it allowed me to employ stars like Tom Jones, Shirley Bassey and so forth – I had them all on, in the course of time. Having been granted the licence, I built the new club, the *Cedar Club*, employing a man called Stanley Kay.

I demolished all of the buildings on the existing site and replaced them with a one-storey building in the yard. Stanley Kay was a nice guy, although I found out later that he wasn't really a builder, he was just a rough roofer, but he knew a little bit about building. I agreed to pay him a good wage, and also make him a licensee, because I needed someone with no history of club raids or court appearances.

George Gardner and a couple of his blokes eventually rescued the situation and built the *Cedar Club* in no time at all. Stanley Kay had put the roof up, but with no 'fall' on it, consequently, we had nothing but trouble all of the days of the *Cedar Club*, with water coming in through the roof. Eventually, I got George Gardner to put a new roof on top of the existing roof, with a big 'fall' on it, so that cured the problem.

While I was building it, I had visitors: former police Inspector Ted Morris, patrolling up Constitution Hill, stopped for a chat about the club and Alan Wyant, my army friend, came across me, on a stroll from town, to the Jewellery Quarter, up Constitution Hill, then helped me with some of the building.

I spent a fortune on the club, and then the great day arrived in late 1962. We had the Lord Mayor of Birmingham and all of the dignitaries there for the opening, all the planning people and the Licensing Authorities. I was shaking hands with all of the celebrities. All of a sudden, this tramp pushed through the door – and ran straight in. We got him out and gave him a few quid; all he wanted was some money and then he was gone like a shot again. What nobody except Roger and I realised, was that the 'tramp' was my brother, Kenny... how about that for timing!

Laurie Hornsby, formerly a Handsworth lad, born 1st May, 1948, is a successful, singer-songwriter, musical historian of Brum, and writer of such musicals as *Wallop Mrs. Cox*.

I'm going to ask Laurie to set the scene for us, because our cabaret is about to start... the stage is yours Laurie.

"I had cause to take the bus into the town centre, as a schoolboy. I'd take particular notice as the bus neared the stop where the *Cedar Club* was situated," Laurie recalls. "The bus went down Livery Street, up to Snow Hill Station, then down to Constitution Hill. I used to travel the 'Golden Mile', which was from the bottom of Constitution Hill, up to the Soho Road. Coming home from town on the bus, from school every day, the bus would come up Constitution Hill. The *Penthouse* opened in 1966, so I wouldn't see that in my schooldays, but the bus would certainly go past the *Cedar Club*. Being only fourteen years of age I'd never ventured through the doors, but it looked such a wonderful place to go! The *Penthouse* was over the top of Tony Green's *Surfside Stop* – facing *Yardley's Music Shop* – which was there at the time, on the corner of Summer Lane; a hundred yards up from there was the *Cedar Club*.

"As you went up Constitution Hill the *Cedar Club* was on the right-hand side, on the corner of Bond Street, just south of the Canning Factory, where they made all the brushes. As you went past the George Canning factory, and on to Great Hampton Row, on the left you'd see Kenyon Street. On the right was a little club called the *Marmoset Club*, which I'm sure Eddie remembers – God knows what went on behind those doors! It was just before you got to the *Church* pub. The *Ridgeway Georgian* opened shortly before the *Cedar Club* – round about 1960. It used to have this big canopy on the front, and neon lights on the walls. I think they had Strip Shows there. That was on the corner of Soho Avenue, on the main Soho Hill, as it was; they *may* have had dancing girls too. Just down the hill you'd get the traffic lights, where Villa Road came on to Soho Hill. Over on the right-hand side was *Tito's Club*, which Bunter (David) Broadhurst had opened, but I believe that Johnny Prescott fronted it; I think they traded on Johnny's name, but it was Bunter's club. The Broadhursts were a scrap metal family. Bunter died unfortunately.

"The first time I went to the *Cedar Club* was 1966, when I was venturing out. I was eighteen," continues Laurie. "I went down with the Jack Woolf brigade for the first time. As I walked through the door *This Old Heart of Mine*, by the Isley Brothers was playing. And it stayed with me because it seemed as though every time I went into the *Cedar Club* after, that *This Old Heart of Mine* would be playing. I was quite a regular, especially with the Reuben crowd. It was as if the disc jockey was waiting for me to come through the door!

"The first lad you'd see would be Ted – 'Ready Steady Teddy' – because he would wait for innocent-looking kids. The beer was a bottle of Export. He used to cadge drinks. He had the speech ready: 'Our mom said: "Can you get us an Export?"' That's how he used to introduce himself. He used to wear the scruffiest evening suit that you've ever seen; you know – with all the ash down the front. Ted did a Tom Jones impersonation; anybody less like Tom Jones would be difficult to imagine!

"In the late 1960s, I played at the *Cedar Club* with *Varsity Rag*. We were a Wolverhampton group, but we'd have been booked through the Astra Agency. We did a couple of nights there, on different occasions. In the 1970s the *Cedar* was the place to go on a Sunday night. I don't know whether they used to open up illegally, because most places were closed on a Sunday night, at that time. Certainly the *Dolce Vita* used to close at midnight on a Sunday night. Everybody went to the *Cedar*; we used to get 'hammered'! It was great for everything. Good social 'craic' – an Irish word, pronounced 'crack'. If you were lonely-hearted you could meet a girl there. There used to be twice as many girls there as men – a situation deliberately encouraged by Eddie!"

Thank you Laurie. Don't forget, ladies and gentlemen, while I was building the *Cedar*, and then getting if off the ground, Hazel was working in an insurance office, so she was bringing money into the home. She was a good lady, Hazel – a very hard worker. She helped me *immensely*, in the early days. I also had a Mini car, which I used to give people driving lessons. So while I was building the club I'd have to shoot off to give lessons, which cost £1 an hour in those days. Having opened the *Cedar Club*, and left the *Bermuda Club* behind me, different people would still come in, trying it on again. But the club was run so tightly, if they spoke with a London accent, they couldn't get in.

I first met Tom Jones in the *Cedar Club*, around 1965. I used to pay him £15 a night – he was *Tom Jones & the Squires*. Meanwhile, Tom had come up with this new song, *It's Not Unusual*. He played it the first night and people went wild – he was absolutely unbelievable! Tom asked me if I could do anything to help him promote the song, so I got hold of Colin Berlin and Barry Taylor, who had an agency in London. I'd done a lot of business with them. I had a guy called John Tully, who used to run my agency for me, called *Fewtrell, Tully and Associates*. John would be there with his secretary. All day long he'd be booking different acts and contacting fans, talking to agents and so on, for my clubs. He was also selling them all over the country.

Tom played at the *Cedar Club* almost every week. The *Squires* were a great backing group. There was absolutely the most *unbelievable* atmosphere that you've ever seen in your life! Everybody was happy, there was plenty of money and the place was the best place ever. People still say that today – it was the best club ever – never any trouble or anything.

I sent Barry and Colin a recording of *It's Not Unusual*. I got them on the phone and said: "This record is absolutely fantastic – it's definitely going to be a Number One." Barry said: "I'll take it, but will you put my wife on at your club?" So I did, but I got Tom to sign a contract saying that he'd perform at my club every week, for twelve months – whatever happened he'd do my dates – one a week.

Everybody at the *Castaways* knew that Tom was going to be on at my place afterwards, so some of the audience would follow him down to my club after: it was spread by word-of-mouth. We were absolutely packed out. So for those twelve months, no matter where he was performing, Tom would drive all the way back to Birmingham, to honour his agreement with me.

He came back to Birmingham quite often – although I can't give you the precise details why. But whenever he was in Birmingham, he *loved* to come to the *Cedar Club*. I used to go to Vegas, to see him perform there, and he'd also come to the *NEC*, in Birmingham. When I was in the audience, he'd invite me to come up on stage with him. I'd say: "No way will you get me coming up on stage with you!" He was a very good friend and he still is today. Later on, when he was playing in Vegas, he used to make me welcome there, get me into hotels, and do everything for me. He introduced me to every star there was in Las Vegas. He treated me like a king. He was a good man – and his son Chris too, who was his manager.

My longstanding friend and right-hand man, Kenny Hatton, first met Jimmy Tarbuck when Jimmy was a Redcoat, at Butlins: "I met him when I was a hairdresser at Butlins Holiday Camp, in Pwllheli, during the early 1960s," recalls Kenny. "Ringo Starr was also playing there, with Rory Storm. Ringo was a drummer in Rory Storm's band. We worked for one season, which was about six months. Then I left, went back home to Birmingham and stayed there for a while. After that I went to Jersey, where I met 'Bomber' – Roger Fewtrell. I stayed in Jersey for six months. Roger left, to go to Birmingham, because Eddie had just opened the *Cedar Club*, so this was around 1962.

"I returned to Birmingham and got a job with Len Fowler, who died recently. *Len's Pitch* was originally in Monument Road. The *Cedar Club* was the only real nightclub in Birmingham at that time, so we started to go there. I met Edward at his club and because we knew Roger, he came to *Len's Pitch* for a haircut, which brought all the other brothers over too. Edward used to park his red E-Type outside. So those years at the *Cedar Club* were great years for me. I think I was about twenty or twenty-one at that time and remained single until I was thirty-four. There was also the *Elbow Room*, with Don Carless and Tony Carr and the *Rum Runner*.

"During the six months that I spent in Jersey, the *Beatles* and Jimmy Tarbuck started to become very popular and then Ringo joined the *Beatles*.

Myself and another fella from the *Cedar Club* visited Jimmy at the *London Palladium*. He was the compere. Jimmy invited me to the *Coventry Theatre*, where he was appearing with Frankie Vaughan. He then asked me if I'd be his Road Manager and I said that I'd love to," continues Kenny. "We travelled all over the world together over the next eight years."

Mark Smith, from the previous chapter, had left the RAF and was working at the *Grand Hotel*: "I was twenty years old then, so that was 1963. I worked in the *American Bar* there, as a trainee barman: I learned how to make all of the cocktails. I used to see Edward occasionally, around the town. The *Cedar Club* was open by that time and I'd go in there quite often. I loved the atmosphere: he always had a nice crowd of people. I lived in West Bromwich, so it was on my way home."

The group, *Things to Come*, came to work for me around 1969. All three of the group will be helping us recall those days. Their drummer, Chris Lewthwaite begins: "I was our negotiator. Although we'd played at other clubs in the suburbs, the first club I went to in town was the *Cedar Club*. They happened to be looking for somebody to fill the Tuesday to Friday slots. Don Fewtrell explained that what they *didn't* want was a live, electric band, blasting the walls down; he wanted a group that would play more quietly in the background. So we fitted the bill. Don said we could do Tuesday to Friday – and away we went. Don's favourite number was *Spanish Eyes*: he often asked us to play that. I don't remember much about Chrissie. We probably only met Eddie five or six times, but it was obvious that he was a man that you didn't cross! We mainly negotiated through Don.

"I was a bit older than the other lads. We modelled ourselves quite closely on the jazz group *The Peddlers* – a semi-jazz, semi-rock trio, who played quite intricate music. We liked that style of music and it suited Les's voice as well. So we did quite well. We were asked to do just general records. We didn't do the weekends of course. They used to have a feature band there on a Saturday might. Sunday night was good, because we weren't working, so we could 'jam' it: get on stage with each other; we had a lot of fun. There were a lot of talented musicians jamming there, including Russ Abbot, who had that superb band called the *Black Abbots*, with a wonderful lead singer, who could pitch higher than Paul McCartney.

"Down the inside of the club was a dining area; the bar was in the middle. I'd be up on a sort of raised platform, at the back of the stage, with the drums. Every month to six weeks or so, they used to have a special meeting in the restaurant at the back, which was at the side of the bar. They would draw the curtains across and we were told to play very quiet stuff for the next hour or so. Normally it was where customers would have basket meals – you know – soup-in-a-basket!

"You saw the very dignitaries arrive. There would be Eddie, Don, and the Chief of Police. The other guy was Greek and I was told that he was the Head of the Mafia in the Birmingham or Midlands area. So we were well aware that these things were taking place, although we obviously didn't know exactly what it was. But there was certainly a good strong association between Clubland and the police, which kept everything peaceful.

"There was a push button, which rang a bell in the reception area. Being raised up, I could see fights starting and things like that. If I saw a fight starting, I pressed the button and warned them in reception. People wondered how the doormen got there so quickly! This was in the days before the Licensing Laws were more strict, so anyone could run a Casino if they wanted to. Eddie had a roulette wheel and a Black Jack table. While I was playing the roulette wheel, I'd occasionally be there with a stocky Greek gentleman. Let's just say that I became aware that he was wearing a gun holster! We managed to play a whole string of night clubs around Birmingham in the course of time."

Les Hemming continues the story: "The *Wellington Kitch Band* had just finished their long-standing residency at the *Cedar*. They gave us a try and that led to a residency that lasted just under a year; we did a couple of sets a night. The DJ there had a funny arm, poor guy. He used to open up his set every night with the Norman Greenbaum song, *Spirit in the Sky*. It was his opening signature tune, and he also finished off with it.

"The musicians in our band were Chris Lewthwaite on drums, Roger Shropshall, who also had a recording studio in Balsall Heath; he was known as 'Bone', because he was a long, lanky type and looked like he needed a good meal! He played the Hammond Organ, quite well. I sang, and played bass guitar. We had a guitarist-singer named Steve Evans, a very handsome guy; he looked great and had a great voice, but he would be the first to admit that he wasn't the greatest of guitarists!

"Eddie had a mystical aura about him, inasmuch as he was often front of house; big 'Meet-and-Greet', big welcome; lots of energy, lots of dashing, good-looking guys. He was immaculate looking – a dedicated follower of fashion – to quote the *Kinks* straight off! Endearing and greatly-loved – couldn't have been a better nightclub owner. So that created a magical mystique, which became part of the character of the *Cedar Club* and the other clubs that he owned… and the Fewtrell Family and their legend.

"We were on until midnight; the DJ finished at 2am. Then certain people were invited to carry on beyond that. The popular legend used to be that the *Cedar Club* really opened when it closed! There was an incident when we were performing our first set of the evening, on stage at the *Cedar*. From the stage, which was set quite high up, you could look right through the club, to the front door, where Eddie would be standing – front of house. You can find out what happened next, in Chapter Thirteen.

"It used to be the habit for up-and-coming artistes, who are now national and international household names to frequent the *Cedar* – Tony Iommi, Bev Bevan, Jeff Lynne. All of these guys went on to become great stars, so we were quite in awe of them. I'm still quite friendly with a few of them, to this day. Tony Iommi started *Black Sabbath*. Ever the opportunist, Eddie would find out who was appearing at the *Night Out* and persuade them to do a late night turn at the *Cedar Club*."

They didn't need much persuasion, as I knew them so well!

"The likes of the *Black Abbots* and Tom Jones performed there," continues Les. "Bob Monkhouse took the stage once. Russ Abbot, of course, went on to have his own show. Eddie even had quirky little shows like the *Morgan James Duo*, who some people may remember. They were brilliant; they would plug in to our gear. We didn't mind too much, because we could have a break and, I suppose, see how it *should* have been done!

"Although he wasn't the tallest man in the world, Eddie seemed to collect around him a harem, if you like, of beautiful women, whom he had persuaded to come to the club; at least half of them were as tall as we were! They were very glamorous, beautiful women; very sophisticated," remembers Les.

"These were the Rock n' Roll days and there was no better place to be than in the *Cedar Club*. That's where it was happening, as far as we were concerned. There were various legends that would come up, about how if you ever crossed the Fewtrells you could finish up as part of the fabric of a motorway stanchion, on the M1. There was no foundation for believing this

– it was just put around – it was all part of the mystique. But that absolutely terrified us, so we really were very good people indeed, when we were working there!"

Roger Shropshall, the group's keyboard player's first love was Rock n' Roll. "The first record that really interested me was *Whiter Shade of Pale*. After I'd heard that, which completely knocked me out, I was able to buy the same instrument that they used on that, which was a Hammond organ. I joined a band that was later known as *Chicago Hush*, in the summer of 1967. I stayed with them for about a year. We were a Psychedelic band: we all wore flowered suits, which I suppose looked rather ridiculous!

"Then we joined the Reagan Circuit. Mrs. Reagan was an Irish ballroom owner. She owned the *Ritz* in Kings Heath, the *Handsworth Plaza* and the *Old Hill Plaza* in Rowley Regis. They were cinemas; the buildings are still there – probably occupied by Bingo Halls and Indian Restaurants. We played with some well known bands at those venues, including Long John Baldry. Elton John actually played my Hammond organ, although I didn't know his name at the time.

"Eddie was at a different level," continues Roger, "but his brother Don, God-bless-him, seemed to be very insecure, because Eddie was very successful and Don wasn't."

What had actually happened was that I'd improved Don's lifestyle, by taking him out of the factory; moving him to Birmingham, to be in charge of a club, on a very high salary.

"Chris and Les were gambling mad," continues Roger. "They'd sometimes lose a lot more than their wages! I think we were paid forty quid each week, for the whole band. The stage wasn't particularly big. It would be probably half the size of this room. I'd be on one side, on the Hammond organ. Chris, with his drum kit, was raised up, right in front of me, and our bass was close by, so I'd only be able to hear what I was actually playing. If you wanted to do a *deal*, the *Cedar* was the place to go. There was the back room; the restaurant area and so on; it was quiet there – you could talk, but you wouldn't argue with any of the doormen – some of them looked as if they would be able to dismember you with their hands!

"With the Fewtrells you'd got Eddie who was a professional: he'd got the style and the panache – the sharpness; whereas, to me, Don seemed a bit like the school bully. After the *Cedar Club* we moved on to the *Can-Can*. Chris was very good at getting us gigs, which meant that we didn't need to get a manager. Eventually I formed *www.cheapstrings.co.uk*. We've got about ten thousand customers, on the Internet. So that's my future now, and I've been doing that since 1983," Roger concludes.

Alan Wyant remembers: "I first worked at the *Cedar*, doing the coats job and collecting glasses. Eddie then employed me as a waiter. I probably got to know Larry Farrington through Eddie. We knew Teddy before the *Cedar* opened. Eventually I took over the running of the restaurant, as a manager. Sometimes they asked me to go into the Casino, which was at the front of the club, by the Reception, to be a croupier. They'd call me in to settle disputes. It was probably because I was the only one of the staff who understood gambling; the rules, and the various card games.

"Chrissie and Bomber were doing the card dealing, but they didn't really understand the rules that well, so I'd be called in as a mediator. Eddie said: 'This is ridiculous – you'd better go and work in there.' So I was a croupier for a while. During the evening I sometimes worked in the restaurant to begin with. Then when the Casino opened, around eleven or twelve o'clock, I'd work in there. When I worked on the door I was very handy because I knew all of the customers by then. He also knew that I wasn't much of a drinker, so he could rely on me to be sober."

Gordon explains: "I was usually on the Roulette Table, rather than dealing cards, but I'd start the Brag and Poker games off, and then leave Bomber and Chrissie to manage them."

"Harold Wilson brought in the Gambling Commission, to license gambling," continues Alan, "but most of the Birmingham clubs weren't awarded licences. Only three clubs were – the *Midland Wheel*, the *Rainbow* and the *Rum Runner*. I was working at the *Cedar* by 1963, because that was the year of the Great Train Robbery. There was a Cockney fella, called 'Little Johnny Hart', who used to come in. He was in business, round the back of Dale End. He had a warehouse-cum-shop. As he was from the London area we used to tease him, saying that we reckoned he was one of the Great Train robbers!

"I saw Tom Jones at the *Cedar Club* twice. I think Eddie only paid him £15. But Tom put on a fantastic night. The club had its own atmosphere. Even the people who appeared there seemed to just soak it up. Tom was one of them. Instead of just doing three-quarters-of-an-hour, which he was booked to do, he was on all night. You just couldn't get him off. He was having a better time than the customers!

"Eddie became great friends with a lot of the entertainers, like Tom, Russ Abbot, Jimmy Tarbuck and Tommy Steele. If they were appearing at shows around the Birmingham area, he'd invite them back for parties afterwards. I remember Pat Roach too. He was always a good customer – pleasant and jovial; a nice fella. You were always glad to see him when he was in there.

"In the earlier days, when the Krays were still only well known in London, I was in the restaurant. Eddie came up to me and said: 'Look after these five fellas. They're the Krays.' Well, that meant nothing to me. I seated them, asked them what they wanted and they all had steak, which cost fifteen shillings in old money. The twins must have been Ronnie and Reggie. Their older brother was also there, and two hangers-on. I served them. They were just like ordinary customers! I brought them the bill at the end of the night. They all gave me a pound each and said keep the change – which was absolutely fantastic! But to me they were just five ordinary fellas from London.

"Stephanie and her sister were barmaids at the *Cedar*. She was a lovely girl – she fancied Chrissie far more than me. But she and her sister were killed. Her sister had only been there a couple of weeks. Stephanie had been there a while. They left the *Cedar* with Pete, who was one of the waiters. He drove up Constitution Hill in Peter's car; he was dropping them off home. Just up from Constitution Hill, he was turning right at the island. Coming the other way was a fella nicknamed 'Ray the Duck' – which meant that he was Irish. God knows what speed he was doing, but he was driving a Jag, with another fella, who I think was called Michael. Anyway, they hit Peter's car, sideways on. Peter only had a Hillman Imp. His car rolled and killed all three of them. The story made front page news. It happened around 1966. Such was the impact that the Imp ended up just twenty-five yards from the *Cedar Club*. Another tragic accident involved Mavis, who was the love of Bomber's life. Bomber was going with her in the *Cedar* days."

Bomber explains: "Mavis Taylor was a singer with the *Colin Hume Orchestra*. She was driving to Nottingham, on 17 May 1967, to record a *Come Dancing* programme, with the band. She pulled out to overtake another vehicle, when a lorry hit her, full-on; she was killed – outright. She was only twenty-six. Her passenger, another musician in the band, survived the accident."

"Stevie Wonder is my big 'claim-to-fame'," continues Alan Wyant, "because I cut his meat up for him! He was known as 'Little Stevie Wonder' then, because he was only a young kid in the sixties. He played the *Cedar* and came in the restaurant. I served him to a steak. He was sitting on his own, so he said: 'Would you mind cutting my steak up for me?' So I always joke with people: 'That's my big claim-to-fame!'

"I was at the *Cedar Club* until 1968. There were no till receipts at the bar in those days, but Eddie was always far more suspicious if the takings were higher than the receipts showed. He was less suspicious if the till had less money in. So he must have had some way of checking.

"Marianne Faithful appeared at the *Cedar Club*, but she wasn't the right person to appear at the *Cedar*. When Eddie booked Dakota Staton, he didn't actually know much about her. I was able to explain to him: 'She's only about the third best jazz singer in the world!' Dakota was booked for the week and she was fantastic! When she was on there, you could hear a pin drop! She did about an hour.

"Little Kenny Baker came to the *Cedar* a lot. They used to pick Kenny up and stand him on the bar! Tony Britton the actor came in one night. He was a really nice fella. I believe you can tell a lot about a person's personality by the way he treats a waiter. Harry H. Corbett came in one night too. What surprised me about him is that he was nowhere near as tall as he looks on the telly. He looks tall because that Wilfred Brambell must have been a very tiny bloke.

Alan continues: "The *Small Faces* were a recording group, in the 1960s. You know how crafty Eddie is – he's a bit of a 'boyo'! I think we all know that. The *Small Faces* had played at a gig somewhere in Birmingham. All the groups had heard of the *Cedar*, so when they'd finished their own gig, that's where they'd make their way to, as customers. Eddie brought the *Small Faces* into the restaurant where I was and said: 'Give them all a steak.' After they'd all finished their meal Eddie said: 'While you're here lads, how about playing for us?' So he got the show for the price of eight or nine steaks – that's Eddie all over! I met Eddie's two sisters, Phyllis and Violet: they came in the *Cedar*, very occasionally. One of them was married to a fella called Bill.

"I went to Gordon's wedding. I didn't actually go to the service, because they had the Reception at the *Cedar*. I was laying the tables and getting everything ready." Gordon recalls that Steve Gibbons and the *Uglys* played at the Reception.

Eddie, c. 1948, with three of the four younger brothers whom he helped to care for. John, who is three years younger than Eddie, is not in the picture. By kind permission of Gordon Fewtrell.

Fewtrell Family Party, includes, L-R: Eddie, Gordon, Mrs. Cartmale – (Eddie's gran), Johnny Fewtrell and Norman Field. By kind permission of Rebecca Fewtrell.

I

Donald Fewtrell's wedding reception, at the Stork Public House, end of Lozells Road, Birmingham, early 1950s. Photo includes, seated on the far left, Agnes Fewtrell (mother), Frankie Fewtrell, and Gordon, with his back to the camera. By kind permission of Gordon Fewtrell.

"Was it something I said guys?!" Frankie and Eddie, doing their best to bury Gordon in Bournemouth sand. Paul, Frankie's son, is in the lower left-hand corner. By kind permission of Rebecca Fewtrell.

Eddie and Hazel, opposite the Hall of Memory, on their wedding day, 20 June, 1956. Hazel made her own wedding outfit. The American Buick, in the background, was owned and chauffeur-driven for the day, by Eddie's friend, Alan Fowler. By kind permission of Rebecca Fewtrell.

Eddie and Hazel's wedding, from L-R: Johnny, Frankie, George (father) and Eddie. The couple were married at Broad Street Registry Office, close to where this photograph was taken. Johnny was Eddie's Best Man and vice versa. By kind permission of Rebecca Fewtrell.

The wedding group includes, to the right of Hazel: Johnny, George, 'Lottie Pot', Vera, Frankie and Beryl Hindley, one of Hazel's two sisters. Her other sister is to the left of Eddie. By kind permission of Rebecca Fewtrell.

Johnny Fewtrell's wedding to Joyce Mucklow, at Quinton Church, 1960. Eddie was his Best Man. Hazel and Eddie are either side of the bride and groom. Two of Phyllis' daughters are the other bridesmaids: Pat is on the far left and Val is on the far right. By kind permission of Rebecca Fewtrell.

Val Garrington's wedding (Phyllis' daughter). L-R, back row: George, Phyllis, Billy Wheeler (Phyllis' second husband). Front row: Val, and Billy's mom. By kind permission of Phyllis Wheeler.

Paulette, on her wedding day, with George Fewtrell to her left and Rebecca as bridesmaid, c. 1966. Paulette was Chrissie Fewtrell's first wife. By kind permission of Daniel Fewtrell.

Left: Hazel and Eddie in Brighton, with animal friends. The parrot messed up Eddie's jacket! By kind permission of Daniel Fewtrell. Right: Frankie and Vera Fewtrell. Sadly, Frankie died suddenly, at the age of thirty-eight. He and Eddie were joint owners of the Bermuda Club, in Navigation Street, their first nightclub.

Vera and Frank's two sons, Mark and Paul. Mark died when he was a young boy, but Paul is a very successful businessman, based in Bangkok, with offices as far afield as Japan. By kind permission of Rebecca Fewtrell.

Eddie, Hazel and Becky, on the steps of the Victoria Law Courts, Birmingham city centre. By kind permission of Rebecca Fewtrell.

Hazel and Becky descend from the aeroplane, at the start of a holiday in Majorca, Easter 1969. Guess who's carrying the bags! By kind permission of Rebecca Fewtrell.

Birthday party for Becky, appropriately enough, at Rebecca's Nightclub. *Her friend is dressed as Little Bo Peep. On the right is Brenda Humphreys, who was Eddie's secretary. By kind permission of Rebecca Fewtrell.*

 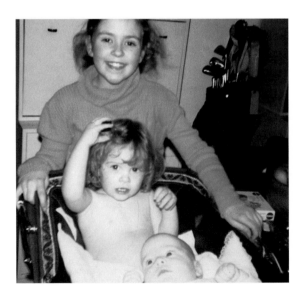

Left: Eddie with Abigail, c. 1972. Right: Eddie and Hazel's three children, Becky, Abigail and Daniel, in Eddie's 'Den' at Anstruther Road, Edgbaston c. 1972. By kind permission of Rebecca Fewtrell.

Daniel with Aston Villa Charity Shield and Cup, at Aston Villa Club. By kind permission of Rebecca Fewtrell.

John Fewtrell, with his second wife, Carrie and their children, Warren and Leona. Warren is now training to be an airline pilot, like John's older son, Matthew (by his marriage to Joyce Mucklow). Leona was married quite recently... how time flies! By kind permission of John Fewtrell.

Family Holidays – Montego Bay: Hazel, Frances Sinclair and Eddie. Frances, who now lives in Perth, Australia, was Becky's Nanny. 'Lord Lebby' was playing the steel drums that night. Over the microphone he remarked: "I see Eddie Fewtrell is in the audience!" He'd previously worked in Eddie's clubs. By kind permission of Becky Fewtrell.

Hotel Cala Blanca: Eddie, with Daniel on his lap, c. 1975. Birgitte, one of the Danish Au Pairs, Hazel and Larry Farrington. Eddie had considered buying the hotel, when it was derelict, and converting it into flats. By kind permission of Rebecca Fewtrell.

Hazel and Eddie on the beach, in Palma Nova, Majorca. By kind permission of Rebecca Fewtrell.

Eddie and Larry Farrington, in Palma Nova. By kind permission of Rebecca Fewtrell.

Daniel, Hazel, Abigail and a friend, in Los Gigantes. By kind permission of Rebecca Fewtrell.

Torremolinos, front row, L-R: Phil, a previous owner of the Elbow Room, Hazel and Eddie. Back row: L-R: Chrissie, Paulette, Vera Fewtrell and Roger – 'Bomber'. By kind permission of Rebecca Fewtrell.

Hazel and a young Abigail, with Chrissie's first wife, Paulette, explore some Italian ruins. They were chased up the steps by amorous Italians! By kind permission of Rebecca Fewtrell.

On board a San Francisco trolley bus, c. 1980, with Norman Robinson. By kind permission of Daniel Fewtrell.

Eddie doing a cabaret number, New York, New York, *with Rita Radvanyi, at Rebecca's Halloween Birthday Party, her 18th, inside the marquee. By kind permission of Rita Radvanyi.*

Eddie and Hazel, dancing at the same party. The decorative silhouettes are just one example of Hazel's artistic talent. By kind permission of Daniel Fewtrell.

We opened one part of the club to begin with. The place was heaving and I realised that the existing building wasn't going to be big enough, so I started building, the other side of the wall, making it twice as big; the roof had been finished on the other side of the yard. The *Cedar Club* was the first one to get a Gaming Licence – with a roulette wheel and everything else; nobody else had got that. Later, the law changed to say that you couldn't have gambling where there was music and dancing; it had to be separated; Harold Wilson brought that in. Legally-speaking, Hazel was the owner of our Casino, but they didn't recognise the legal rights of women then, in the way that they do today.

As we closed one night, we changed into our old clothes: George Gardner, myself, Stanley Kay, Larry Farrington and other people who I knew, were all there to take a wall out. When we came back the next day, the club was twice as big. Where the bar had been against a wall, it now became a round bar. It was the first round bar in the city. Most Birmingham pubs were still very old-fashioned, dating back to the war days. We now had a massive round bar, which was very successful, because the customers could see everyone else, all the way around the bar. Flo' Frost and Hazel were working behind the bar, and Patti Bell; Val Bevan too, who was married to Bev Bevan of *The Move* – you'll meet both of them in the next chapter. The barmaids used to make fortunes, from all of the tips. It was a fantastic club, because nobody was allowed to cause any trouble in there. I'd got about six or seven of the biggest doormen – all controlled.

Frances Sinclair phoned Shirley recently, from Perth, in Australia, where she's lived for years. At the age of twenty, she'd had to put her illegitimate baby up for adoption. She moved to Birmingham, and began working at a hairdresser, which is where she met Val Bevan. Val brought Frances to the club and introduced her to me.

"My first impression of Eddie was that he was a playboy, with a very good sense of humour!" quips Frances. "I needed to earn some money. Eddie kindly gave me a job as a barmaid. I continued to work as a hairdresser during the day. Don was running the *Cedar* most of the time, as Eddie was busy at his new club, *Rebecca's*. I loved Don very much – he was so nice to me – although I know that Val didn't like him. He used to give me a lift back to my rented room in Handsworth.

"There was a fantastic atmosphere at the club. Eddie gave me a twenty-first birthday party. He came in one night with a fat lip and said: 'I wish you girls would wash the glasses properly!' He made us laugh and always made sure that the staff had a meal.

"If the cook didn't turn up he'd say: 'Franny, would you like to go in the bloody kitchen?' I'd say: 'Yes, but I'm not doing omelettes!' I'd make steak sandwiches.

"Sometimes we'd find him parked outside the club in his red Jag, waiting to go in. He wouldn't go in on his own – because of the ghost! I remember that John had a butcher's shop in the centre of Harborne and a pub on the Lordswood Road.

"I only ever worked at the *Cedar* – none of Eddie's other clubs. Sometimes Eddie asked me to baby-sit his youngest daughter, Rebecca. I went back to Handsworth Wood, when Becky was two and stayed overnight, to look after her. I also went on holiday to Montego Bay, Jamaica, with Eddie and the family, as a Nanny for Rebecca, but I never left the hotel, because the Black Panther movement were causing trouble.

"After Jamaica I returned to England in February, with Rebecca," continues Frances. "When we got back it was sleeting. That made me realise how much I missed the warmer climate. Somebody told me about a job working as a Nanny for an American family, in Bermuda. Meanwhile, in 1966, Eddie had promoted me to Head Barmaid at the *Cedar* and I was sharing a flat with Patti Bell, in Lordswood Square. Eddie had the ideal personality for a club owner. He loved being with people, but he also seemed to accept them for what they were and to value their uniqueness. He trusted me with the most precious thing in the world – his daughter.

"I eventually emigrated to Bermuda, met my first husband there and stayed for ten years. I met Eddie again in Bermuda, when he came over for a holiday in 1970. I divorced my husband, moved to Australia and was reunited with Lance, who became my second husband; he was a deep-sea diver. We're still happily married. Lance and I had previously met in Bermuda. Eddie had an almost boyish sense of humour in those days and a very infectious giggle," remembers Frances. "In all the time I worked at the *Cedar* I never once heard him raise his voice."

By this time I had given my younger brother, Chris, a job. So my brothers, Johnny, Chrissie and Gordon were there with me. All three were very young, and to tell you the truth, they were all a problem for me, because I was frightened to ever do anything, because you could not stop them. I used to go in there and say: "You must not fight the customers; you must learn how to handle them. Only fight when it's absolutely necessary." It felt rather like being the lion tamer in a cage with the lions. However, Johnny makes the point that, in order to survive in that kind of environment, they *had* to be able to take care of themselves. We had some close calls, which you can read about in Chapter Thirteen.

I then started to promote bands, such as *The Walker Brothers*, off a guy from London called Barry Gibb. He kept asking me to put his wife on the stage, because I was promoting groups like Carl Wayne; *Danny Lane and the Diplomats*: hundreds of small groups. There were all kinds of bands.

Patti Bell was born in Bradford, but brought up in Rhyl, in Wales. During the 1960s she was working over in Jersey, with two of her friends, Angie and Penny, at the *Chateau Plaisir*, which is on the beach road – Five Mile Road; the fact that she met Angie and Penny led to her working for me at the *Cedar Club*, from 1965, and subsequently at other clubs, over the years. She became an invaluable member of my staff.

"The year before, I'd been to London for the winter and because I'd got on well with Angie and Penny they said: 'Why don't you come to Birmingham and we'll get you a job in a nightclub?' So I did, and I've lived in Birmingham ever since. The *Cedar Club* was the first Birmingham nightclub that I worked in. When I met Eddie I thought he was very friendly and very easy-going, and that I'd like the job very nicely. I'd been working in a club in Jersey. If you were good with people, Eddie didn't mind. He already knew Angie and Penny as nightclub goers.

"It was really good," continues Patti, "because you could be behind the bar, but then you could be doing other things. I remember once, this dwarf said to me: 'Do you want to dance?' The other barmaids were laughing, because in those days you couldn't really dance on your own; you always danced with somebody else. And they were saying: 'Oh, she's dancing by herself!' I don't know why that always sticks in my mind. The dwarf was Kenny Baker, who played R2D2 in *Star Wars*.

"I remember Danny King – he was really good – and some of the big stars – like Tom Jones – before he had a nose job," Patti continues. "I remember once, I was in the Back Bar: that's where some of the 'celebs' used to go. Tom Jones was there. One of his minders was causing a fuss – being really loud. Pat Roach had to take him outside. But the guy was really drunk.

I'm fairly sure that Elton John played at the *Cedar Club*. He played piano, with Long John Baldry singing. The name of the group was something like *Locomotion*. Desmond Dekka played at the *Cedar Club*. *Stray Cats* were really good.

"I liked the *Cedar Club* and *Barbarella's* more than *Rebecca's*, but I don't know why – it's weird! I don't think that I was at *Rebecca's* for as long as I was at the other clubs.

"I often felt a 'presence' in the *Cedar*, especially when I was behind the bar. I'd sometimes go in early, to clean it up. I remember being in the Back Room – you know – where I said that Tom Jones and other celebrities used to go? And I definitely felt something *touch* me, on the shoulder, like a hand. When Don Fewtrell came in and I said: 'Do you know what? Something just touched me on the back!' He said: 'Well, there's supposed to be a ghost.'

"Another time, the lights weren't on… and you know how you're supposed to be able to see cloudy shapes? I'm positive there was a ghost. But a lot of people saw it," concludes Patti.

Gordon remembers: "The fella that owned the building that the *Cedar Club* was in, Mr. Hornick, told me that it had been a leather factory. Fred the Ghost used to wear a cap and a mack. He had hung himself, during the war, by a big leather strap; either because he was having trouble with his love life, or because he'd just heard that his son had been killed. They made the straps and other leather goods at the factory, before it was transformed into a club."

It still looked like a workshop upstairs. The brickwork was in bad shape; I had to replace the cement, a section at a time, to reinforce it.

The Rolling Stones were with me one particular night. The day after, on the Sunday, I saw on the news that Brian Jones had been found, drowned in the swimming pool. Apparently, he wasn't very happy with the band, and in fact, he hadn't been playing with them at my club, the previous night. I'd noticed that he was a bit 'down'. We're getting rather morbid at the moment aren't we? … better lighten the mood!

Laurie Hornsby has already mentioned *Ready Steady Teddy*, who was absolutely *besotted* with Tom Jones. One night, he's standing up there, singing "It's Not Unusual". There was a *Hen Party*. The girls in the party were drunk, so they got up on stage and started pulling at his clothes – pretending that he *was* Tom Jones. Then all of a sudden, they started pulling his clothes off and ripping his hair! They were like maniacs – these women! I saved him, and brought him down; he stood at the side of the bar with me. I couldn't stop laughing!

My brother, Johnny, worked part-time at the *Cedar Club* for a while, because he had a butchers shop: "Eddie had this birthday and I used to cook the turkeys for them and carve them; do a bit of chefing for him. Later on I did do a bit of 'crouping' at the club; we used to earn forty quid, which was a lot of money in those days. Austin Ullah, an Indian kid I worked with down the Birmingham Bull ring, used to play at the *Cedar*. There was Pugh, from Cradley Heath Dogs. Mario from *Da Corrado* – he used to gamble there. There was a bloke there called Jack Evans – the car man. During an interview that Shirley did with him, for *Pat Roach's Birmingham*, our brother Gordon remembered winning a lot of money off Jack.

Gordon elaborates: "During that game of 'Black Jack' I won about £2,000-£3,000 off Jack Evans. He said: 'I've never known anyone so lucky,' and he gave me a fifty dollar bill. It was a long time ago, so I've probably spent it by now!"

There was a poker game with Jack, and some of the other wealthy Jewish players. I used to sit in. This particular game took us four days and four nights; Hazel was a-ringing, all the time saying that she'd booked us in for Spain! I couldn't go, because I was winning all the money. It went to the biggest pot ever! I knew I couldn't be beaten: I finally won it with a running flush of diamonds, against a group of really top players.

"I worked at the *Cedar* more or less from when it opened," continues John. "I used to do door work for Eddie, in the evening, and then I would go straight from there to the Meat Market, to open my shop. I slept under the counter, when I'd put my window on. I was about twenty-six and was married to Joyce Mucklow then. We had a son – 'Matty': short for Matthew – he's an airline captain now, a pilot. He flies Jet 2 from Leeds and Bradford. A new member of his cabin crew said to Matty: 'Oh – Fewtrell – I've heard the name Fewtrell. Do you come from Birmingham?' My son said: 'I do.' He wouldn't talk about it further; being the captain, you see? This guy wanted to know if he was Edward's son. But he said: 'No, John's my dad.'

"I worked at the *Cedar Club* for years and years. There's a photograph there, with all of us on – that's taken at the club. I remember the night that John Kennedy was shot, 22nd November, 1963. The Walker Brothers were supposed to be performing at the *Cedar Club*, but Scott Walker wouldn't go on stage, because he's been on the phone to his mom in America and sworn at her: 'What the effing hell's going on over there!' He was upset because he'd sworn at her. He did go on eventually," concludes John.

'Big Albert', aka Albert Chapman, the owner of the *Elbow Room* remembers: "When I worked at the *Plaza* in Handsworth. I'd go to the *Cedar Club* afterwards. That's where I first met Eddie. I was on the door at the *Plaza*. My first impression of him was that he was a flash bastard! I was a lot younger. When you go in you think: 'Well, that's the gaffer there.' He always had decent people around him. I didn't really get to know him at that point. But as the years went by, our friendship grew. I see his club the same as I've got my club now – the *Elbow Room*. It was that era of clubs, and I still keep the *Elbow Room*, in Aston. I've been there twenty-seven years, this April. The *Cedar Club* was a characters' club. The club game then was totally different to what it is now. There was only a certain element that used clubs, in those days: there were villains, musicians; motor traders... with sheepskin jackets and gold bracelets. Just Townie people really... that's what we used to call them.

"Everyone knew everyone. When I first went there I was a lot younger, although people thought I was over twenty-one, because I was on the door. Of course, you're in awe of a lot of these people – at that age, because you think: 'How the hell have they done that?' Then over a period of time you get to know them and you become part of the circle. I was originally a boxer. Pat Roach and I used to spar – and Ron Gray," continues Albert. "I just used to do it for fun; I was an amateur. I served my apprenticeship as a butcher."

Ron Gray, former champion boxer and a highly successful entrepreneur met me in 1963, when Johnny Prescott brought him to the *Cedar Club* and introduced us: "We used to train at the *Trees*, in Hockley," Ronnie recalls. "I'm not sure whether Johnny had a party, or whether Eddie put it on for Johnny, after one of the fights, but we all ended up at the *Cedar Club*. Of course, whatever night you went there it was just absolutely packed all the while – it was very hard to get in. It was the place where Birmingham people wanted to be – it had a terrific atmosphere.

"Everybody liked Eddie. He used to like the boxing; he began learning the sport at the age of thirteen. He always remembered you when you had a bad fight, or when somebody knocked you down... never the night that *you* knocked someone down! But we had some good times with Eddie.

"The reason that Eddie was Number One was that at every club of his, when you walked through that door, the atmosphere hit you – that's why his clubs were always full. You could have the most beautiful place, but if it doesn't have atmosphere, after the first official opening, people don't come back. Of course, my old pal Pat Roach was in the *Cedar Club* a lot; we'd have a great chat about what had been going on. Whatever night you went, there was somebody there that you knew. That's why it was so popular. In those days I wasn't one to remember bands; but it was always good music, good entertainment," observes Ronnie.

My good friend Rita Radvanyi and I met over forty years ago: "Eddie's sister-in-law, Paulette, who was married to Chrissie, worked as a beautician, with a friend of mine," recalls Rita. "Paulette invited my friend, Audrey, to go to a cabaret at the *Cedar Club*. At first I thought that was Edward's first nightclub, but then I found out that he had the *Bermuda Club* before that. We saw a great show, *Georgie Fame* it was, and Paulette introduced me to Edward and Hazel. As you'll discover in the *Cupid* chapter, I met my husband Nick at the *Cedar*. Eventually, Hazel, Edward, Nick and I became very good friends, through the children, and even spent holidays together. We had a wonderful few years."

Chapter Six

BEV, CHUCK, STEVE
AND FROGGIE

Our cabaret continues, with additional artistes, from the Cedar Club and beyond. So, ladies and gentlemen, allow me to introduce Bev and Val Bevan. They will be followed by Chuck Botfield, Steve Gibbons and Raymond Froggatt – all of them outstanding musicians. Raymond is joined by his lead guitarist – Hartley Cain. Brian Yeates, a musician-turned promoter, closes the chapter. Brian has staged the 'Brum Rocks Live' shows over the last two years, featuring Bev, Steve, Laurie Hornsby, Danny King and Trevor Burton.

As Eddie's been working overtime in our book so far, he's going to take a walk round, checking that everything's in order. Then he'll grab a seat at the bar, and enjoy a tonic water, while the aforementioned musicians entertain you; he never drinks alcohol while he's working, you see? We'll just have speech marks at the beginning and end of each musician's set, as there's no commentary from Eddie. The exception to this is where Val and Bev are in conversation and also Froggie and Hartley.

The 'Move Online' website describes Bev as: 'Co-founder and powerhouse drummer behind two of the UK's most famous and respected bands, The Move and the Electric Light Orchestra.' It also refers to 'Bev's awesome live reputation, which began in earnest in the 60s.'

His musical career began around 1959-60 when he and some school-friends formed a band at Moseley Grammar School. There was another band there already, called the Strollers, two of whom became the Fortunes, two years later. Bev and his fellow musicians experimented with a range of names for their group, changing them almost weekly, but eventually settled for 'Ronnie & the Renegades'. While still at the Grammar School they played every weekend at the 'Las Vegas Club' in Birmingham, in Summer Row, by the Ice Rink.

They were only school-kids – just literally fifteen or sixteen years old, but they'd be there a couple of nights a week, until two o'clock in the morning! The place was full of drug dealers, prostitutes, drag queens: it was horrible. But they were happy to play anywhere. So they had a taste of Birmingham nightlife, even before they left school – before they were at the 'Cedar Club'. Bev had his first set of drums at fifteen. He lived with his mother, above a toyshop and mobile library, in Sparkhill.

"The whole area has changed – unbelievably," comments Bev. "When I was there in the 1950s and 60s, it was a hundred per cent white, with a few Irish immigrants. I left Moseley Grammar School, along with Jasper Carrott and we were both best mates. Me and Jasper had a conducted tour of the school last year… on TV. It was on *Central News*. They were showing us what they'd done to it, and everything.

We both got a job at the same furniture store, which was the Beehive. Jasper stayed there for about three years, but I was only there one year. I'd already made my mind up that I wanted to be in a Rock n' Roll Band, so I was just killing time and keeping up the payments on my drum kit. The minute I had the chance to turn professional I did.

In 1963, Denny Laine asked me to form a band with him, which we called *Denny Laine and the Diplomats*. We all had platinum blond hair and wore mock black crocodile skin suits! That lasted until the end of 1964, when Denny left to form the *Moody Blues*. We carried on without him, with a couple of other lads from *Gerry Levene and the Avengers* – they joined us instead, to make up for Denny. But it never worked and the band just folded, around Christmas 64.

I had to get a job again – at Keane & Scott, as a furniture salesman. The only two places that I ever worked were the Beehive and Keane & Scott. I was working in the store when Carl Wayne came in to see me, in July 1965. *Carl Wayne and the Vikings* were about to go to Germany on one of their month-long stints.

Eddie had previously become their manager, re-christened them *Carl Wayne and the Cedar Set*; paid for their outfits and all of their musical equipment, then sent them on German tours. That was in 1965, around the time that Tom Jones' record *It's Not Unusual* was released. Eddie's been kicking himself ever since, because he turned down Tom's request to be his manager – he was already managing Carl's group and couldn't afford to do both! When I joined the group, on their very last tour of Germany, Eddie was no longer their manager because he was too busy with the other clubs.

Carl Wayne and the Vikings had been going for some time, before I joined them, but Carl and Eddie were still very close. So I did this German stint with the group, which was incredibly hard. There were no days off, but we earned thirty quid a week each, which was a fortune, because I was only earning about £9 a week, in the furniture store.

We came back in August or September 1965 – that was when *The Move* was formed. Roy Wood, Carl Wayne, Trevor Burton and Ace Kefford asked me to be the drummer in the new band. Carl had by far the best leadership qualities in the group, in a business sense, rather than a musical sense. Eddie became absolutely invaluable to us: he let us use the *Cedar Club* any day that we wanted to. He'd just give us the key and we'd open it up and go in and rehearse, every day.

Mike Alexander recently described Carl as the best male vocalist in a group that he's ever heard. He *was* magnificent. Singers, like Robert Plant for example are absolutely brilliant at what they do, but you can't imagine him singing Sinatra stuff… whereas Carl could actually sing anything. When Mike became his Musical Director Carl branched out – he was trying to change his style. He was always changing his mind about things: he was an absolute bundle of energy. When he left *The Move* he said: 'I'm going to be the next Joe Cocker – I'm going to form a Rock Band; like Rod Stewart.' But within a month I read in the papers that he had decided that he wanted to be the next Engelbert Humperdinck! – and do the cabaret scene. It's a shame that he didn't succeed; he was an incredibly talented singer.

Eddie would say to Carl: 'Show me your date sheet for this month.' There was masses of work then, in 1966 – all the pubs, clubs dance halls, ice rinks – we played them all. That's about four years after the *Cedar Club* had opened. Eddie would say: 'Whatever nights off you've got, you can play at the *Cedar Club*.'

The first show that we ever did was the 20 something of January 1966 and our first-ever gig was at the *Belfry*. It was a double-header. We did the *Belfry* and then we drove down to the Cedar *Club* and did a second spot. That's a very big day for me because that's the first time that I met Val. So the first ever night that *The Move* performed was the night that I first met Val. You'll discover more about this in Chapter Nine, entitled *Cupid*.

We were scattered all over Birmingham. I was in Sparkhill. Ace Kefford, the bass player, was in Sutton Coldfield; Carl Wayne and Roy Wood were around the Castle Bromwich area and Trevor Burton was in Aston. I was the only one from South Birmingham. The *Cedar Club* was the best nightclub that I've ever been in, because it always had a great atmosphere. We used to see it at its best and its worst. As Eddie used to give us the key, we'd go in around mid-day and open the place up. There was that awful smell from the night before: stale beer, spirits and cigarettes. Sometimes we were in before the cleaners!

There was a lot of cedar wood panelling – hence the name of the club, and a circular bar, right in the middle. It had a decent-sized stage up in the corner, although not a big one. It was quite elevated too, which you didn't always get in clubs; sometimes you had to stand on the floor in those days. So you could always see who was playing and the sound system was quite good too. I think some of the weekday nights probably weren't so good, but come the weekend the place was jammed!"

Val explains: "I was Val Taylor in those days. Tuesdays and Thursdays were always busy nights because the Townies used to meet up at the *Albany* and from there they used to come into the club; they never used to come in until about ten you see, and then it would really liven up. They always had a band playing; there were no discos of course. They had to have live music; so Tuesdays and Thursdays were very busy nights. There were all sorts of *characters* in the club. Billy Sutton was one of them. He was great. He used to do the market, with the stockings, at first. Always odd stockings, of course! He was hawking really, wasn't he? Then he went on to the flowers; he was a great character. Eddie's brothers were all 'hard-nuts': Chrissie was always fighting.

"When we were there Don was the Bar Manager," continues Val, "so the Casino must have come later. I wasn't *that* keen on Don, to be honest. He was hiring and firing like mad. I don't know whether I should say this but one of the Coventry girls who was his girlfriend worked there. If she wanted anybody sacked or 'gone', so that she could have the best position in the bar, she'd just tell Don and he'd bloody sack them! She wasn't very kind, so quite a few of the girls had to be fired. I was one of them in the end. He was firing them right left and centre: it was a shame. So I then went to work at the *Rum Runner*.

"Eddie, on the other hand, was a very kind – a very generous man. He'd always help anybody out. When I wanted a car, because I was earning quite a bit of money, from my day job and at the *Cedar Club*, he actually took me to Measham's – to choose a car, as they were coming through. I liked this Triumph Vitesse, so he bid for it, because I didn't know how to do it; he organised the finance. So he was brilliant and that's how I got my first car ever. He was always very fair," observes Val.

Bev agrees: "Eddie was the nicest of all the brothers… definitely. There's this quite famous story about the Kray twins coming down to take over – which shows that you didn't want to cross Eddie. But I'm not sure that *The Move* would have got off the ground without Eddie's help – we were always eternally grateful for that. All the rehearsals and all the gigs he gave us – just to get the band off the ground. The *Cedar Club* is by far my biggest memory of playing any of Eddie's clubs. I did play at *Barbarella's*; I think it was probably a charity night, in the 1980s. But generally speaking, it was mainly the *Cedar Club* – the *Cedar Club* and *The Move* is a hugely strong link.

After Eddie helped *The Move* to get started, Tony Secunda discovered us in 1966 and actually came to the *Cedar Club* to see us, because we were there so often. It all happened in that one year, so that by the beginning of 1967 we'd actually left the Birmingham scene completely.

We became one of the hot bands in London and switched from the *Cedar Club* to a residency at the *Marquee Club*. That was in Waldour Street in London and was *the* main club in London. *The Who*, *Cream* and Jimi Hendrix were all discovered there. Tony Secunda, our manager, secured a Thursday night residency there for us. Within six months we'd signed a major record deal and we'd had a hit record. So by January '67, exactly a year after I'd met Val at the *Cedar Club*, we'd got our first hit record – which was *Night of Fear* … our lives changed completely then.

In 1966, we were just a touring band. Then in 1967 we had big hits with *Night of Fear*, *I Can Hear the Grass Grow*; *Flowers in the Rain*. The following year we had *Fire Brigade*; *Blackberry Way* was in 1969. I don't think we ever played the *Cedar Club* again after 1966, but we still returned to the club as customers. In fact if we'd done a gig in Nottingham, or somewhere reasonably close to Birmingham, we'd go back to the *Cedar Club*. We had a lot of Jam Sessions there, when we went back.

In contrast, London was and still is the place to see and be seen. You have to go there to be seen and when you're playing at the big London clubs, you literally would see Mick Jagger, Pete Townsend, Paul McCartney, Eric Clapton et cetera, in the audience: you're not going to get that in Birmingham. Some of the London customers were other celebrities too; they wanted to check out new bands and see what the opposition was like.

Of all the groups I belonged to – there was *The Move, Black Sabbath* and *ELO* – which was by far the biggest band: we sold millions of records and played massive venues all over the world. But actually my most *enjoyable times* were with *The Move* – those very years that we've been talking about – before we'd actually made it. I think it was because 1966 was such an exciting time. We'd been in bands before – all of us – and never really been very successful. But we always knew that *The Move* was going to make it, so it was a case of waiting to see what was going to happen next.

In 1967 it was even more so, because we'd got a hit record. Suddenly you're on *Top of the Pops* and you're rubbing shoulders with people that have been heroes of yours for years; suddenly they're your contemporaries. Then you start getting another hit record; you're making your first LP. Then you're being asked to perform outside of Britain, and you start doing foreign tours. We did a major tour in '67, with Jimi Hendrix, *Pink Floyd* and *Amen Corner*: that went all over Britain and we did some other shows in Europe. That's when you know that you're really on your way and you think 'Wow!'

We performed with an orchestra, with *ELO Part II*. That was in the nineties. It wasn't a particularly successful band: it was just on the back of *ELO. ELO Part II* finished in 1999. Right now I'm back to Square one – I do mainly *Move* stuff, with *Bev Bevan's Move*; we do all the old material now. We work around Birmingham but also all over Britain and Europe too. We do the *Jam House* and we've been doing this *Brum Rocks Live*, which is Steve Gibbons, Danny King, Trevor Burton – these are all *Cedar* people. We did the tour last year and we're doing another load of gigs this year. There are ten in May. Just around the Birmingham area. It's a very good show actually. We do places like Sutton Coldfield Town Hall, Solihull Theatre, Lichfield, Tamworth, Worcester, and Redditch. We'll be doing the show next year too. In the final chapter, Shirley will be telling you about a recent *Brum Rocks Live* show, which she saw on 29 May, this year.

Bev Bevan's Jukebox has been on Saga Radio for five years – ever since Saga has been around. It ends at the end of this month – it's being taken over. It's been bought by GMG Radio and is now – Smooth Radio 105.7 FM. When we started out as schoolboys, it was Elvis, Little Richard and Ray

Charles who were our favourites; that was in the late 50s – early 60s. When we started with *Denny Laine and the Diplomats* we were big *Beatle* fans really. We were a supporting act for the *Beatles* at the *Plaza* in Old Hill, West Midlands, in 1963.

As I was the drummer in *The Move*, I didn't do very much singing: I just had this very deep voice, but I had party piece – even at the *Cedar Club*. I used to get up and do *Zing Went the Strings of my Heart*... the old *Coasters* style of doing it. The rhythm guitarist, Trevor Burton, can play drums, so he took over for a bit. So just for that one number, he'd play drums and I'd get up front and do the singing.

I plan to stay with *Bev Bevan's Move* for a few more years. I like being on the radio. I do Musical Reviews for the *Sunday Mercury* – it's all music-related. As long as I can just keep my hand in and do bits and pieces. I was in *Black Sabbath* in 1983-84 and went back in 86. Tony Iommi, one of my best mates, is off touring on the road, for a couple of months; which I'm kind of envious of, in one way, but the reality of it is that I don't want to be living in hotels. I don't mind the odd night here and there, but... the weeks and months on the road that I used to do, I'd find very difficult now.

Val carried on working at the *Cedar Club*, when she met me. "It was great for both of us," she explains, "because we were both working the same hours. I used to give Bev a lift home, so he got home a bit earlier. I lived in Great Barr, so it was quite a distance to cover between there and Sparkhill. But you never thought about it in those days because there were hardly any cars on the road; no traffic queues and when you're younger you drive everywhere, don't you? I moved to the *Rum Runner* in about 1968; afterwards, I worked at the *Ambassador's*.

"They were great days and the *Cedar Club* was definitely the best club in Birmingham – wonderful – there'll never be days like that again. It was just so fantastic. The atmosphere at the *Cedar* was very special, because it wasn't as big as the others. So you got everybody around the bar – and everybody knew everybody.

"I didn't know what I was doing when I first went to work there, but Hazel would say: 'Go on – get behind the bar!' Everybody loved Hazel; they were a great couple. Hazel was an *avid* reader. She introduced me to some of the American writers – Harold Robbins and so on. She used to pass books on to me. We didn't have time for Girlie Nights, because we were always at the *Cedar Club*, but we'd have chats together and I used to go up to her house. She lived just off Hamstead Heath, to start with; as I lived in Great Barr, it wasn't very far. I used to baby-sit for her, with her eldest daughter, Rebecca. Hazel was a great mate. Of course we drifted apart when I left the club, got married and stuff. Bev and I got married in 1970. But Hazel was smashing!"

Brian 'Chuck' Botfield is our next entertainer to take the stage. The origins of the *Rockin' Berries* go back to the late 1950s when Brian 'Chuck' Botfield, born 14 November 1943, Birmingham, and Geoff Turton, born 11 March 1944, met while attending Turves Green School, Birmingham and playing clarinet in the school band.

Laurie Hornsby explains, in *Brum Rocked On*:

'A good measure of Chuck Berry material was always guaranteed in the performances of Longbridge's *Rockin' Berries* – hence their name. They had started in 1959 as the *Bobcats* – a skiffle band at Moseley Art School, where pupils would marvel at the ability of Brian 'Chuck' Botfield. Here was a lad who could strum the chords to *Diana*, without once looking at his fingers. They spent a fair amount of 1961 and 1962 in Germany, honing their skills and singing *Along Came Jones* in ten gallon hats. During their early days they were fronted by 'Mr. Dynamite' – Blues artiste Jimmy Powell.'

Chuck explains: "In the early days most bands were a mixture of skiffle and Rock n' Roll. The reason we became the *Rockin' Berries,* was because I used to go over to the café opposite the school, to eat my lunch, because I didn't like school dinner. They had *Johnny be Good* by Chuck Berry, on the juke box there; that's what really started me playing guitar, because before I passed for Art School I was at Turves Green and I was in the orchestra. I was a clarinettist. I used to have private lessons and I was also playing with the Birmingham Youth Symphony Orchestra. I was being trained for it at the Birmingham and Midland Institute, which I hated!

My mother played the piano and my dad played the fiddle. My parents wanted me to stick with the clarinet, but I made my first guitar from a hobbies kit – it was virtually unplayable! My parents relented; we went to Woodruff's Music Store in Birmingham and they bought me a guitar. I started to play with the Skiffle Club and I'd strum along with the *Bobcats*. I'd listen to jukebox records of Buddy Holly and Chuck Berry playing the guitar, and realised that I didn't really like skiffle. When I left Moseley Art

School the *Bobcats* ceased to exist. There was a local group in West Heath called *Archimedes Deal*: I think they were named after a firm that Mark Johnson, the bass player worked for. They were looking for a lead guitarist, so I joined them and I suggested the name the *Rockin' Berries*. The original *Rockin' Berries*, after the Art School, had Christine Perfect on the piano, who became Christine McVie of *Fleetwood Mac*, because she went to Moseley Art School. She was my first pianist – which nobody really knows about, and she never mentions it. Our first gig was at the *Cofton Youth Club*, in Cofton, which is just up the road, between Longbridge and Rednal. I was an apprentice commercial artist. I mentioned to a friend who I worked with that we needed a piano; he said that his parents had got one.

We went into cabaret when we began to tour Germany; you played eight hours a night, with a fifteen-minute break. Like Bev – we had a tough time there! You played the first two sets, from 8 until 10, with hardly a break; then it would drag off at about two o'clock in the morning. For the last half hour or so it would be half empty. To entertain ourselves, if it was virtually empty, we would wear cowboy hats. But that started to pull the crowds in, so the club owners would ask us to make it a part of the act.

We began to branch out into comedy and impersonations; we found out that the Germans really liked that. So when we came back to England we continued to do that sort of thing. We did two records for Decca, and then we did a gig at the *Whisky-a-Go-Go Club* in London, where P.J. Proby saw us. We were doing *Four Seasons* stuff, which regular bands didn't do. By that time *Beatle mania* was on the go and that's really why we came back to England. We'd played with the *Beatles* in Hamburg, but two years down the line we were still working for a German agent, whereas the *Beatles* came back to England and became famous with their Album, *Love Me Do* and their Number One, *Please Please Me*.

So we thought we'd try something similar with our career. We were touring, but we'd already recorded a record for Pye, which was called *I Didn't Mean to Hurt You*. Meanwhile, we went to this party with P.J. Proby, at the *Marquee*, in London, and met an American record producer called Kim Fowley. He played us *He's in Town*. He said: 'You can have this record, but I must tell you that within three weeks, it's going to be released in this country.' We were already negotiating with Pye, so we went to their A & R guy and explained that we'd already got this record called *He's In Town*.

He said: 'That's a great record,' booked us in the studio the next day and rush released it. Within four weeks it was Number One in Scotland. The record was released in October 1964 and went to Number Three in the charts.

We followed *He's in Town* with *What in the World's Come Over You?* It tickled the charts, but proved not the wisest of choices. Both of our major hits, *He's in Town* and *Poor Man's Son*, we found for ourselves. *Poor Man's Son* made the top ten in May 1965.

We also recorded *Walk Away Renee*, which Pye Records said wasn't commercial; six months later it was Number One, by the *Four Tops*. We'd already made a similar recording to the *Four Tops*. The way we discovered it was that Terry Bond, our drummer, met a girl called Renee, when we were in Bermuda. She was from New York. We went over there and after we got back to England, she sent this record, written and recorded by the *Left Bank*, called *Walk Away Renee*. Terry played it to me and I said: 'What a great song this is.' We took it to Pye and recorded it, but they said: 'No, we don't think it's strong enough,' and they put it on the shelf!

In those days I think a lot of bands, apart from the *Stones*, were ruled by the record companies. John Schroeder liked all these 'lovey-dovey' songs, and he didn't think it was *Berries* material, as we'd 'heavied' it up a bit. Whereas if it had been released it could have altered our career. *Funny How Love Can Be* was written by Carter & Lewis. They didn't think it was commercially viable and put it on our Album. Carter & Lewis heard our version, formed the *Ivy League* and recorded it, so that was another Number One! So that was two Number Ones missed, by Pye Records.

After our hit records we were managed by Morris King, who also managed Tony Hatch and Jackie Trent and the *Walker Brother*; coincidentally, Tony and Jackie visited the *Cedar Club*. We did a charity show at the *London Palladium* and we had a number called *My Baby's Got a Transistor Radio*.

Our front man, Clive Lea, used to impersonate Norman Wisdom. So because it was a theatre, Morris suggested that we did it. Bernard Delfonte said afterwards that he didn't realise that the *Berries* entertained – he thought we were just a pop group. Kingey said: 'No, they entertain too.' So that's how we were then given a *Sunday Night At the London Palladium*. Then they booked us for a summer season in Great Yarmouth. That was our launch into Variety.

The *Rockin' Berries* really started to take off from the mid-60s onwards, around the time of the hit records. At Great Yarmouth we were second on the bill to the *Bachelors*. In May 1965, we made our debut in ATV's *Sunday Night at the London Palladium*. At the end of our stint in Bermuda, myself and Terry Bond went to New York for new material – that's where the *Walk Away Renee* story comes in. Laurie Hornsby's book contains the following comment from me:

'We had four great years after *He's in Town* and *Poor Man's Son*. No complaints from us.' In 1967 we were in Blackpool, at the North Pier, with Des O'Connor and we were honoured by being asked to do the *Royal Command Performance*. So we did that in 1967, and I've got the actual certificate that we were given. It was attended by the Queen and Prince Philip.

Although I *have* been up on the stage and played there, we never actually performed at the *Cedar* as the *Berries*, but we *were* regular customers. At the time I had a Chevrolet. One of the doormen used to take great pride in saying: 'Next time you come, just come to the door and I'll park the car!' That was one of the only clubs in Birmingham at the time.

In our heyday, during the mid 1960s onwards, the members of the group were Roy Austin on bass; Geoff Turton on guitar and keyboard; myself on lead guitar; Clive Lea who was the front man and vocalist, After Germany it changed: Clive started to go solo – he was a Billy Fury-look-alike. He won an Elvis Presley of the Midlands Competition before he joined us! When Roy left, in 1965, Bobby Thomson joined, so by the time we came to do the Palladiums, that was the band: Bobby Thomson and myself, Terry Bond on drums, Clive Lea and Geoff Turton on the lead vocals.

It was through our show business connection, having done a summer season with Jimmy Tarbuck, that we were introduced to one of Eddie's brothers, by Tarby, because Eddie liked people in show business. I knew Kenny Hatton from doing the summer season in Yarmouth. He had a dog, an Alsatian and he couldn't find anywhere to put it. I'd rented a house in Gorleston-on-Sea, number 4 Clarks Road, which became quite famous at one time. We thought it would be a good idea to have an Alsatian in the house – as security. So I put Kenny up and that's how I first met him. *Barbarella's* was the main club of Eddie's, where we performed, although we used to do *Rebecca's* as well. That's all for now, because Steve Gibbons is waiting in the 'wings.'"

"Thank you Chuck...good evening ladies and gentlemen. I grew up in Harborne and attended three of the schools there, completing my education at Station Road Senior School. The first band that I joined, as a temporary singer, was the *Dominettes*, in 1959. I was an apprentice at the time, so it wasn't as if I'd given up my day job to do it. We had two residencies with the *Dominette's*: the *California* pub in Weoley Castle, every Thursday, and the *Palace Theatre*, Redditch, which was once a fortnight.

In those days I was earning more money, from doing two or three gigs with the band, than I was with my day job. We played at venues around the city centre, including the *Sicilio Coffee Bar*, at Five Ways Island, Edgbaston around 1960-61. Also a youth club in Ladywood – at *Saint Vincent Hall* – those were two more residencies. The beauty of doing a residency was that you could leave your equipment there; it became a sort of staging post! Wherever you played around the city, you would eventually end up with a residency, which became a sort of headquarters. A member of the group would collect the money, at the door.

Musicians were a pretty friendly fraternity: they would help each other out. Another residency was the *Firebird* in Carrs Lane, which no longer exists. We started a Tuesday night residency there. There was a famous Birmingham musician and jazz player called Dan Pawson, He was there on Friday night. Trevor Emeny was another modern jazz musician.

The *Grotto Club*, in Bromsgrove Street had that look about it ... you were never quite sure whether it was legitimate or not. Next door to it was the *Black Swan* Club, which is now long demolished. You entered the *Grotto Club* via a back alleyway; there were pickaxe handles over the door! I was still playing with the *Dominettes* at that time, in the early 60s. The entrance was really seedy. It was a wooden door with a spy hole – and barbed wire around the top. It was frequented by local businessmen – from the city centre, I guess. There were lunchtime sessions and evening sessions. The entertainment was provided by strippers. We used to play our own music and we backed the strippers for their twenty-minute spot, with pop hits of the day and Evergreen Standards such as *Shadows* music, or even *September in the Rain*. There was an ante-room and a bar.

At clubs, as opposed to nightclubs, we'd approach a pub owner, explaining that we had a band and could we use the upstairs room? The arrangement, which was usually accepted by the landlord, was for us to do the door, which we would run ourselves and he would take the bar. It was a very good arrangement, because he would have a room, which normally wouldn't get many people in, but because of the burgeoning scene with Rock n' Roll in the city, anywhere where there was a band playing, you'd get a crowd of kids.

I first met Eddie at the *Cedar Club*. He rang up the agency that I was managed by – Carlton Johns; their offices were in Wake Green Road, Moseley. Eddie said: "We're looking for bands to play at the *Cedar Club*. I was with a band called the *Uglys* and he rang to book us to play there. We were the *first* band to ever play at the *Cedar Club* – and it was fantastic. It was full of late-night clientele and good-looking women! Handsome blokes, dressed in good suits: a good cross-section of the Birmingham club life community. It was very exciting and obviously a good place to play. It was also a good rendezvous, where musicians would arrive from their various 'gigs' around the city; they'd all head for the *Cedar Club*, because that was where they knew that they could get a late drink and listen to the music.

There were basically three groups of people at the *Cedar*. They tended to be made up, firstly, of the well-suited and booted kind of young guys; either successful businessmen or entrepreneurs from around the town – there were quite a few of them. There were also the more 'run-of-the-mill' kind of guys, who'd just come along out of curiosity, or to just have a few drinks, and meet the girls. The third group would be the musicians. Eddie was great with musicians. I think he realised that if you got young musicians in the place, then you'd automatically get the girls there too. It was a great combination, There was very little aggravation, apart from outside forces; people of all shapes and sizes got along together.

It's been described it as a very intimate kind of club, but that was the nature of Birmingham anyway, wasn't it? Probably not so much nowadays – but certainly in the 1960s; there was much more of a community feel about it. When you think about it, nightlife was a new thing for Birmingham people. The pubs used to close at ten o'clock; it was a very restrictive society, at the beginning of the sixties. People like Eddie Fewtrell were the pioneers of breaking down a lot of taboos.

Although Eddie wasn't au fait with Rock n' Roll himself, he'd got this charismatic, powerful persona, and was very good at networking, and helping groups to develop; so he was able to provide a setting in which people could enjoy that kind of music. So he didn't need to know that much about the musical side of it; it was just the fact that he was a really good promoter. Music promoters and managers are not necessarily good at recognising the good, bad or indifferent of musicians, but people like Eddie can spot a trend – what sells and what doesn't: that was his talent.

The *Uglys* evolved from the *Dominettes*. There had been some personnel changes, but we changed our name somewhere around 1961. The only hit that we had with the *Uglys* was a song called *Wake Up My Mind*, which I *think* was a Number One Hit in the Australian charts. I remained in the *Uglys* until 1968. This was a time when several of us were looking for a new direction. Trevor Burton left *The Move* and Keith Smart then replaced Jimmy Holden as our drummer. We decided we would pool our resources, with a fella called Tony Secunda, who was *The Move's* manager. So then Tony said that we'd got to change our name and we were wracking our brains about what to call ourselves. One of the guys came up with the name *Balls*.

The line-up in those days, when we were still calling ourselves the Uglys, consisted of Dave Morgan on the guitar; Keith Smart on drums; Richard Tandy on piano, myself and a guy called Willy Hammond, who left to join the Royal Air Force. Thirty per cent of the songs that we did were original, because I'd co-written them with Jimmy and Bob. Then there'd be some Chuck Berry, some Bob Dylan. Later we formed the *Steve Gibbons Band*, which is still in existence. We play all over the country; our next gig on Thursday is in Chester. I was always the lead singer with every group I belonged to. I've had no formal training so I tend not to think of myself in those terms of bass or tenor. I can read a chord structure, but I can't read or write music. I think that's true of most musicians of my generation. We followed the same path, if you like, though Rock n' Roll.

For *Brum Rocks Live* we're did some dates in May 2007, mainly around the Midland theatres; we're doing a third series of shows next year. Basically, it's a trip down Memory Lane, but it was instigated by the *Brum Rock* book itself, written by Laurie Hornsby, which is about Birmingham music from the 1950s to the mid 1960s; a subsequent book, *Brum Rocks On* is about the 1960s to the 70s.

I think probably what gives Birmingham its particular nature is that there were so many big firms, such as the B.S.A and Cadbury's; so that any generation of kids that left school, around ten per cent of them might go to the same firm as their father's. At one time it was known as the 'city of a thousand trades'. People used to live in the city centre. My mother attended Severn Street School, which is where *Edward's No.8* was situated. So there was a very strong community, from the city outwards. It puts me very much in mind of a village. You could be in a certain part of town and you could ascertain where someone was from by the school they went to; you would say: 'Oh, so-and-so went to that school.' So there was always a link between someone from across town – or whatever. There was that same link from the working situation, football teams, and so on.

It was great for us, as local rock musicians, to be promoted within a hospitable and familiar environment; that situation applied for a good ten years until the end of the 1960s. We'd play lots of different functions in the suburbs, but then the bubble burst and it became very difficult to function, as a band. To hold a band together professionally was extremely difficult – there just wasn't the work there.

I played at all of Eddie's clubs. I did the *Cedar Club, Rebecca's, Barbarella's* certainly. I also did *Edward's No.8* and *Boogie's. Abigail's* was a cabaret club. I never played there, although a good friend of mine used to – Slim Simons, who was Mike Alexander's drummer. Slim has passed away now; he lived quite near me. I remember him playing with Brooke Benton. The *Cedar Club* was the catalyst – the one that launched Eddie's chain of clubs.

The *Whisky-A-Go-Go Club* was by the corner of Navigation Street and Hill Street, above Chetwynds, the tailors; next door to Woodruff's the music shop, and just fifty yards from the *Bermuda Club*. The *Whisky-A-Go-Go* was a very important part of the Birmingham music scene, because you had fashion, the instruments and the gig, all within a few doors of each other. Now, over to Raymond Froggatt. It was great when you did a guest spot recently on the *Brum Rocks* show Froggie, on 5 October 2007, at Birmingham Town Hall. The Fortunes, the Rockin' Berries and Robert Plant were amongst other stars in the show."

"Cheers Steve! Ironically, it was illness that originally got me involved in the music business. When I was nineteen I caught tuberculosis. I had to go away for a while and I couldn't go back to my old job. I'd always fancied myself as a bit of a singer, so I put an advert in the paper, when I got well, in the *Birmingham Mail*. 'H' came along with a band and asked me to join them as a singer.

Hartley Cain, aka 'H,' was about fifteen or sixteen when we first met, and we've been working together ever since. It's been fantastic really. The other members of the original band have gone to other parts of the world. Louis joined the *ELO* – our bass player; our drummer went to live in Canada. Our first band was called *Monopoly*. Our motto was: "Don't play it, listen to it!" Dear boys! But the racket we kicked up in those days, you'd probably never listen to us again!

We did the kind of music that everyone else was doing. Because of our young age, we thought we were pretty cool, so we turned it up – very loud! But we went all over the world, so we must have been alright. Hartley lived in Mansfield Road, in Aston the same road as Eddie's family, when he was a boy – how about that for a coincidence?"

"I was born there in 1947," explains Hartley. "My house was at the back of a backhouse. We had no bathroom; we shared a toilet. It was a typical inner city Birmingham house. My Gran lived over the road. She still had her shelter in the garden. Our back garden backed onto Albert Road, which was the back of Eddie Fewtrell's family house. My dad mentioned the Fewtrells a couple of times, as being a big family; and the fact that you wouldn't mess with them!"

"The *Cedar Club* was a completely new experience for everybody in Birmingham," remembers Raymond, otherwise known as 'Froggie', "because there had never been anything like it. It was not just a place to drink, but a place where you could actually be *seen*. Established artistes of real quality played there; who you would normally have to go down to London to see, or up to the Northern Theatre Clubs – which were very good. So there was nothing like that in Birmingham at all – until Eddie Fewtrell.

You *do* get a following from people who come from just your town, when you're learning your trade. But, before you go out to *another* town, you'd better be pretty good at it... because *they've* got no love for you whatsoever! You might just as well be a picture on the wall. They could be totally disinterested. But if you're good at your job, every audience is the same. When they show you some compassion, or you touch their hearts in some kind of way, with your music, it's because you're good at it; if you're not, you'll never reach them.

Luckily, people warmed to me that way, quite early on. Don't forget that we never really moved out of the city, for about six years; purely because, in those days, you had to have a London agent, to sell you in different areas of the country and maybe abroad as well. The first time we left our town, we didn't just go to Leamington Spa; we went to the South of France – the French Riviera. We were still a very young band – but we were okay. I was about twenty-two at that stage; 'H' was about seventeen. 'H' has always been a lead guitarist. He'll tell you that he's hopeless, but he's actually very good. He's one of the very best guitar players in the country; one of the very few people that the American guitar players really love, as well. He's a *great* player – but he will never tell you.

We were ambitious – not for fame – but because we wanted to *go* everywhere. We went to Paris and were playing at the *Locomotive Club* there, long before anyone else. A lot of people were going to the clubs in Germany: the Rock Clubs in Hamburg, and so on. But we went for the culture – we went to Paris, Nice and Amsterdam – all those sort of places; which were great places to go to, when you're young; and *they* were Rock Clubs too. We remained rock musicians until we ran out of steam… and got too old to rock!

We didn't have much say in changing from Rock to our present style – it was the business that did that. We were with Don Arden – Sharon Osbourne's dad. Fortunately, Don liked me. I knew artistes that he didn't like, personally, but as long as he could make money out of them, that was okay. I liked Don too – I thought he was great; he was a proper show business mogul. He had no friends, but he didn't care. He was a very good music man; he'd get you in anywhere and he would spend anything on you. But you just had to respond to him and give him something that he could sell. That's all that he was interested in: having something to sell that was of interest to the market.

Performing at the *Cedar Club* was astonishing, because you were working with something other than a pub room. Most of us young bands were on the same circuit and we did places mostly like the *Elephant Lounge* – and all the pubs that there were. Chetwynds tailors – there used to be an all-night session above there, where all the bands played. People like Elton John, would come up and play with a London band, – and do those sorts of places. Roger Shropshall described an occasion when Elton John played Roger's own organ. When Elton did that, he was with a group called *Bluesology*: there were about eight of them, including Long John Baldry. Rod Stewart was singing with them. The bass player became well known later too. John Mayall, with the Blues Band, used to travel around a lot too.

What the *Cedar* also had … I don't suppose this will have occurred to anyone else… was that it was a great place for electronic sound. It was difficult to play *loud* electric music, in a lot of places; but you could play reasonably loud in the *Cedar* and it sounded nice. In many places it used to *deafen* people. Perhaps all of the wood absorbed a lot of the sound? It might have been as simple as that; and the bar was round, so the sound went straight across the bar, instead of into a wall. It was a great place. I remember Gordon Fewtrell selling his old brown Daimler to me.

Eddie had his regular customers at the *Cedar*. One was 'Ready Steady Teddy', who everyone keeps telling you about. He must be dead now. He was great! He was there every night, wearing a dickey-bow… Ready Steady lived alone. He told me once that the bailiffs came one Sunday morning, to take his cooker away, because he hadn't paid for it. He said: 'Well, you can't take it for another hour, because I've got a rice pudding in it.' They would have to wait, so that he could have something to eat!

Music publishers say to me, although I don't really know what it means, that my music 'travels'; so one of my songs could be done by a Japanese person; a South American band… or somebody classy, like Gladys Knight. We moved to America, for two or three years, around 1977-78. Don Arden called me over there – we lived in Nashville."

"But I got fed up!" interjects H. "I just didn't like America. It was 'Have a nice day!' all the time. I was glad to get home. Going back to the *Cedar Club*, beside Eddie, Johnny Prescott always used to be there."

"Well, if there was a girl involved I'm not surprised, because Johnny was one of the handsomest men that you've ever seen. When he was a kid, he was a real Paul Newman – a real film star-looking chap. Johnny was a nice guy, but a really good boxer too. There were only little scuffles like that; you get that in families, don't you? But a lot of people gathered there. Most of them were just ordinary members of the public, but amongst them all were the Townies – and they had a yard somewhere – and rings with diamonds on them, that the Rag Men had. They were all *those* sort of characters.

There was somebody for everybody. Then there were people like us and Ozzy Osbourne. Ozzy was always at the *Rum Runner*. He was courting Thelma, one of the barmaids there.

Brian Yeates is an Entertainment Consultants and Promoter. He and his son, Ashley, run *Brian Yeates Associates Ltd*. Brian started playing in a band called *Mickey Harris & the Hawks*, when he was in his teens; then they changed the name to *Mark Stuart & the Crestas*. He became Mark Stuart, the lead singer... the stage is all yours Brian!" concludes Froggie.

"We played all the main venues and that was when we started to play at the *Cedar Club*. We were playing at the *Bournbrook Hotel* when Don Fewtrell hired us," remembers Brian. "We finished at the *Bournbrook*, because in those days they closed at half ten, on the dot. We got our gear out, drove up the road and went into the *Bermuda Club*. We had a good time and so did the audience, so we were offered various dates to play. But being youngsters and having day jobs it was a bit too much for us. We couldn't do those late hours. So we didn't play there again.

The next time I met up with the Fewtrells was at the *Cedar Club*. They opened that and we played there. That was such a successful club that everyone wanted to be associated with playing there. We had quite a few dates there. The *Crestas* lasted for two or three years, then I had a break and decided to go back and form a bigger band – the *John Bull Breed*. When we had two sax players there were seven of us. I played the *Cedar Club* when I was with the *Crestas* and I also played there with the *John Bull Breed*.

I became an agent and we were a very busy office; we were booking bands, from everyone who was performing at the *Cedar Club* and at all the other clubs around. We were dealing with other agents too, and people who were booking, so we got busier and busier. Eddie and John had established their own agency, which John Tully was running, so I did a lot of business with John. A lot of the stuff that we booked in went via their office. But I used to pop into the club anyway and show my face, because you were always made very welcome.

Birmingham was growing, with the bands and the nightclub scene. We had lots of pubs, as venues for the bands. We had pop groups on at the Youth Clubs that were opening up, so it was a busy scene in Birmingham. I would think that it was a lot busier there, for the pop bands, than in London.

I think Eddie was unique. Obviously, other cities have had club owners, and in Birmingham, too, others have opened them. But no one has lasted as long as Eddie. Other people opened clubs, but as their clubs finished, *they* finished. Eddie *did* sell out, but he came back and opened another series of clubs. I've known him from those early days, right through to the present day. He has the magic formula. He knows how to make people welcome.

The clubs were right; he booked the right entertainments and he wasn't frightened to spend money, to book the big acts. Of course, the other things was, in the old days, when live touring shows used to play the *Odeon*, New Street, Eddie always made sure that someone went up there to see them, to invite them back to the club.

When we played at the *Cedar Club*, Bomber used to get up and sing with us, and several of the other bands. He had a good tenor voice. He was more of a ballad singer, rather than a Rock n' Roller. He was good enough to join a band. But of course, he was working in the clubs, so he had the option to get up and sing with bands when he liked. He was a nice guy."

Nowadays, Bomber is a Financial Advisor – a director of First Select Asia Ltd; also a Representative Ambassador for the recently-formed Fairfund Foundation – a non profit-making organisation, which protects the interests of Third World countries. He is very widely travelled. He still sings in his own clubs, over in Thailand, and visits the UK around three times a year.

"On one occasion we'd been out playing somewhere and we didn't have any money with us," continues Brian. "Eddie saw us and said: 'Are you lads not drinking?' I said: 'We haven't got any money.' So he said: 'Well, have what you want. You're playing here next week, so I'll take it out of your wages.' When we played there the following week, he paid me the full money. I said: 'We owe you for the drinks last week.' Eddie said: 'It's good of you to say that… but you can have them on me,' or words to that effect. Then again, I thought that was nice of Eddie… and I've always remembered that. We never had to worry about payment," concludes Brian. "Eddie was a pleasure to deal with. He always made me welcome… and my family."

Chapter Seven

THE OPPOSITE LOCK
AND OTHERS

Eddie's back as your MC again, recalling Birmingham Clubland and the so-called 'Competition', in company with Laurie Hornsby, Don Maclean, Les Hemming, Chris Lewthwaite, Roger Shropshall, Steve Gibbons and Froggie.

Eddie pays Martin Hone a visit, soon after Martin opens The Opposite Lock, in Gas Street, in 1966, followed later by The Factory, which became King Arthur's Court. Martin compares and contrasts his own club with Eddie's, and recalls how he and Eddie later joined forces to solve certain licensing difficulties.

"John Reeves was the owner of the *Castaways*," recalls Laurie Hornsby. "He opened this club in a warehouse, down the bottom of Bradford Street, which was an absolute 'gas'… it was like being shipwrecked! It had a sandy carpet with footprints in it, but the *Dolce Vita* killed it, because they opened up in 1968; it was the first 'chicken-in-the-basket' club, in Birmingham.

"It was an old gym and faced the *Corinthian*, at the top of Hurst Street, on the corner of the Ringway. But it was ultra ultra cabaret. They put on – more or less the same stars, the same celebrity names that John Reeves was putting on at the *Castaways*. Ted Rogers the comedian; the *Baron Knights* – those kind of middle-of-the-road acts, that everybody, at that time, would be prepared to go into the town centre and see. They ran the shows, twice-nightly, for a week. You could get a meal for half-a-crown… chicken-and-chips and so on.

"So it knocked the *Castaways* for six," continues Laurie, "because they were trying to serve a la carte. People didn't really want it; they wanted jugs of ale and a standard that was just a little bit up from the Working Mens' Club at the top of the road. The *Dolce Vita* knocked the *Castaways* out of business really."

Laurie is the ex son-in-law of Don Reuben, Dave Reuben's son. Don's daughter, Julie, was married to Laurie; sadly she died from a brain tumour. Both of the Reubens were good friends of mine, as you'll hear at other times in the book.

Laurie continues: "Dot, who had been Don Reuben's partner, before he was killed, was looking for something else in life, about a year after Don died. John Reeves closed down his *Castaways* club. There was no romantic tie between him and Dot. John had a lady, and with what money he got out of the *Castaways*, he bought a boat, down in Southampton. They sailed down to the Canary Islands, with this fella who was going to show him how to navigate; by which time John felt confident enough to navigate himself, to the West Indies: the three of them did the Columbus Run.

"When John reached the West Indies, he started these Beach Barbecue Parties in 1968/69, where he filled the boat up with Bacardi, using a car battery to fire up the record player, and the speakers. So he was doing a disco on the beach, for all the American tourists and whatever, and made a fortune! While Dot was helping him, she picked up with a multi-millionaire American hotelier, who owned one or two hotels in Florida. She married him, a couple of years later, divorced him, and out of the settlement he gave her a hotel in Florida, which she sold. She came back to England and bought one of those big London hotels, in the road where the *Royal Lancaster* is at the bottom of the Bayswater Road; it's just as you're getting into the West End. So she ended up owning one of the prestigious London hotels.

"Shirley tells me that she asked Bernard Manning if there was an equivalent of Eddie Fewtrell in Manchester – owning a chain of nightclubs, as opposed to two or three. But he said that nobody else had the flair to build them up on such a scale and with such variety. There was a fella up in Leeds, wasn't there – Peter Stringfellow? But he just had *Cinderella Rockefeller* in Leeds. Then he opened *Stringfellows* in London. So I think it's true to say that there's not actually been anyone else in the U.K. quite like Eddie, or if there is, he was definitely the first in! Ray Berrows had two: he had the *Rum Runner* and then he had *Snobs*.

"We did gigs in the pubs and clubs in the London suburbs. London's always been totally different. If you were blindfolded, then driven to London, when you took the blindfold off you'd know you were in a London pub. It's the layout and the general atmosphere: it's totally different," observes Laurie. "The same applies to the London clubs."

Steve Gibbons played at London's famous *Marquee*, in the 1960s – two or three times, as the *Uglys*: "Then I subsequently went to play there, about a dozen times, in the 70s, as the *Steve Gibbons Band*. It used to be in Wardour Street," remembers Steve, "but it eventually moved to a different location. In the 1980s, I played at other London venues. Most of the memories I've been recalling, in earlier chapters, have been about the 1950s to the 70s, but nowadays pubs can more or less present themselves as clubs. I remember the scene in London, certainly during the 80s, when I was struggling to survive. I had a hit record, just before that: *Tulane*, which was a Chuck Berry song. So during the 80s there was a thriving pub scene, which dissipated somewhat during the 1990s. *Tulane* was released in 1977, on the Polydor label, and in the USA on the MCA label. Patti mentions it, elsewhere in the book – with some of the lyrics."

Returning to Brum, Les Hemming who now runs *Hemmings Leisure*, met his first wife, Maggie, when she was a dancer at the *Cresta Club*: "I fell in love with her bottom, when she was dancing around to *Viva Bobby Joe*!"

Don Maclean enjoyed working at the *Castaways*: "I always thought that it was great. I'm amazed that it didn't last very long. There was a genre of going to clubs in those days. In that era, young people didn't go out drinking so much. They didn't go into pubs so much – that's where your dad or your uncle went; old age pensioners went there! Youngsters went to clubs – I think that's pretty relevant. The *Castaways* was a great place to work. You really felt that you'd arrived when you did cabaret there.

"I also worked the Bailey Circuit, all over the country and thought they were marvellous," Don continues, "including the *Dolce Vita*. The manageress of the *Dolce Vita* was Sheila Ismay – Dave Ismay's former wife. It was a great place to work, with a nice stage. If other performers were on there, my wife Toni and I used to make sure that we went to see them. It was a place I knew really well.

"One night we went to see Kathy Kirby; she was always rather a strange lady. At the *Dolce Vita* the artiste was announced and entered through a door, a sort of panel, which was flush with the back of the stage. The announcement was made: "Ladies and gentlemen, Kathy Kirby, the musical star," and she entered through this door. The door was then shut behind her.

"She sang her opening number, but then she suddenly looked at the audience and said: 'I know what you're all saying about me. I know what you're all thinking. Well, I can tell you now – it's not true!' She went into a rant and she started to cry. She ran to the back of the stage but couldn't get through this door, because it needed to be opened from the opposite side. She stood there banging on the door. It was unbelievably embarrassing! Then somebody opened the door and off she went. There was an announcement: 'Miss Kirby will be on stage in another fifteen minutes,' or something, but I don't think she ever came back on.

"But of course, the best place we ever had was the *Night Out*. It was the best nightclub in the country; it was fantastic! I did *Crackerjack*, from 1972 to 1977. Towards the end of that period, around 1976, I worked the *Night Out* for a week. Business there was always good, no matter who was on. It was one of the highlights of my career, being Top of the Bill at the Night *Out*, for that one particular week of shows."

Chris Lewthwaite recalls a very memorable night, in 1970, when *Things to Come* played the *Dolce Vita*: "It was right underneath where the Ringway crosses Hurst Street. There was always a major band on; on this particular night it was the *Hollies*. When they took a break, we filled in for about twenty-five minutes, until they did their second session; them we came on at the end. Some notable things happened that night. I was aware of the *Hollies*' equipment up the side corridor: they must have had thousands of pounds-worth of equipment, to make sure that they had all their sound equipment right there were various engineers with head gear on, and so on.

"They were magnificent, but then they went off. The curtains closed, then opened again, then we went on. Les absolutely panicked. He said: 'We're not going to play rock music. We'll play jazz – *Peddlers* numbers and that sort of thing.' Understandably, he did *not* want to follow them! But we did alright and they played again. It was amusing, because the World Cup was on at the time and it was in Mexico.

"Bernie Calvert, of the *Hollies*, was a nice guy. We were listening to the World Cup on the radio, in the dressing room. What the audience didn't see was that Bernie, who was a football fanatic, raced up the corridor and opened the door of the room that we were in, to find out how the game was going, because England were playing. Then seconds later, he casually walked back onto the stage, picked up his guitar and started playing again!

"In our second set, after the *Hollies* had gone off, our speaker, at the side of the stage, fell onto the table where the boss was dining with some guests. Needless-to-say, we heard no more about any further work at that place… another disaster!"

Martin Hone has been involved in entertainment of one kind or another, from the age of eleven; Don Maclean and Kenny Lynch are just two other examples of a range of people in our book, who started early in the business too. "We all started like that," observes Martin. "Their destiny was to go on to become famous comedians or musicians; I became quite well known on the After Dinner Speaking Circuit; with highlights of addressing substantial groups of black-tied businessmen at the *Savoy* – and goodness-knows-what! Within me was a wish to entertain – I think that's the 'Servant Heart': that's where my service towards people at *The Opposite Lock* came from: there was something already within me, whereby I wanted to please. Being a comedian… there's *nothing* more wonderful than to hear people laughing. I was quite good at the time, but then that pull towards motor racing became more important than making people laugh; so I took the fork in the road that took me into motor racing."

As former owner of *The Opposite Lock*, in Gas Street, and *The Engine House*, at Tardebigge, Martin recalls the difference in clientele, between *The Opposite Lock* and my own clubs:

"What *The Opposite Lock* set out to do was to provide a rendezvous that would satisfy what was probably a more sophisticated person, who we didn't feel was being catered for, at that time," Martin explains. "There were plenty of clubs satisfying the various strata of the city; we had a particular interest in loads of sport, from which I had been pursuing motor racing, as a racing driver for many years. I was also very interested in jazz.

"My racing, across Europe, had introduced me to very good food, in a considerable number of countries: Germany, Italy and France. I was very keen to see improvements on the Birmingham scene. In those days, 1966, you couldn't really get a decent meal after half past ten anywhere. There was no restaurant facility of any status, outside of perhaps a club. The *Ambassador's Club* was into rather grand flambé dishes, and was liked in Edgbaston, but the majority of the clubs didn't focus on food at all. They focused on getting people in, putting booze down their necks, sending them home at a time, depending on their relationship with the police, in between two and six o'clock in the morning.

"We attracted people who wanted to find an environment that interested them – particularly motor sport and motor racing. They were pleased to come, talk motor sport and rub shoulders with famous racing drivers who came to the club. There were the motor racing driver forums; motor racing film shows; visits to the circuit that we did from the club; also, jazz aficionados: people who understand and like jazz cover three of the strata of the Birmingham make-up. Invariably we attracted a clientele who would enthuse about the quality of the music. It also provided us with a clientele who had good taste in food.

"The Bistro Restaurant (*Le Bistro*) that we opened, served from eight o'clock in the evening to two o'clock in the morning, It suddenly came alive, with people who wanted a rendezvous with nice music, a nice clean atmosphere; didn't want to be involved in any fights or aggression, gambling, drugs or girlies. *The Opposite Lock* fulfilled all of that.

I had a chef who cooked the most wonderful Scampi Provencal. Every time he made it, it was *perfect*, but I can hear *now*, the voice of one particular very sophisticated client, out with his lady, having supper, when we invited him to enjoy the Scampi Provencal, his words were: 'I'm not going to eat any of that foreign muck!'

"Remarkably enough, we *did* find ourselves in the niche to which I had let my 'gut' lead me – although I had never run a club, bar or restaurant of any sort; it was just a gut feeling that there were sufficient people like ourselves – on a different strata of the Birmingham society, which included everybody from the general working man; middle class working man, through to the professionals: the lawyers, doctors, surgeons; many of them came over from the Queen Elizabeth Hospital. A lot of sports people came in.

"We were probably the *first* club to welcome professional black people. The stars that we promoted, from Salena Jones to Count Basie, Earl 'Father' Hines and Colman Hawkins were internationally famous black people; Elaine Delmar, Doris Troy, Dakota Staton. You never saw their colour – all you saw was the talent... and you got to know them as human beings. This was quite a breakthrough in 1966, because there was still the heaviness of racial prejudice towards black people.

"People then came to the club singly, met each other, enjoyed a bit of dancing on the floor, the House Trio, the discotheques that we ran, which were not ear-blasting things until the very early hours of the morning, when we turned the volume up a bit. But by that time, love was in the air: a considerable number of people, over the years, wrote both Patti and I invitations to their weddings."

It will come as no surprise Martin, when you read our *Cupid* chapter, to find that many couples found happiness at our clubs too. I understand that your life changed dramatically, in 1978, due to the corruption that was happening in the city?

"We had our eyes opened to the corruption that every entrepreneur had to face, yourself included; each person made his own individual choice about how to deal with it. I had two years of the most miserable hell; it was absolutely soul-destroying. In retrospect, however, it was one of the biggest favours that ever happened to me, because it brought me to my knees. And I've been on my knees ever since – in the nicest possible way!

"Here was a man who was sitting on something of a pedestal, because people were applauding all my initiatives; they were applauding all the famous people we brought into Birmingham. My plans to bring road racing to Birmingham; they were applauding plans that we were making for Film Festivals and Jazz Festivals. I became a quasi-celebrity in the town. It's remarkable for such a large city, that it's actually a small town! It's amazing how a single person's name can actually start to become famous.

"However, I did find to my cost, that there was no value in being famous or being thought of as being important. Being on my knees led me to the Church and my wonderful spiritual awakening, and Christianity, which has helped me now, over many years of endeavours, to stay on that very fine and thin road, hopefully keeping me away from the corruption of the world."

Martin sold *The Opposite Lock* in 1978; *The Engine House* in 1980 and then finally the restaurant, *Waterside House*, which was in Gas Street, in 1995. He's been in business, in one form or another, for forty years, since he opened *The Opposite Lock* on 21st December 1966. His paths and mine have crossed, from time to time, as we challenged the licensing laws of the day.

"By 1966, the World Cup year, Birmingham City Council had started to wake up to the fact that if they were to attract tourists they'd got to start thinking about offering something, because as a city, we'd failed miserably; we didn't have an Eiffel Tower, a large river, or anything particularly attractive architecturally, to bring people to the city," Martin continues. "A giant machine began to evolve, to start turning Birmingham into the pulsating city that we have today. I became very active in city matters and served on a considerable number of committees. I became Chairman of the Birmingham Conference, which eventually turned into the Birmingham

Convention and Visitors Bureau, when we linked with the City Council, of which I remained a main board director, for over twenty-five years. But I was brought close to my knees regarding how to make this big machine turn... and what it needed.

"As far as the night life was concerned, we needed to reappraise the existing licensing laws, which had satisfied World War II and the post-war years, but now the country had begun to get back on its feet. London enjoyed a Metropolitan title. Although we were a 'metropolis', the city of Birmingham at that time was not known as a metropolitan borough. So Birmingham had, down the line, a second-hand licensing law; although they were all supposed to be under a national banner, there were double standards, nationally.

"The 'forty-eight hour law', I was able to demonstrate in Parliament, when we started to get under way with a movement to remove that one, by describing the night that we had *Count Basie and his Orchestra* in the club. Bill Basie's multi-millionaire Texan friend arrived on the doorstep, greeted us, and said: 'I want to see Bill Basie.' I said: 'Well, you can't come in, because you're not a member.' 'Ok, I'll buy a membership.' I said: 'Yes, but then you've got to go away for forty-eight hours.' 'Whadya mean? I've got to be back in Houston tomorrow!' So we used that as a demonstration of the farce, that we were having to work under. After eighteen months that particular law was changed.

"We came together, as a group of nightclub owners, when a new ruling dictated: 'after half past ten only waiter or waitress service.' We had to put waiters between the barriers and the bars, to carry out anywhere near the sort of service we wanted to give our clients.

"We weren't *all* rip-off merchants: many of us had businesses based upon giving a service. To that end, I started to come into meetings with you, Eddie. Up until that time as you know, we'd held each other at arm's length: you went about your business, I went about mine. I was not a nightclub goer: I didn't go up into the town and visit nightclubs. I didn't have a need, because I had a very good club myself. The difference was that a lot of people ran nightclubs, whereas *The Opposite Lock* was a club, which happened to be open at night; this is the irony of it all... so I became dubbed a 'night club runner'!

"So it wasn't unusual for people to understand that perhaps you and I should rub shoulders. In fact, I can't remember ever being entertained by you until you opened the very sophisticated *Abigail's*, where you were promoting a jazz star, Salena Jones, who I had brought to Birmingham for the previous five or six years. Salena was very good in a cabaret room and you invited Patti and me to a very nice table in your very nice club, where we enjoyed some fellowship and the music.

"Other than that," Martin continues, "I'm sure you'll agree, we didn't pursue any social meetings; but I have to put on record that in the endeavours to bring about the changes in the licensing laws, you were always willing to back me; always prepared to pay your 'corner'. You helped Birmingham in backing the various other entrepreneurs, who eventually brought about the licensing law changes, which took several years... and supported us all the way."

I was Chairman of Club Watch, the official organisation where club owners liaised with the Birmingham police, whereas Martin was involved with A.L.N.E.

"Yes, A.L.N.E. was the 'Association of Late Night Entertainments'. It drew together a number of the other entrepreneurial licensed club owners in the city, because we *knew* that to get the City of Birmingham into a proper position, as far as the licensing laws were concerned, we'd have to set up meetings in London, to eventually get laws changed. It was a quasi-name that drew us together for lunch, every now and again, in the *Castillane Restaurant*, within the *Midland Hotel*.

"I often used to be amused, when I looked around the table, at the thought of what would happen if the devil were to drop his net now... because they were a marvellous bunch of entrepreneurial pioneers, who had been working very hard. Nightclub running is a very hard business; long long hours. Members included the Berrow Brothers, who ran the *Rum Runner* club; the Morralls – Harry Morrall, now deceased, who ran the *Ambassador* and the *Rainbow Club*; Billy Cutler was also very much involved with us when we founded the Variety Club of Great Britain, in Birmingham, which was one of the long-term charities that were created.

"The Birmingham Variety crew consisted of Fred Crowton, MD of Mitchells & Butler; Harry Cressman of Bristol Street Motors; Chris Bryant of Bryant's Buildings; Doug Ellis of Aston Villa Football Club; Len Matthews of ATV – he was Lew Grade's right-hand man; Israel Cohen: I think he was S & U Stores, in those days; together with myself. These were the founder members of the Variety Club of Great Britain. The crew in the Midlands eventually grew into a very substantial money-raising organisation into which many then came on board, and supported the initiatives to raise money for mentally handicapped and disabled children.

"During the course of running *The Opposite Lock* I had a considerable number of other interests on the go. The pursuit of bringing road racing to Birmingham, which started in 1966, eventually brought me to organising events on the streets of Birmingham. *Festival Services* came into being in 1970. We ran the first Birmingham Motoring Festival on the streets of the City Centre of Birmingham in 1970, closing down New Street, Corporation Street and Colmore Row twice a day: eleven o'clock in the morning and three o'clock in the afternoon, for fourteen days; bringing racing cars and drivers to the city, to try and demonstrate that a road race would bring tourism. So my business life, by the time we came out of the clubs, in 1978 and 1980, was already established with the company that we've run to the present day."

Various people who're helping with this book have been comparing the differences between Birmingham, Manchester and London nightlife Martin, but you could do the same comparison between the London scene and any other major UK city really.

"Yes, the successful entrepreneurs of the fifties and sixties hadn't got anywhere other that the *Rainbow and Ambassador's* clubs, to spend their money. The Brummie man used to take his 'Fancy Lady' away from Birmingham, straight down to London. He was going to do the 'Mr. Big' and have his happy weekend with her, before he returned back to the wife and kids. This was an exercise that was very much part of the Brummie culture – particularly those men who'd made money and became famous out of their business endeavours."

Do you remember about three months after you had opened *The Opposite Lock* – that I suddenly arrived – unannounced?

"Yes – the Fewtrell family were famous in Birmingham and had this rather heavy image, because the *Cedar Club* and certainly the *Bermuda Club* in Navigation Street, were known as places where you could expect, if you went looking for that sort of excitement, a bit of 'trouble'… and these men were capable of handling this sort of 'trouble'. So when I was informed that you were actually in Reception, with a number of men, I came down to greet you. There was a sense of: 'Oh my goodness, are they coming looking for trouble?' Or it could simply be a visit where we could get to know one another; but there was a feeling of apprehension in my heart. You were surrounded by a number of men all of whom, to me, looked quite large!

"You introduced yourself to me, we had a drink. You asked if you could have a look around and I showed you around. Eventually, we ended up back at the Reception. You'd weighed it all up and we hadn't got many people in, on that particular night – it was fairly quiet. So our converted stable block didn't actually look as if it was offering very much. The musicians were playing and the bar was well lit; the waiters were waiting to do business in the little Bistro Restaurant. But there was no real evidence of a 'buzz' in the building. It would have been difficult for anybody to weigh up exactly what we had to offer.

"I remember to this day your immortal words, as you said: 'Where's the gambling?' I said: 'Well, we don't have a gambling room.' You looked at your pals and they looked at me. You said: 'Well, when do the girls come on?' I said: 'We're not doing Girlie Shows.'

And you stood… and quizzically tried to weigh it up: 'Well, what are you offering?'

I said: 'There's a nice lounge here; there's a House Trio and you can go to the bar; you can have a nice meal and if you're interested in motor sport, you can come to one of our film shows or forums.' You looked me in the eye and said: 'I'll give you three months.'

"Well, bless you for that, because what you hadn't really taken into account was that there were sufficient people in Birmingham who wanted a quiet, more sophisticated place, and happily, that's how it turned out."

Shirley tells me that she was a customer of yours, both in the club's early days and in its closing stages. In fact, she and her husband David met there, in May 1978, when she was twenty-nine. Whenever she was there, it always seemed to be teeming with people.

"Yes, it was amazing. After two-and-a-half years, the news had got around; we'd got a reasonably 'in-your-face' type of advertising. We told people what was on; by that time we had made enough money to start attracting the further-up-the-ladder stars. So an advert came out that said:

'Step on the gas to high speed Gas Street and enjoy a touch of *The Opposite Lock*. Tonight, presenting one night only, Miss Marion Montgomery, and the Brian Lewis Trio.'

"They were known from London: we'd made great friends with Pete King and Ronnie Scott, of the *Ronnie Scott Club* and we worked in unison, to bring American stars across the Atlantic.

"Mike Alexander took up a residency; again, we had great admiration for his musical ability; he was a very good pianist. He led a very good House Trio, which was the format in those days. He was capable of backing the itinerant one-man stars, in particular, the sax, trumpet or guitar players – or whatever. Talking about guitar players, Barney Kessell came to the club; Muddy Waters; *Cannonball Adderley and his Messengers. Dudley Moore and his Trio*; the *Roy Budd Trio*; the *Blossom Dearie Trio*; the *Mike Carr Trio*; *Dakota Staton, Doris Troy*; *the Peddlers* – who had a great following; the *Roland Kirk Quartet*: he was a legendary blind jazz saxophonist, who I used to book for three or four weekday nights, because we didn't need jazz at the weekends. Roland was reputed to be able to play forty-five wind instruments.

"By this time they started to come because of what we were offering; there was the first sign and trickle of people coming up from London. The *Holiday Inn* was built by now: it was just the other side of Gas Street Basin, in Holliday Street – very close by the club. So all of a sudden we found that we had succeeded in reversing the flow of men and women going down for their 'naughty weekend' in London; they were actually coming up from London, staying at the *Holiday Inn* and spending a considerable amount of their time at *The Opposite Lock Club*.

"So we had started to reverse the trend; not only of not losing our own people, away to London. And coincidentally, you mentioned earlier Bernard Manning's comparison of Birmingham with Manchester. Manchester had an even bigger advantage, compared with Birmingham, as far as nightlife is concerned, because it was four hours away from London, by train or by car.

"Manchester, because of its geographical position to London, built its own nightlife, which drew in from Liverpool and Manchester; they had a big enough conurbation of people to actually fill the clubs; you knew where to go to if you wanted food, entertainment, or to meet up with someone of the opposite sex. Manchester's night scene spawned a considerable number of entrepreneurs, who went on to build national groups. We actually met some of those, in our licensing endeavours. The Bailey Club organisation, for instance, which eventually came to Birmingham, and planted a very substantial club in the middle of Birmingham, also supported the Birmingham initiative, to get licensing laws changed.

"Although there wasn't any way that that which we've seen today on Broad Street was going to happen in the sixties or the seventies, we were, nevertheless, pioneering: I was the bloke at the top of the pyramid; other guys were behind me, supporting and financing me; they used me as their mouthpiece.

"I suppose that anybody looking at my life would say that it was multi-faceted, because it never changed. Making people laugh, and joking was very important to me. For the many years that I ran my nightclub I'd do my own spot. Mike Alexander will remember, many times, having to put up with my getting up on stage to introduce him, then not getting off myself, for twenty-five to thirty minutes, trying to throw new jokes at people and testing them. I always used to try to find something that would appeal to people and used their intellect. I recall many of them not even understanding the jokes – and me having to explain them to them, before they got the point!

"As the business took off, we took over the four-storey building, behind the stable. We converted the ground floor into *The Factory*, where we used to accommodate the younger people, with more of a pop scene, which I wasn't particularly good at, because I didn't see much sophistication in the pop scene, in those days. But very famous names came down Gas Street – I looked it up the other day... *incredible* the names that came into there: *Fairport Convention*, *Moody Blues* and *Pink Floyd*, who played for £125 and Joe Cocker, who I noticed the other day, we paid £75!

"By the early 1970s Duckhams had shown great interest in our racing team, and we became the national team for Duckhams Oil Company Promotions. We had the *Art Gallery*, which was a walkway to a beautiful door, which lead you into *Martin's Room*. Many art exhibitions were held in the *Gallery*.

"*Martin's Room* was a V.I.P. Gold Card Room, if you like, on top of *The Opposite Lock* Member Club Card. If you had *that* card, then you entered into a very sophisticated domain, which I designed and decorated. I went all over Britain to look for the furnishings for the room. My family were specialists in oriental carpets and I needed two carpets of twenty square yards, which had got to match. The colour scheme was leaning towards a Georgian Green: very pale and easy-on-the-eye, with Georgian Green hide leather

Chesterfields. We had very sophisticated antique furniture; it was a lamp-lit room, with these beautiful carpets.

"On Opening Night, we invited all the sophisticated Hoi-Polloi of Birmingham, to come in their black ties. By this time we'd attracted many of the film-stars: the *Carry On* Team. My friendship had grown with Jack Douglas and Des O'Connor, into links with the *Carry On* Team. To have all of them down there: Barbara Windsor, Bernard Bresslaw, Sid James, Jack Douglas and all of them, made it a great Opening Night in 1972.

So there I am with my beautiful wife, Patti, in her lovely Gina Fratini gown. Simon Livingstone was photographing everybody; the sophisticates of Birmingham were there, smoking their cigars. I'd worked *hard* to put this room together – it should have given people real pleasure. There were these Rajbik carpets, which were two-and-a-half inches thick; hand-made, hand-carved beautiful Indian carpets, but as I looked around, a man dropped his cigar onto the carpet... and just ground it in! I looked at my brother, Ian, and I said: 'You know, I don't think this is going to work' – because that sophistication which we *thought* we'd attracted, had still got a long way to go. *Martin's Room* was a successful extension eventually, but at first it frightened Brummies to death – it looked too good!"

Comedian Don Maclean began to make headway in the entertainment scene from 1964 onwards. He recalls: "*The Opposite Lock* was the place to be seen. It was for young trendies, but it was also a little bit bohemian – it was jazz. The ambience was fabulous. I got to know Martin Hone and became very friendly with him. *The Opposite Lock* would have still been with us now, if it hadn't been for certain circumstances, which challenged Martin at the time. I was there at the opening night of *Martin's Room*.

"It was wonderful. You lounged around and you felt very decadent. Then he had *King Arthur's Court*, where he performed a lot of the time, as King Arthur. He was very good, because it suited him. He did a lot, did Martin. The two of you, Eddie, had a funny relationship, because you were sort of in competition with one another, but you seemed to appreciate each other.

"I heard Martin make a very funny speech in one of your clubs one night Eddie," Don continues. "The gag that got the biggest laugh was that he was trying to arrange to get the QE2 into Gas Street Basin, so that he could run it down, and the tidal wave would completely engulf *Abigail's* from the canal ... and you would just sit there and laugh at anything like that!"

I think it's fair to say Martin, that in some respects, you and I definitely had a common cause.

"Yes, the common cause was firstly, to run a successful business; to keep our families fed and mortgages paid, but also to work to improve the image of Birmingham. Although we didn't ever develop a close, social friendship, I think it's fair to say that we did have common respect for each other. I certainly can go on record as saying I had great respect for you and the manner in which you serviced *your* clientele, which helped me look after my clientele. When we meet today I'll very happily shake hands, probably give you a hug, and say: 'Well, those were some interesting years, weren't they?'

"The scene in the fifties and sixties was really born out of what we were able to see, in the back row of the *Warwick Cinema*, or the *Olton Cinema*, in the black-and-white films showing the gangster films or whatever. I think that my romanticism for all of that came out of watching a *very* romantic film. It was either Clark Gable or Cary Grant; seated at one side of a round, candlelit table, having supper with a beautiful woman facing him, across the table.

"There was a jazz trio playing in the background and a little dance floor, with people there. That image was so romantic that it stuck in my mind. I wanted that for other people. It could have been Claudette Colbert or Jean Simmons as the leading lady. I fell in love with Jean Simmons, as a boy! I don't think I lusted after her; it was just that she had the most beautiful face. So I think that that element in your clubs Eddie, where you had the gambling wheel and you had to be quiet if the coppers were around – it's straight out of movies, which gave people a buzz of excitement: 'Blimey, this is happening in Birmingham!'"

Raymond Froggatt and 'H' recall performing at Martin's club.

"Although *The Opposite Lock* was normally a jazz club, we played our kind of music there: *Roly*, *Red Balloon* and others – and Bob Dylan songs. Martin just wanted us to play what we always played – and we'd bring a following in as well; they didn't have their frogs with them – that came later! We played there around 1974. It was shortly after that that I got involved in writing songs for Cliff Richard. It was rather classy for us, to do *The Opposite Lock*. There was always somebody famous in there; not necessarily a singer, but maybe an actor or some racing drivers, because it was a racing driver or rally people's place.

"I remember doing a Rock n' Roll Revival Show there for charity once. We had Birmingham City Football players dressed up as Elvis. Most of them still looked like footballers, to be honest, but one or two of them were okay. We had a really great night, because Robbie Plant, the *Led Zeppelin* player was there, to sing some Rock n' Roll too – and off course that was our 'bag'. We had a really great night and raised lots of money for charity," remembers Raymond.

Les Hemming comments: "I'm sure that Eddie would be willing to acknowledge that Martin Hone was his competitor. Although Martin was quite pleased that Eddie catered for some of the clientele that he preferred not to have in his more sophisticated club, meanwhile, back in the world of Rock n' Roll, I think that Eddie got the best of the deal; because a fair number of the people that normally follow jazz had probably got a fiver in their pockets, whereas people that follow casino entertainment would have several fivers! That might have been an interesting analogy, which probably suited Eddie quite well!

"Our big break, as we saw it at the time, with *Things to Come*," Les continues, "was that we got a gig at *The Opposite Lock*. We were the warm-up turn for the *Maynard Ferguson Big Band*. In our band at that time we'd actually managed to attract Nick Pentelow and Charlie Grima, who went on to join *Wizzard*, so that eventually broke up the band.

"Martin used to put on things like the *Count Basie Orchestra*. He was quite phenomenal, to bring such acts over. Anyway, we had our moment. We all congregated at the bar beforehand. That's when we realised that our lead singer had got this most horrendous, glowing boil on the end of his chin! And there we were, about to go on, with the eyes of the world on us – as we saw it. So we had to put plenty of stage makeup on Steve's boil!"

Roger Shropshall confirms: "We did two auditions there: one for Martin Hone and one for Jeff Turton. *The Opposite Lock* was my favourite club of all time. Jeff was about to become a solo singer and was looking for a backing group to tour with. He'd had loads of hits with the *Rockin' Berries – Poor Man's Son* and so on. He left the group and had quite a few singles as *Jefferson*. He'd had one record in the Hit Parade at about number twenty-five, that was *Colour of My Love*. He took one look at what we had to offer; waved and blew a kiss… and he was gone!"

Martin observes: "The American influence on our lives, to me, is traumatic, because I think the American cop films that we see on television today have brought us the most horrendous problems; mentally deranged young thugs. The killing, the suffering, the violence was never a part of the Birmingham scene in the 1950s and 60s, until the London boys came in. We went through a period, particularly when the *Mulberry Bush* was bombed, by the I.R.A. We then had to go through checking people on the door."

I can pinpoint exactly when that was Martin. It was Thursday night, 21st November, 1974. As you can imagine, that was a traumatic night at our clubs too. Patti Bell recalls that we had distraught parents phoning us – and all *sorts* of things happening – like searching for bombs!

"Right. We *did* find guns and knives in people's pockets, but we had never suffered from anything like that," continues Martin. "That shook me! Like a lot of things shook me – I did a lot of maturing in those days. A working class kid, suddenly finding himself rubbing shoulders with city councillors and the like; I had a lot of growing up to do. In actual fact, in retrospect it was the best education that I could have wished for... living life. I'm certain that a university could not have given me more."

Chapter Eight

REBECCA'S AND BARBARELLA'S

Eddie's oldest daughter, Rebecca, is born in 1964. Rebecca's Nightclub, named after her, opens in 1966. John Fewtrell is one of the new managers. Rebecca's Brasserie also opens and the two establishments later becomes Boogie's. Rebecca's is on three different levels – the Cabasa, the Blue Soul, and the Sin Bin; Barbarella's eventually becomes three rooms, all on one level: the Top Bar, the Datachick, and the Take Two Room.

Councillor Ken Hardeman died only recently, on 17 July, 2007. Just four months earlier, during an interview for Eddie's book, he recalled showing Eddie premises, which later become Barbarella's. The club opens in 1972, in Cumberland Street, just off Oozell Street, near the Tax Office.

Mike Alexander plays sophisticated music in the Take Two Room and comperes the shows above. Chuck Berry's performance at the club takes a dramatic turn, and Jack Jones plays 'hard-to-get'! Talent competitions produce a winner, who later becomes a star. Tony Orlando, uncharacteristically, encounters an impossible audience. Additional memories provided by, Tony Christie, Kenny Lynch, Froggie, Patti Bell and Steve Gibbons.

John Fewtrell transfers from Rebecca's, to help manage Barbarella's. He is subsequently succeeded by Kenny Hatton, formerly Jimmy Tarbuck's Road Manager. Kenny introduces Jimmy to Eddie and they become lifelong friends. Bob Price, former Chairman of the Birmingham Licensing Committee, summarises Birmingham's licensing regulations and Eddie's role in relation to them.

Adam Faith and Richard Branson are amongst the talent-spotters who frequent Barbarella's, eager to sign up new talent. Many up-and-coming pop groups perform 'Showcases' at Barbarella's.

Hazel was desperate for a child. She lost the first one, named Anthony. That's why we got married – because she was pregnant. In the meantime, we went without children for five or six years. Then, when I was in my early thirties, we had a baby girl, who we named Rebecca Marie Fewtrell. Rebecca, otherwise known as 'Becky', was born on 29 September, 1964. For the first seven years of her life it was just her, Hazel and myself – before the other two children were born.

"My parents had a very loving relationship, at that stage; we were very close," remembers Becky. "Every time we'd visit friends and family, I went with my mum and dad to see them. When my dad came home from work, I was always pleased to see him. I'd rush into his arms. Sometimes I'd have been having a bath – and I'd be soaking wet! He was a very loving kind of father. I always had lots of attention, from both my mum and my father. He always seemed to be around – I never felt that I was missing him. He'd be at work when I was asleep.

"My first family home in Hamstead was very modern. We had an open-plan staircase – just planks of wood, with gaps in between. The house was built next to a church, with a graveyard, which I think my mum wasn't too pleased about – I think she thought it was haunted! Dad kept fruit machines in the garage. Mum and dad took the handle of the inside of my bedroom door, because I used to sleep-walk a lot; they were worried that I might fall down the stairs!

"I attended Edgbaston Church of England School, between the ages of four and seventeen. I must have been around seven, when we moved to our second house in Anstruther Road, Edgbaston; a short while after the Majorcan holiday photo was taken – where I'm descending from the plane with my parents – that was just before my sister, Abigail was born, in 1972; they decorated the nursery, ready for her."

By 1971, I was increasing the number of clubs. Things were going well, financially, so 36 Anstruther Road was a fairly big detached, with a large garden. When Rebecca was young she used to bring frogspawn home – she liked watching the tadpoles change into frogs!

"I used to love that – and butterflies. I remember an incident that happened at the new house. It had snowed rather heavily and I was playing with my friends, who lived across the road," recalls Becky. "We were throwing snowballs at each other. I threw a snowball at the brother and sister: I think they were twins. I hit the boy in the face; then the father of the boy threw a snowball at me, with a brick inside it – pushed it in my face! My father was very angry and he went over to see him. It was terrible! Obviously the boy was upset, but his father's reaction was very 'over the top'. My father was very protective of me. I didn't play with them again after that. After 36 Anstruther, we moved to Fitzroy Avenue. Daniel and Abigail were both there then. Then Norfolk Road was the last family home."

Bob Price and I first met in the 1960s, in his capacity as Chairman of the Birmingham Licensing Justices.

According to Bob, "The Licensing Act of 1964 enabled for the first time licences to be granted to 2.00 am, outside London. Prior to 1964, there had been no late night drinking outside of London. So the new 1964 Act was to encourage cabaret and dining with alcoholic drinks, until 2.00am.

"Initially, when the Late Night Licensing came in, premises were able to operate under what was then known as a Special Hours Certificate, catering for cabaret acts, dining, dancing and drinks until 2am. Now several of these places opened and were granted licenses in the 1960s. Eddie Fewtrell was one of the very first in Birmingham to be granted the Certificate, followed by people such as the Bailey Organisation, in Newcastle-upon-Tyne and Mecca. The Baileys had the *Dolce Vita* in Hurst Street, and the *Cavendish*, in the new *Swan Centre*, at Yardley, which is now to be at least partly demolished, I gather.

"Late Night Licences were granted to *all* of Eddie Fewtrell's establishments, over the years; firstly of course, because they complied with the law and they satisfied the Licensing Authority's stringent structural requirements. These were in place to ensure that the premises were safe, convenient and run properly, to protect the clientele: contrary to the view of certain people at that time, the disgruntled applicants, who thought that they were getting a raw deal – they weren't being given a raw deal at all! All the hearings of the Justices and the Licensing Committee complied with the legal requirements and every case was dealt with very fairly, on its merits, with evidence being given, on oath, from both sides of the application.

"Over the years, we had *Barbarella's* off Broad Street, *Rebecca's* and *Abigail's*; two were named after Edwards daughters, in addition to *Edward's No.7* and *Edward's No.8*. Edward's secret ambition must have been to be an impresario, and over the years he brought many stars and groups to his clubs.

"*Abigail's* in Hill Street, (the premises are now a casino) was a super, very high-class cabaret club, providing international acts such as Brook Benton from the States, and from the UK the *Pasadena Roof Orchestra*. The standard of catering and service was top quality.

"Later on, as you will have been informed, by other contributors and by Eddie, he booked Shirley Bassey for a sensational Charity Night at the *Birmingham Metropole Hotel*. The demand for Cabaret Dining Clubs gradually declined and the gaps were filled by discotheques, with much lower overhead expenses, to satisfy late night drinking. With the new Licensing Act of 2003, with much later pub opening, the trade has changed yet again. From the early beginning, to the present day, Edward Fewtrell has survived and indeed maintained a predominant role in Birmingham's nightlife.

"The Licensing Committee used to meet every two months and often we had up to a hundred applications. Now these weren't all for nightclubs; some of them were very small applications, for Off Licences. But there would be several adjourned hearings. From time to time there would be another two or three applications for late night drinking nightclubs. No one person could be granted licences on a chain of premises; each establishment would have to be registered in a different name. For that reason there was individual, personal control and one person responsible for each premises. Multiple Licences for holders, were not granted; so you could not have two people or more, as joint licensees of a premises, because if there are any problems who do you blame? Who is responsible?"

It's important to mention that Bob did his Committee work, totally voluntarily, for twenty-two years. Also, if these licences were actually granted, it considerably increased the value of the property.

Rebecca's was two factories, knocked into one. It was built before *Abigail's*, and was the very first one, after the *Cedar Club*. There was a lift that went all the way down to the *Sin Bin* in the basement. I put steel prison doors across the front of the lift shaft, down in the basement, so it looked like a prison cell. If anyone misbehaved they were put in there for a while and we played the record, *He's a Sinner*. On the opening night, for a bit of fun, we locked a Chief Inspector in there. Unfortunately, the lock jammed and it took us over an hour to get him out. He was convinced that I'd done it on purpose, but luckily, he'd got a good sense of humour!

Gianni Paladini worked for me for fourteen years. My brother, Johnny, was the manager of *Rebecca's* too.

"When Edward was there he used to look after the *Cabasa*," recalls John. "I used to be in the *Blue Soul*, which was the middle room; Bomber was in the *Sin Bin* and Chrissie used to run the door."

I used to go to America, Las Vegas, for example… and take the family, so many of the ideas that I used in my clubs, came from America. Also, the idea of putting ice and lemon in the drink, and serving them cold; at that time in England they used to just slap in the drinks.

Froggie remembers when I put Bob Marley on, at *Rebecca's*. "I was there that night, with Joe Cocker. Joe was on the following day. Unexpectedly, there were absolutely thousands there… and you couldn't get them in. There were crowds outside too and they had a tannoy system outside, so that other people could listen too. They wanted to be near Bob and were quite content to just sit in the street; so they put these speakers up.

"Although *Rebecca's* was a small club," continues Froggie, "I had some great nights there. Eddie, quite bravely, put us on with the *Birmingham Symphony Orchestra* around 1972 or 73; we always wanted to do that and we did it twice – first of all in the *Belfry*, which was a great success. So we decided that it would be nice to do it in town, but who would be game enough to put it on? But Eddie Fewtrell said: 'Yes, we'll do it!' It was absolutely jam-packed to the rafters. We'd got all these quite posh people…amongst all this glitter. With any kind of pioneering thing like that, you're going to get 'spoilers', but Eddie was more concerned for the welfare of his customers, rather than his own particular safety, We've worked all over the world – and you don't always feel safe! But tell Eddie – I always felt safe in his clubs."

Froggie wrote loads of songs for Cliff Richard: *Going Away, Big Ship; Rainbow Eyes.*

"I was in London with Cliff last week," he continues. "We went down to the American Embassy, at Wingfield House, as guests of the American Ambassador. He said some nice things about my contribution to American music. I had my photograph taken there, with Cliff," explains Froggie. "I've also written for Gladys Knight; David Lloyd Arnold; the *Dave Clarke Five*."

I had David Bowie on at *Rebecca's*. He had a Number One Hit – *This is Ground Control to Major Tom*. Thousands of people had bought the record, and the place was packed, but he took that long coming on, everyone had got that drunk, that he was singing away and nobody was listening! I paid him thousands of pounds to do it too. He sang it, put the mike down, and came off, saying, "Well, nobody's listening to me!" I said: "I shouldn't bother about that. It's me who's paying you. I'm the one who should be feeling depressed about it!"

Becky remembers: "Around 1970, when I was about six years old, dad took me to *Rebecca's* after school – to his office, on the top floor. The whole of the top floor was the office, but partitioned off, behind this door, was another room, where he stored all the Lost Property. I sat on the floor of this room, almost buried in handbags and coats – trying on all the old make-up. When I think about it, I cringe! There were fur coats – the lot. My father had a shock when I came from behind the door, with my face daubed with make-up!"

I sometimes took my children to the clubs in the daytime, during the school holidays. That top office floor overlooked Severn Street, because *Rebecca's* was on the corner of Severn Street, as opposed to *Rebecca's Brasserie*, which fronted on to John Bright Street.

"When I was young, it didn't really register," continues Rebecca, "but as I got older people would say: 'Did your father name *Rebecca's* after you?' I'd feel really proud and say: 'Yes he did!' It was great really.

"Daniel, my mother and myself were quite artistic, whereas Abigail was more on the academic side. My father had artistic tendencies too – certainly in terms of the colour, design and layout of his clubs. I left school when I was seventeen. Although I had been doing three A Levels I decided to go to Bournville Art College instead and did my Art A Level there. Then I went on to Sheffield Polytechnic, to do a three-year degree, in Silver-smithing and Jewellery. I did some secretarial training too, although I only worked in the Jewellery Trade, for about a year. There was a Fewtrell jewellery company in the Quarter; the owner, Mickey Fewtrell, is related to my dad's father's brother. Abigail, my younger sister, lives in Devon; she's more academic; she teaches English and French, and she's performed in plays. I was going to the clubs before the Punk era. It was still quite normal. If I went to another nightclub Nobby walked or drove me there.

"We stayed with Jimmy Tarbuck in the Home Counties, when I was very young; before my brother and sister were born. Jimmy's two daughters were there. They were quite close in age, and much older than me, but I remember playing with them. Pauline Tarbuck, Jimmy's wife, was very nice. They were all very down-to-earth. They had a massive garden, with a swimming pool and a very nice house. Cilla Black and Ronnie Corbett were amongst the guests there too. I used to go to Val Bevan's house quite a lot – mum took me over, to visit them; Val showed me her horses. Sometimes she came over to baby-sit, when we lived in the Hamstead – Handsworth Wood area.

"Mum and dad would think of names for the next club and discuss suitable décor. Mum thought about the colour schemes; the décor and things like that. Dad would pick all the furnishings and carpets. In the earlier days, they were definitely a team effort. Being a few years older than Abigail and Danny, I saw more of the positive side of their relationship; when they were getting on really well. I never heard them argue, or have a cross word. They were always laughing – my dad was permanently laughing; it was such a happy time."

Councillor Ken Hardeman was a former owner of the *Celebrity Restaurant*, the *Pickwick*, in Needless Alley and then two more places, out in Worcestershire. Over the years we became good friends. More recently he became owner of the *Brasshouse*, on Broad Street. He was one of the founders of the Birmingham Convention and Visitors Bureau, with myself and the other club owners.

"By then I knew that Eddie was a major player in the nightclub scene that was Birmingham," observes Ken. "I claim, justifiably, to be the man who created Eddie's opportunity to *Barbarella's*. I opened the door on that premises, but I didn't create any special terms. All I did was to open up an opportunity for him, in the early 1970s, when I was sitting on the Estate Committee.

"Eddie wanted to find a property, so we went to look at a building in Oozell Street, just off Broad Street; that was when I first experienced his visionary approach. It was an ex-engineering, scruffy-looking, dirty place. Eddie walked in and his eyes lit up – almost immediately. He wandered around: 'Oh I can see this. I'll have this room here, that room there.' And of course he repeated that, for some of his other clubs. Eddie and I met socially," concludes Ken. "We would go to events and he and his family would be there – his brothers and their wives."

When we converted *Barbarella's*, it was a major piece of work. We had seven days to do it, although everybody said it was impossible. We had people, myself included, working all night long.

Froggie recalls: "I was there with Eddie, whilst *Barbarella's* was being done up. He was always 'hands on'. It was important to Eddie, what it would be like for the customer. He catered for all kinds of people. I always thought that Eddie had a wonderful vision. He took me around the bar; it had been open about a week. There were some alterations, which weren't quite right, in the Top Bar. Then all of a sudden, a car reversed straight through the wall. Some drunks in the car park, on the other side of the wall, had slapped the car into reverse – and it ended up behind the bar! Eddie said: 'I don't know… they'll do anything to get in without paying!'"

Joe Frazier & the Knockouts were actually Top of the Bill, with a girl singer. Joe came on later, after Froggie. We saturated the market for weeks before, with lots of press releases and large advertisements on buses; so thousands turned up on the Opening Night. We had national TV coverage, with lots of prime time advertising – around the time that Coronation Street went out.

Kenny Lynch remembers one evening in particular, at *Barbarella's*, when Joe Frazier was coming to see what the room was like, where he'd be performing. "When I finished my act Joe was sitting at a corner table with Eddie; about seven people altogether," recalls Kenny. "Joe started telling me stories about Cassius Clay. Apparently, the two of them were really the best of friends. After training Joe would say: 'I'll see you up in Howard Johnson's for a coffee, but don't start getting stupid man!' But as soon as Joe walked into Howard Johnson's, Clay would say: 'Oh God help me – Joe Frazier's in here!' Joe would say: 'Sit down man, for Christ's sake!' Every time I think about Eddie, I remember that he was the fella who introduced me to Joe Frazier – who told me all these fantastic stories."

Joe had a Bouncer, named Nick with him, on the opening night – a great big black guy. He was twice the size of Joe Frazier! A nuisance boxer, from London, kept jumping on the stage and interfering with the star. Joe was a fantastic singer – and dancer. This boxer was pretending to fight with Joe, but he was spoiling the show. So Nick got up, picked him up, carried him off and put him some distance away, in the restaurant – a long way away; he'd got three or four other nuisances with him. So I took them down in my car, to *Rebecca's* and put them in the *Sin Bin* bar, with a lot of girls around them.

But suddenly, they were back again! By three o'clock in the morning everybody had more or less gone. Frazier and his team were in a raised, higher part of the restaurant, having a party, with waiters waiting on them, but this London boxer was still upsetting things. Big Nick said: "Eddie my son, no trouble at all. We are the champions of the world – not these guys." He just picked him up; the other two guys with him put them outside the door; called them a taxi, to take them back to London. They kicked the door, for about twenty minutes, but of course, it was all reinforced. We switched the bells off, so that we couldn't hear these fellas outside ringing them. Joe and I had a lovely night, and he invited me to come over to America. I said; "You won't remember me, amongst all those millions of people." He said: "I will Eddie. I shall never forget you."

Musical Director Mike Alexander worked for me, on and off, from 1971-1976, and then later, at various times.

"My association with Eddie began when I left the *Ambassador's Club*, in Augustus Road, Edgbaston, which was owned by Harry Morrall," Mike explains. "I'd been working there for two years, until 1970/71, with my own jazz trio – a bass player called Colin Motié and a drummer called Slim Simons. Harry decided to end the *Ambassador's Club*. After a week I got a call from Eddie, to go and be his Musical Director at *Barbarella's Club*. There was a special room called *The Take Two Room*. Eddie said: 'Now, this is your room.' That's where my trio was going to play, for a more sophisticated audience than, as it turned out, they were getting in the main discos. His friends, his wife and family came too.

"I remember going to Crane's – the piano shop that used to be by Lewis's. They'd got this refurbished, nine-foot Steinway, in the main room upstairs. This smart-arsed salesman said something like: 'It's £8,000.' Eddie said: 'Well look, I'll toss you a coin for it.' The fella agreed and he got his own coin. They tossed it for half the price – £4,000, Eddie called 'heads' and won the toss, so he got the piano for half price. He also got the guy to throw in an adjustable piano stool, worth about £120!

"So the piano was delivered to the *Take Two Room*," continues Mike. "I was also compèring the shows in the main room above; shows like the Everly Brothers were great on stage, but they wouldn't speak to one another off stage; they had to have separate dressing rooms. Ike and Tina Turner came there too, before their marriage split up; they were Number One – fantastic.

"The first week that I started at *Barbarella's* Eddie had booked Salena Jones, for a cabaret in the *Take Two Room*. We had this new piano. Salena wasn't happy with my drummer, and unfortunately we just did not see 'eye-to-eye'. Another week, Eddie provided an orchestra for her. She came out to perform the opening number. I'd got a different drummer at this point, as she didn't like the other one. She started to sing in the wrong key. She eventually got it, but not without some huge embarrassment at first. A successful MD needs infinite patience. Often, with the best will in the world, if an artiste *does* make a mistake, then the Musical Director has to assume the responsibility.

"Monday, Tuesday and Wednesday were always pretty quiet," continues Mike. "So we decided to run talent competitions there. We'd advertise in the local paper. It is actually true that a man won one of the competitions by playing the spoons. It's just that when people used to ask Eddie what had happened to the man who played the spoons, he'd make a joke about it, saying that he was now in Hong Kong, trying to win a trip back! An eighty-year-old woman won the Hot Pants Competition. She was up there, giving it plenty, and everyone could see that she was so old that they were clapping as hard as they could, so that she would win. So she was winning week after week. Jimmy Tarbuck sometimes helped Eddie with the judging.

"The thing that I *really* remember about the talent show was that quite a scruffy girl came in. She was about seventeen, wore a denim top, denim jeans. Her hair looked as if someone had stuck a bowl on her head and cut round it! I said: 'What do you do?' She said: 'I play the piano and I sing.' I said: 'Okay then.' I didn't have time to do auditions. If they brought us music, we'd quickly glance at it, then we'd play it and they'd go and sing. The girl I described performed her songs and I was very impressed. I asked her if she'd got a music publisher, adding: 'I think that's where your fortune lies – writing songs – music publishing.' As it turned out – that girl was Victoria Wood! I never saw her again, from that day to this, to tell her: 'Hey, I was right!'

"We had Chuck Berry there, on tour with the *Roy Young Band*. I was only involved with the one show that evening. Chuck came for an afternoon sound check. That evening I couldn't get him on until about half past eleven. He played 'til twelve o'clock, then came off. I went on stage and said: 'Ladies and gentlemen, Chuck Berry,' expecting him to come back on and do a bit more," recalls Mike. "Then all of a sudden a bottle and a glass went over my head; they started to break the club up!"

For an audience viewpoint of this, see Sheila Williams' letter, at the end of Chapter Nine. Meanwhile, behind the scenes, when the audience became impatient, I rushed to find Chuck, who was just outside the back door, with his guitar. Nobby Nobbs was holding him back. Nobby said: "He said he's going – he's had enough! The band is refusing to back him, because of what he's done to them." I said: "Well come on in. Leave it to me – I'll sort the band out."

I looked at Nobby, and then looked at the woman with the bag, because she had all of the money in there. I looked at Nobby with my eyes – and he knew what my eyes meant, straight away! So Nobby had the girl mugged by ones of the boxers, and off he went. Chuck was nearly in tears: "My money's gone and my guitar's gone!" I said: "Come back in here and I'll sort it out." I sat them all down and got the band to agree to back him, for the second show.

I asked Chuck where he'd been going with all of the money and he said: "Well, I forgot!" I said: "We'll get the money back. We'll soon find out who's had that." Of course, I knew exactly where it was. When he was back in the office he was shaking like a drug addict. I said: "Sit down and stop worrying. Your guitar will come back and your money will *definitely* come back. You go on and when you come back your money will be here." This was the thing he was doing all the time – charging extra, to do the False Tab. He expected another four hundred dollars: two hundred from the first show and the same amount for the second show. It was totally out of order.

We stalled until about eleven o'clock. I said: "If that money doesn't come back, I will pay you again. But if you don't go on again you're going to get nothing and I'll cancel the show." All of a sudden he jumped up and decided to go on; which I knew he would. He did exactly the same act for the second show. His guitar was back, but not his money. When it came to the False Tab, he stayed back again, saying yet again that he wanted another two hundred dollars. So I promised that would be sorted.

He went back on again, then I said: "Come back up the office now." Nobby and one or two of my men were standing round. I counted all of the money out for him again in one pound notes, saying: "Right there's the money, less the extra four hundred dollars that you were trying to get off us. We've had to pay a reward of £500 to get the money back." So we charged him the £500 – which he was so pleased to pay! The next day he was in Scotland, and the evening papers following his performance read: 'Riot at Chuck Berry's Show.' He'd done the same to the band again and the audience rioted. That was the trouble with Chuck Berry – he was so mixed up and unpredictable. But I brought him back two years later and he did the show – and this time he behaved himself!

"I remember another time at *Barbarella's*," continues Mike, "when Eddie *desperately* wanted to get Jack Jones, because he was the ballad singer of the day. He was coming in seven days' time and Eddie decided to make it a really special gig. Although the main room held two thousand people standing, he wanted to have everybody sitting, so he knocked the back wall out of the room. There was another disco behind that. He built the floor up in the disco room, so that it was about eight foot high, knocked this wall through, put tables and chairs in this back room, so that people could look through the hole in the wall, at Jack Jones on the stage, which would give him another hundred seats or so. He did all of this in a week!

"Then on the morning that Jack Jones was supposed to come, we had a telephone call from Harold Davidson, Jack Jones' booking agent, to say that he wasn't coming. We decided to get some more acts together, during the day. Eddie found a few of his people; I found a few of mine. We'd got a fantastic show on the night, with about six different acts, including Tina Charles, the *Fantastics*, Freddie Starr, plus an 18-piece orchestra as well. We hadn't told anybody that Jack Jones wouldn't be there.

"When people arrived that evening Eddie said: 'Look, I'm sorry, we've been let down, but we've got a fantastic show for you; this is who we've got on.' The place was *heaving*. Hardly anybody turned away. So instead of paying their ten or twenty quid for two, people came in free to see the show. We offered to give them their money back for their tickets, if they had pre-booked, but very few of them chose to do that. So that was a fantastic night, with Freddie Starr and the other people who were on.

"The other Jack Jones story is when he was appearing at the *Odeon*, in New Street. Eddie phoned me that morning and said that apparently Jack Jones wanted to see if *Barbarella's* was worth working in the future. This was a Saturday night. He was going to come later, after he'd done his own show. Now, you can imagine, this is a disco that we're talking about. Eddie has got tables on the dance floor, candles in the middle of the table, tablecloths, chairs et cetera. He's playing Tony Bennett, Jack Jones and Frank Sinatra records on the disco. These kids are coming in, thinking that they're coming to a disco, when all the time we're trying to create the right effect for when Jack Jones comes in. So all of these kids are wandering what the hell is happening!

"Eddie's wife, Hazel, his brothers and their wives; friends and their wives... they're all in evening dress, ready to have a chat with Jack Jones, in the *Take Two Room*, where my trio's playing. So I suggested to Eddie that

Chrissie and I should collect Jack in the Rolls Royce. Chrissie drove the car, and parked it down the side of the *Odeon*; we were the only Rolls Royce there.

"We went in the Stage Door at the back," recalls Mike. "I saw Jack Jones' manager, but he said: 'Oh, I don't know whether Jack Jones is going to do that!' Jack Jones comes off stage, goes into his dressing room. Chrissie and I go into his dressing room, saying: 'If you'd like to join us we can take you back in the Rolls Royce.' At that point Jack Jones was going out with Susan George, the actress, who was apparently staying in the hotel with him. So Jack turned to me and said: 'Well actually, I don't feel very well. Susan's not feeling very well either tonight – she's got a cold – so I'm not coming.' Well, I could hardly contain Chrissie, because he wanted to hit him!" remembers Mike.

Chrissie was a bit wild – I had to watch him all the time. If they'd done something to me, he'd just want to hit them. The trouble was that, allegedly, Susan George was going out with somebody else, who was in Birmingham. She was around *Barbarella's*. I could be wrong, but I was under the *impression* that Susan George didn't want to come back with Jack, to *Barbarella's*, because we knew who she was going out with.

"Anyway, we told Eddie that he wasn't coming, but that he'd given me a signed photo to give to him. Eddie threw it behind the bar," continues Mike. "I've never seen *Barbarella's* cleared so quickly, as it was that night. They cleared everything out, put the disco records back on; so Jack Jones let Eddie down twice."

The second time that Jack let us down, I went down to the Odeon and got some placards, and I had two girls standing outside, saying: "Jack Jones – fulfil your obligation to *Barbarella's*." The funniest part about it was that Jack had sent me tickets to go and see the show. They were using Servin Veger, a fantastic American PA system; the best there was, in those days. A lot of artistes asked specially for it. I actually installed it for *Frankie Valli and the Four Seasons*.

I installed a sophisticated tape system too, which meant that you didn't need particular musicians, because certain sounds were incorporated into the system. So they'd got this very expensive system on at the *Odeon* during the Jack Jones Show – the same as we'd got in *Barbarella's* and *Abigail's*, but it was tuned into the same radio frequency as the local taxis. We were sitting in the *Odeon* and Jack Jones was singing a ballad. You could have heard a pin drop. All of the girls were swooning – even my wife was a-swooning –

because he was a fantastic singer. Then all of a sudden, the sound came across: "A taxi for *Barbarella's* – Mr. Fewtrell – straight away!" And I tell you what – I slid down in the seat and I thought: 'I've got to get out of here. I hope no one recognises me!'

"Around the time that we did the Chuck Berry show Eddie booked a band called Tony Orlando and *Dawn*, which included a couple of girl singers," continues Mike. "They were the biggest selling recording artistes in the world, at that time, having sold eighteen million records, in twelve months. They had hits with *Tie a Yellow Ribbon* and *Knock Three Times*. They were absolutely fantastic, but there were only two hundred people that particular Tuesday, because what nobody could have foreseen was that there were three World Title fights – on that one night. So the audience were mainly boxing people, who'd been to see the fight at the Villa ground. Then they were going on to the *Odeon*, to see Muhammad Ali and Joe Frazier. They didn't want *any* music – they were drunk anyway. All of these boxers were up in the *Top Bar* at *Barbarella's*, laughing and joking and taking no notice of Tony at all. He was a well-built guy himself, from the Bronx, in New York and he had no fear.

"He ran off the stage, up the stairs to the bar, slammed his fist on the bar and he *screamed* at these people: 'I expect you to listen to me. I'm going to make sure that I entertain you. I've never been treated like this in my career. I'm not going off this stage, until you show some appreciation!' They all looked at him as though he was mad. Anyway, he went back on stage, sang a few more songs, and they showed a little bit more appreciation of him. He did approximately an hour and fifteen minutes, then went off to the dressing room. I went backstage and said: 'I'm sorry Tony. It's just a bad night.' He said: 'Mike, I've never had an audience like that. I've sold eighteen million records in twelve months. We normally get standing ovations. I'll never forget this gig!'

"At the end of the *Barbarella's* days, Carl Wayne asked me to be his Musical Director. I left *Barbarella's* around 1972/73. Carl and I toured for about eighteen months, mainly in this country, with the occasional trip abroad to do a Song Festival – in Yugoslavia and Bulgaria, where Carl's popularity could have made him a huge star. But there was a currency issue at the time, whereby it was difficult to take money out of the country.

"So, in chronological order, I worked as a Musical Director for Carl Wayne, between 1972 to 1973. After that I returned to Eddie and worked for him at *Abigail's*. From 1976 until 1979/1980 I worked for *Peters & Lee*; then Freddie Starr – for about ten days! After that I worked for Shirley Bassey for a total of fifteen years. That was for two different periods: firstly from 1980 until 1988; secondly, between 1990 until 1995/96. From 1994 to 1999 I was Musical Director for *Pebble Mill*. Also in 1999 I worked for Jane McDonald. Following that I worked with Gary Wilmot, who has become a close friend," concludes Mike.

Tony Christie and I first met at *Rebecca's* nightclub in 1971, when he'd had three hit songs, including *I Did What I Did For Maria* and *Las Vegas*. He was on there for a week and Billy Fury was on the same bill. Tony was born Antony Fitzgerald, in Conisbrough, South Yorkshire. His mother was English, but his father's side of the family are Irish. Sean Fitzgerald, his son, became his manager just over three years ago. Sean is responsible for getting Tony back into the UK, although he'd been living in Spain for fifteen years. Work had dried up in the UK, but Tony was doing wonderfully well everywhere else on the Continent.

"We were having a drink in the bar at *Rebecca's*," remembers Tony. "For some reason Bev Bevan was in that night. He joined us for a drink. I'd changed my surname to Christie, because I saw the film called *Darling*, starring Julie Christie. I thought the name had a nice ring to it. Eddie said: 'I want you to come down to the bar after your performance. Billy Fury's there; he's having a drink.' He'd make sure that none of his artistes were bothered.

"One particular night, I finished up staying at Eddie's, rather than driving home, because at the time I was living in Sheffield. I think they parked my car up for me too. Eddie said: 'Oh don't worry about that. My mates will park it at the Fire Station opposite.' I stayed with Eddie and Hazel that night. They were quite young, and had one child – Rebecca. There was standing room only at *Rebecca's* when I performed there on stage. People filtered through from the other floors when it was time for the Cabaret Spot."

Tony did the show upstairs, in the *Cabasa*, where we would put the Artiste of the Week.

"The place would be quite empty before midnight," continues Tony. "The show began about 12.30 or 1 am in the morning, when everyone had got to the nightclubs. Suddenly, the place was jam-packed... heaving! It was a great atmosphere, with the entire audience swaying and singing – and joining in; especially to my 'up-tempo' songs.

"I'd got a good reputation, before the hits records. I was already a 'name' on the cabaret circuit. *I Did What I Did For Maria* was number 2 in the Charts in 1971; *Is This The Way To Amarillo* reached number 18, so I had three Top Twenty hits that year. *Las Vegas* reached 16 or 17.

"I met my wife, Sue, when she came to see me in a show, in 1966. Generally, I did my show, then drove home to Sheffield. We'd got a little boy, Sean, who was three years old, and my wife had just had a little girl. Antonia is my eldest daughter. She married a French man and they have two children. They live in Brussels – he works for NATO, so both of the kids are bi-lingual. They can switch from Spanish to French – and they're only five and six. She's got a boy and a girl: The girl's called Tais; and her son is Paddy, named after my dad. My youngest daughter, Sarah, is thirty-one and she's a Headmistress at Matching Green Primary School in Essex. She lives in Thaxted and she's got a little boy, called Isaac. Then Sean, my eldest, is married with three kids, including a baby daughter.

"I always had a band with me. We could interchange musicians if we needed to, with a good rehearsal. I knew Mike Alexander, because at the time he was playing for Carl Wayne. We used to meet at motorway service stations at three o'clock in the morning, coming back from gigs. That was before he left to manage Shirley Bassey.

"I was at the *Dolce Vita* before the hits. Des O'Connor came into the club; he was doing panto. That was about 1968. I was headlining at the club and Des came to see me there. Then we got a phone call from Des O'Connor's agent, asking me to do the *Des O'Connor Tonight* show, which was televised from the *London Palladium*. So suddenly I was doing a major TV show – from the *London Palladium*… live – which was frightening! It was a great date."

Tony took part in a Charity Event, with Marti Caine, Bev Bevan and *Cannon & Ball* and lots of others – in Birmingham. Most of the artistes there were working in Birmingham at the time. Although his popularity waned in Britain, through most of the 1980s and 1990s Tony maintained a successful singing career in continental Europe; especially in Germany, with a sing-along style. In 2002 *Is This The Way To Amarillo* was used in the comedy series *Peter Kay's Phoenix Nights*, leading to a resurgence in his popularity. The song was then re-released on 14 March 2005, to raise money for the Comic Relief charity and reached number one in the charts – outselling all the first release's chart run put together.

"People forget that when that was released my album was already at number three in the charts," explains Tony, "before that single was re-released. Of course when *Amarillo* came out, my album went straight to number one as well. So within a few weeks I had a number one album and single. What Peter Kay did with the track, when he made that video, was pure genius! It just grabbed a whole generation of kids."

Tony released his new album, *Simply In Love*, on 6 November 2006, to excellent reviews; 2007 has been even busier.

"I'm going to have to pull back a little," he explains. "You can take booking after booking – and then you panic – because you're overbooked! I was in Australia and New Zealand in January and February 2007. After that I did a UK tour between April June too – just a mini tour this time, because the record company insist that I have to be limited; so I just put ten or twelve days together, with a small band.

"Generally, club owners keep their distance, but with Eddie and I it was a *genuine* liking for each other; once I got used to his Birmingham accent! Even though he had this reputation I thought: 'I can't see you being a 'baddie'! I think he's one of those people who could be a friend for life – but also, you wouldn't want to make an enemy of him! But you'd like him on your side. He put the hours in – and he wouldn't ask anybody to do what he couldn't do himself. I got the impression he was 'hands on' – managing the bar; checking the cellars," recalls Tony.

In 1972, Kenny Hatton started to work for me, as a bar manager.

"When I finished with Jimmy Tarbuck, Edward gave me a job at *Barbarella's*," recalls Kenny. "*Barbarella's* was the first big club in Birmingham. It was a tremendous place, with three big rooms, the largest of which could hold well over two thousand people. We had all the big names – *Queen*, Lulu, you name it; they were all there.

"As you went in, there was a big long entrance. To the right of that was one of the three rooms; each room had its own name. At the top of the entrance, you'd walk along to the biggest of the three rooms. Turning right, you'd go along another passage to the third room. The queues used to be from the front door, right out onto Broad Street, because nowhere else provided such a range of live bands – it was just incredible! All the pop groups, like *The Move*, for example – they used to play for Edward at the *Cedar Club*. Roy Wood and Jeff Lynne had become big stars; they used to play at *Barbarella's*. Some of the big American jazz singers were there too. Edward sometimes used to phone up and say: 'We're going to the *Belfry* at Sutton Coldfield.' They had a little disco there on a Monday night, so I'd pick him up and we'd go there.

"Some nights he'd decide to go down to London. I'd drive him down there, with Gordon and Jane – his brother and sister-in-law. He said: 'We're staying at the *Hilton* and we're going to see Frank Sinatra. He took us to one of the famous festivals in London too. That was on the Sunday. We had lunch in Hyde Park, came back to Birmingham, and then it was back to work.

"I met Cathy in 1976 and we got married in 1978. She worked part-time in Reception, at the club," explains Kenny. "During the day she was a nurse. We had our wedding reception at *Barbarella's*, which was great. *Barbarella's* was probably the largest of all. Gary Holton used to perform there on a Sunday night, with his band – *Heavy Metal Kids*. Gary began work on *Auf Wiedersehen Pet* in 1983, so his performances at *Barbarella's* pre-date that. He didn't act 'the big star' – he was very modest," Kenny concludes.

After working for me, Kenny managed several pubs for M & B, including some in Birmingham, Bournemouth, then back to Colmore Row and finally *The Old Royal* in Church Street. Then he rejoined me, as you'll see in later chapters.

Jimmy Tarbuck was in *Barbarella's* one night, at the raised bar. People went hysterical when celebrities were about, so the doormen formed a moving bodyguard, to put a bit of space between the celebrity and the public. I had a roped off area, usually at the end or corner of a bar. I had a specific space by the stairs, otherwise people drove you mad. You cannot believe! You get a place with three or four thousand people in it, all doing everything they can to get to them. They rushed the stage, when Joe Frazier threw his shirt off. Coming back to Tarbuck, I hadn't had time to organise bodyguards around him. I reached the bar and just cleared the people out of the area, and put some stools across. Meanwhile, two guys forced their way in and began manhandling him. You could see that Jimmy and his wife were becoming frightened, so I was forced to clip the guys – very quietly – and then get them out. When I go to Portugal, Jimmy will bring it up again. He's never forgotten it, because of the professional way I handled it.

One of the best audiotapes that *Queen* ever recorded was done at *Barbarella's*. When Buddy Greco performed *McArthur Park*, the club used to be packed out everybody went very quiet: it gave me goose-pimples – all the way down my back. So when I bought this big Steinway I asked Mike Alexander to practise *McArthur Park*, until he could play it as good as Buddy Greco. People used to ask: "Is that Buddy Greco playing over there?"

I knew the guy at the *Night Out* very well – I used to go there a lot, with Jimmy Tarbuck and others. The guy phoned and said: "Eddie, Jack wants to come over to see Buddy Greco." Jack was wary of me; as we've explained, he'd pulled some strokes on me. I said: "There's no problem at all. I'll wait for him and take him in."

I took him to the private bar and asked if he'd like a drink. He said: "I'd love one." So I said: "Jump behind and have what you want." So he served me and Hazel to a drink. I said: "Here you are Hazel – we've been served by Jack Jones!" We had a laugh about it, this-that-and-the-other. He said: "Is Buddy on?" I said: "Yes, take him a drink."

So he got a drink in his hand and he was walking up. I walked up behind him, to put Hazel on my table, which I was also going to put Buddy Greco on. But before he got there, Buddy Greco, sitting at the piano, saw him, got the microphone and said: "Ladies and gentlemen, Jack Jones – hi Jack!" Then he stood up, brought him on stage. So Jack's up there with Buddy, and they started singing together. There was champagne at my table; my missus was a bit drunk and she was always a bit of a show-off with the other girls. When it came down to one or two ballads, Jack started singing to some of girls at my table. My missus took her shoe off – she had millions of pairs of shoes! She poured some champagne into her shoe, gave it to Jack Jones to drink – and he drank it! He turned round – and I swear to God – he said: "Is there anything else I can do for you my dear?!" He thought she was my girlfriend you see? My missus turned round and said: "Yes, you can give me the seventeen grand that you owe my husband!" I was so embarrassed, because I was just pleased that he was up there. He smiled away – but he left her alone after that!

During the *Cedar Club* and *Barbarella's* days, we used to give our customers a ticket, each with a number on it, as they came into the club. Then after one or two months we'd draw the winning ticket out. The ticket owner would win a new car; the second prize might be a gold watch. Don Carlos – Carlos the Cook, off *Crossroads*, would present the prize. It was all good publicity for the clubs.

I had a girl come in who was topless, but wearing a coat, when topless was never heard of before. As the press came in, she had to throw the coat off, come straight to me and I'd pretend to push her away. But when they took the photographs, it looked as if my hands were on her boobs. Consequently, when I was having my Sunday dinner – (I hadn't had time to see the papers) my missus came up, with her boobs hanging out, to serve my dinner! So I said: "What's all this then?" She said: "You like bare tits, don't you?!" I said: "What do you mean?" And she showed me the paper. I was on the front page and apparently I was on all the mens' toilet doors for years. It looked as if my hands were on her!

Big Albert has in turn been a road manager and an agent for various groups, including *Black Sabbath*. He recalls: "A record company would send people called A & R – for 'Artistes and Repertoire'. They came out regularly, looking for new products. Edward's was a great showcase for them. He had lot of main acts on, but also a lot of the local bands used to play there. The bands would play for nothing, willingly, just to be seen. That's still happening to this day. In fact, you *pay* to go on tour with some of these bands."

I didn't like the Punk scene one bit. The public demanded that they should go on, but by this time no council would allow them to. So we had to announce their appearances through a sort of code: 'Appearing at *Barbarella's* – SPOT'. People didn't know what it meant, but it actually meant: '*Sex Pistols* On Tour'. Only the fans knew what it actually meant so there'd be a whole network of telephone calls and messages between the fans, informing each other exactly where the concerts were. We used to get thousands of fans at each show, but in the end I stopped putting them on, because it was far too dangerous and we were risking our licence. But before we stopped it, they'd performed for us lots of times.

Patti Bell remembers Georgie Fame being at *Barbarella's* and Alan Price. Also, John Walker, of the *Walker Brothers* – "We used to talk about the music scene and fashion," recalls Patti. "He was really nice. I was on the door quite a lot in there too." Patti and Steve Gibbons were together for sixteen years. They have two sons, Jake and Dylan, whom we mentioned in an earlier chapter, about the parties at my house. Dylan DJs and makes music tapes; Jake is in a band and promotes other bands. Nowadays, Steve is with his new partner, Susy, and they have a daughter.

After working for me, Patti became a clothes designer. She opened a shop, with William Bray, in Hurst Street, Birmingham; he died tragically – in a road accident.

Left: Eddie's first nightclub, the Bermuda Club L-R: Gordon, Hazel, Don Giles, whose father helped Eddie and Frank to build the club. By kind permission of Rebecca Fewtrell. Right: The legendary Bermuda Club, c. 1958 L-R: Lenny Smith, Don Reuben, Eddie, Don Butler and Larry Farrington. By kind permission of Rebecca Fewtrell.

Eddie's favourite photograph of Hazel, taken in 1961. By kind permission of Rebecca Fewtrell.

Left: Eddie has been lumbered with Simon Smith's Amazing Dancing Bear! ITV Sport's commentator Simon Smith left his pet bear in Reception, during a visit to the Cedar Club. By kind permission of Daniel Fewtrell. Right: The Fewtrell brothers line up in the Cedar Club Reception Area – perhaps they're looking for the bear?! From L-R: Frank, Chrissie, Donald, Gordon, Johnny Edward, Stanley Kay, and Roger. By kind permission of Johnny Fewtrell.

The brothers and Stanley again, this time, outside the Cedar Club, in 1965. If you look closely, you'll see it's the same evening as the previous photo. From L-R; Frankie, Donald, Edward, Stanley Kay, Gordon, Johnny and Chrissie. Eddie's E-type Jaguar is in the centre. By kind permission of Johnny Fewtrell.

More early days at the Cedar Club. Closer examination shows that the man on the far left, is the same person as the guest on the far right of the top photo on page II. Could someone please identify him? Back row, L-R: Edward, Val Taylor and Frankie – partially hidden; Robert Lisle. Seated, front row: Flo Frost, Donald, Vera, Jimmy Lisle, Hazel and June Lisle, Rob's ex-wife. By kind permission of Gordon Fewtrell.

Eddie at the Cedar Club, with members of the Nightriders and the Vikings; do you recognise any of them. By kind permission of Mike Lavender.

Left: Dave Reuben, Eddie and Hazel, at the Cedar Club. Dave's son, Don, was killed in a tragic motor accident. By kind permission of Rebecca Fewtrell. Centre: Johnny Prescott was a well known figure at the Cedar Club. He and Chrissie argued over Paulette, who eventually became Chrissie's first wife. Eddie and Johnny were good friends; he was a frequent spectator at Johnny's boxing matches, accompanied by Paulette. By kind permission of Rebecca Fewtrell. Right: George Fewtrell, at the Cedar Club, has a definite 'twinkle in his eye'! By kind permission of Rebecca Fewtrell.

Left: L-R: Bomber, Johnny, Joyce Mucklow, Jane and Gordon Fewtrell. Hazel, Flo Frost and Jimmy Lisle – one of Jane's two brothers. By kind permission of Rebecca Fewtrell. Right: 'Ready Steady Teddy', a Cedar Club 'character', on his way back to camp… only kidding! By kind permission of Roy Edwards.

Left: Patti Bell, on Reception, during the early days of the Cedar Club. She became an invaluable member of Eddie's staff, in several of his clubs. Photo by kind permission of Patti Bell. Right: Mike Horseman, in disc jockey mode, at the Cedar Club. Mike, who later became a professional photographer, has loaned us a great selection of photos for our book. By kind permission of Mike Horseman.

Left: From L-R: Bomber's first wife, Peggy, her friend, Maggie Forte and Bomber, at a Fancy Dress Party, at the Cedar Club. By kind permission of John Fewtrell. Right: The second opening of the Cedar, following Georgian-style refurbishment and the removal of the island bar. From L-R: Peggy's sister, Peggy and Bomber. By kind permission of John Fewtrell.

Left: Ken Hardeman: photo taken from Ken's advertising poster, when he was standing for election in the Newtown Ward of the city, in May 1966. By kind permission of the late Ken Hardeman. Right: Mark Smith, award-winning cocktail maker, pictured at the Albany Hotel, Hurst Street. By kind permission of Mark Smith.

Left: The Rum Runner, 1980. From L-R: Mike, with lady friend; 'Whiskers' – a retro clothing salesman. Sue Buxton, a girlfriend of one of the disc jockeys. Simon Le Bon, of Duran Duran, is behind her. Photographer: Paul Edmond. By kind permission of Mike Horseman. Right: Syd Clegg, and his wife, Cynthia, with friends, Doctor Nick Radvanyi and his wife, Rita. Photograph taken at Penns Hall Hotel, Sutton Coldfield, the Birmingham Markets Annual Dinner Dance, c. 1976. By kind permission of Rita Radvanyi.

The Castaways, during the 1960s. L-R: Eddie, Hazel, Sue – Bomber's second wife, and Bomber; Gordon Pinson's wife, Lorraine. Gordon Pinson, Frankie Warwood and his wife, June; Peter Price and his wife. By kind permission of Rebecca Fewtrell.

A Jack Solomons Dinner-Boxing Show, for the World Sporting Club, held at the Grosvenor Hotel, London, during the 1970s. From L-R: Stan Bailey (circled); Tom O'Boyle, Bill Coleman, Brendan Joyce, Martin Connelly, Bill Cutler, Alan Manning, John Rischmiller, and Don Fewtrell. By kind permission of Brendan Joyce, from his private collection.

XL's Nightclub, c. September 1992. From L-R: a Birmingham City football fan; Pat Cowdell and Chrissie Fewtrell. By kind permission of Mike Horseman.

Left: Bunty Broadhurst and family, at the refurbished Cedar Club. By kind permission of John Fewtrell. Right: Fashion designers, Jane Kahn and Patti Bell. Boy George and Simon Le Bon are valued friends and customers. Patti has also designed for Pamela Stephenson, Fiona Richmond, Bucks Fizz, Roy Wood and Sue Pollard. By kind permission of Patti Bell.

Left: Patti Bell, with Sid Vicious, in Barbarella's Top Bar. By kind permission of Patti Bell. Centre: Eddie bought the Savoy Hotel in John Bright Street, then converted it into Abigail's, a high class nightclub and restaurant, with international acts and bands. The club, which also provided valet parking, opened its doors on 25 February 1974. Club brochure from John Fewtrell's private collection. Right: Abigail's, c. 1975, named after one of Eddie's daughters. L-R: a friend, Barbara Atkins, Eddie and Leamington Jack, as sheiks, and a girl in a Hawaiian outfit. By kind permission of John Fewtrell.

Abigail's, c. the 1974 opening. Eddie is in the centre, then from L-R: Bomber, Val Taylor (who became Val Bevan – Bev's wife); Ricky Rickaby; Jane and Gordon Fewtrell. By kind permission of Rebecca Fewtrell.

Left: Eddie and Tom Jones first met at the Cedar Club, in 1965, shortly before It's Not Unusual rocketed him to stardom. Later, when Eddie visited Las Vegas, Tom treated him royally, and introduced him to the stars. Photograph by Alan Johnson of Harborne, who took many of Eddie's photos, especially those of celebrities. Right: Muhammad Ali signs a pair of boxing gloves for Eddie, which were later auctioned for charity.

Left: Buddy Greco performed McArthur Park to packed audiences, at Barbarella's. Eddie asked Mike Alexander to perfect the number, until, eventually, customers couldn't tell the difference! Right: Eddie, in his 'Flower Power' days, flanked on either side by Bernie & Mike Winters. Photograph taken in Barbarella's office, by Alan Johnson of Harborne.

'Smokey' Joe Frazier & the Knockouts were top of the Bill, at the Opening Night, of Barbarella's. Joe enjoyed the experience so much that he invited Eddie to watch him box in America. Froggie was also on the bill.

Lulu & the Luvvers, at the Cedar Club in 1963, when Lulu was fifteen. 'Shout' had just been released. By kind permission of Rebecca Fewtrell.

Early 1960s – Mark Stuart & the Crestas. L-R: singer Brian Yeates aka 'Mark Stuart'; 'Big Tom' on drums, Archie Edwards – rhythm, and Brian Collingwood on bass. By kind permission of Brian Yeates.

The Move, in 1966: from L-R: Trevor Burton, Bev Bevan, Ace Kefford, Carl Wayne and Roy Wood. By kind permission of Bev Bevan.

Left: The Rockin' Berries, L-R: Chuck Botfield, Clive Lea, Bobby Thomson, Terry Bond and Jeff Turton. Photo taken in the mid 1960s By kind permission of Chuck Botfield. Right: Raymond Froggatt is one of five musicians who recall their memories of Eddie's clubs in Chapter Six. Around forty years ago, he formed the Raymond Froggatt Band. They were, from L-R: Lou Clark, Lou Abelthorpe, Froggie and H. Cain, 1969. By kind permission of RBM CONCERTS.

Left: Smith & Jones: Laurie Hornsby and guitarist John Caswell formed a singing duo whose name derived from a TV series. Managed by Martin Hone's company, Olé Ltd, they were regular performers at The Opposite Lock. By kind permission of Martin Hone, John Caswell and Laurie Hornsby. Right: Pictured outside Martin's Room, at The Opposite Lock, Gas Street, from L-R: Marion Montgomery, Martin Hone, Jack Douglas, Martin's wife, Patti, and Millicent Martin. By kind permission of Martin Hone.

Left: Marion Montgomery and Richard Rodney Bennett. Marion appeared regularly at The Opposite Lock, and also at Eddie's clubs. By kind permission of Martin Hone. Centre: Joan Armatrading, backstage at Barbarella's. By kind permission of Mike Horseman. Photographer unknown. Right: Salena Jones, in the main room at Barbarella's. By kind permission of Mike Alexander.

Left: Shirley Bassey and Mike, with a message that speaks for itself. By kind permission of Mike Alexander. Right: Sean Connery and Jimmy Tarbuck introduced Kenny Lynch to golf when he was in his thirties. From L-R: a golf professional, Bruce Forsythe, Max Bygraves, Ronnie Carroll and Kenny. Associated Tyres Golf Tournament at Stoke Poges, in the late 1960s. By kind permission of Kenny Lynch.

Left: Comedian Don Maclean starred with Mandy Rice-Davies, in A Bedful of Foreigners, in 1984. Don recalls various Birmingham nightclubs for our book, including the Cedar Club and The Opposite Lock, with anecdotes and observations about the entertainment scene in general. By kind permission of Don Maclean. Right: Dave Ismay, with Marti Caine. Dave first met Eddie at the Cedar Club, as a young police constable, before he became a comedian. His tales about the entertainment scene and about comedian friends such as Bob Monkhouse, Larry Grayson, et al, make lively reading! By kind permission of Dave Ismay.

Jack and the Beanstalk pantomime at the Alexandra Theatre, Birmingham, c. 1975, starring Jimmy Tarbuck. Dancer, Carrie Smart (who became John Fewtrell's second wife) had the dubious honour of playing the front half of the pantomime cow, while her cousin, Jill Jones, pictured right, drew an even shorter straw! See Chapter Nine for further details. By kind permission of John and Carrie Fewtrell, from their private collection.

Left: Four Stars Golf Tournament at Moor Park. Jimmy Tarbuck, Ronnie Corbett, Henry Cooper and Terry Wogan (not in photo) staged the event. Kenny Lynch is seated with Henry, in the audience. By kind permission of Kenny Lynch, from his private collection. Right: Kenny and 'Tarby' at a Birmingham nightclub – a double act that was destined to last for over forty years. By kind permission of Kenny Lynch.

Left: Victoria Wood was discovered by Mike Alexander and Eddie, at a Barbarella's talent competition, when she was a student of around seventeen. She won the competition. Mike, who predicted that she would go far, has yet to see her to say: "I was right!" Photographs by kind permission of Mike Horseman, seen here in the photo booth with her. Right: Bernard Manning, pictured with Sir Alex Ferguson, the manager of Manchester United. Bernard posted the photograph to us, immediately after my interview with him. Chapter Ten – 'Comedians', opens with Bernard; he and Eddie were very good friends. He will be sadly missed by many. By special permission of Bernard Manning, from his private collection.

"Then Jane Kahn joined me, recalls Patti. "I met her at Mike Horseman's. We set up a fashion shop, Kahn & Bell, in 1976, in the same shop, in Hurst Street. First of all it was just 'Retro' clothing. When Jane and I got together, the Punk scene was evolving, so we then started designing Punk clothes. Afterwards we went into the more Romantic era. Jane met someone out of Tick 'n Tock, and went to live in London. We had a shop together on the King's Road, but it became too difficult in the end – us both being in different cities. I went to live in London for a bit – left Steve. Then I came back, about a year later."

A Birmingham Mail newspaper article, dated 28 June 1989, featured Patti, describing how she designed for Pamela Stephenson, Simon Le Bon, Fiona Richmond, Bucks Fizz, Roy Wood and Sue Pollard: 'Strippers, sauna girls, gipsies and transvestites regularly call at her shop at 72 Hurst Street, to buy her outrageous creations.' Simon Le Bon and Boy George remain good friends of Patti's.

"We knew *Duran Duran* from the *Rum Runner*, so Jane and I started making clothes for them," Patti continues. "They actually wore them on stage. Before I opened my business, I worked at *Rebecca's* in Severn Street, then *Barbarella's* after that. I remember Freddie Starr at *Barbarella's*. He came over to the till, at the reception desk – probably because I was quite 'dishy' then. I think he was a bit of a ladies' man. He picked up my apple, ate half of it, then put it back! He was having helicopter lessons at the time. I remember meeting Buddy Greco: he was a real gentleman; a scholar type. He said: 'You look nice.' I introduced him to Steve. People get the idea that musicians are big-headed, but often they're just the same as everybody else.

"I was there the night that Chuck Berry was performing," recalls Patti. "I just remember these massive bodyguards, on stage. Chuck had them there to try and freak Eddie and other people out, but obviously, that wouldn't work. They were standing there at the side of the stage, while Chuck was performing – big 'Heavies'. It's mad isn't it? Steve had a Chuck Berry song in the Charts – *Tulane*: 'Tulane and Johnny opened a novelty shop. The goods were behind the bar – the cream of the crop.' (Meaning drugs, you know?) But it was a shame, because Chuck was a fantastic performer – doing all that Chicken Dance across the stage... fantastic!

"When we were barmaids at *Barbarella's*," Patti continues, "the customers used to give us money: 'Have a drink for yourself.' Chris Lambrianou gave me a coin, then realised that he wanted it back. It had a very special meaning for him... it was to do with something that he'd done for the Krays. He said it was his 'Lucky Coin'. Kenny Hatton explained the situation and I gave it him back. There was never any unfriendliness about it. Chris Lambrianou also asked me about one of the other barmaids. He came up to Steve and said: 'Could I speak to Patti about something?' The gangster thing – if you want to call it that – wasn't *like* that. They behaved like gentlemen," recalls Patti. "If they were going to do something they'd take somebody to one side; they wouldn't have a big punch-up like football hooligans!"

According to Steve Gibbons, "*Barbarella's* was a fantastic place. It was big enough to accommodate all tastes. As you walked through the door, you went past the Reception area, which either Chris Fewtrell, or one of the doormen would be in control of. Patti Bell would be collecting the money.

"Sometimes the doormen would look to Patti for advice: 'Is he okay?' Quite often it would be a musician, who the doormen knew nothing about. If she'd seen the band the musician belonged to play there before, it could have been six weeks previously, she'd remember them. Patti and I were together from about 1967 until 1983. Eddie would move people around, so she was sometimes a barmaid too, or on the roulette wheel. My very first album was *Short Stories*. On the sleeve of the album are pictures of myself and Patti – and Dylan, as a baby.

"It was so great for bands to go there. If you'd already played there, you didn't have to pay to go in. It was a special privilege. There was also a huge Reggae following in Birmingham; the *Cabasa* played mainly Reggae at one time. Then there was the main room, where you could see people like Freddie Starr. There would be the House Band – Mike Alexander and so on, so there was a real cross-section of stuff," recalls Steve.

"I finished working for Edward on 19 August 1979," explains John Fewtrell. "*Barbarella's* closed down on 20 August, the following day. I know this because my daughter was born on the day it closed."

Chapter Nine

CUPID... AND VOICES
FROM THE PAST

This chapter opens with a romantic meeting between Val Taylor and the celebrated pop musician and broadcaster Bev Bevan, on the first night of The Move's performance at the Cedar Club. Following this, Rita Radvanyi recalls how she also met her future husband, Doctor Nick Radvanyi at the club, around 1968/69. *Gordon Fewtrell relates how he met his future wife, Jane. Eddie explains how his brother Chrissie, now deceased, met both of his wives at the Cedar. John Fewtrell and his second wife, Carrie, met at Barbarella's.*

This first section is followed by 'Voices from the Past' – extracts from letters and e-mails we have received over the last few months, from other people who met at Eddie's clubs or worked for him, or knew him in some other way. Presented in alphabetical order, according to surname, they are as follows: Andy Cashmore; Kate Cook; Pam and Keith Dawes; Des Fitzpatrick; Mary Green; Stevie McCarthy; Pam Robinson; Lucy Wallis and Sheila Williams. As space is at a premium in the book, because there was such a proliferation of material to include, sadly, we have been unable to publish all of the correspondence that we received. Eddie and I offer our sincerest apologies to those whose letters we have been unable to include.

Patti Bell was playing Cupid, the night that Val and Bev Bevan met at the *Cedar*:
"I think *The Move* were on stage, with Charlie Wayne, and I said to Val: 'Come on, never mind those straight guys. Don't you fancy somebody in a band?' because I was interested in Charlie Wayne. I said: 'What about Bev – he's gorgeous!' Val said: 'Oh, he's quite nice.' Then I told Carl that Val liked Bev, so he came over to the bar and chatted her up – and they've been together ever since. It's *mad*, isn't it Eddie?"

Val explains: "I suppose it *was* all down to Patti Bell really. Eddie asked us all to work in the bar: Fran, Flo, Patti, Hazel and myself. The one girl, Flo

Frost, always worked the one end, where she got the most tips really, with the mohair suit people – they all wore mohair suits: the 'Townie' set. Patti always wanted to work on the other end of the bar, opposite the stage, because she loved the groups: she wasn't into mohair suits!

"The pop groups only drank Coca-cola – they never drank alcohol. Bev came up to the bar and ordered a coke. I said to Patti: 'Actually, he's quite nice – he looks clean!' Of course, she was ecstatic that I'd even *looked* at anybody in a group; she'd been trying to get me to go out with someone in a group for weeks! Patti loved Carl – I'm not sure whether she went out with him for a little while. When Bev sidled up to the bar, I can't remember our exact conversation, but in the end I said that I'd give him a lift home, otherwise it meant that he'd got to jump in the group's van; he didn't have any other transport. He was nearly always the last one to be dropped off – at about five o'clock in the morning."

Rita Radvanyi remembers: "I was going to the *Cedar Club* with a girlfriend one night. We were sitting on high stools up at the bar, having a drink and chatting away. It was an 'island' bar, which was circular: it curved all the way round, providing a good view of everyone seated there… which was great. Syd and Nick were on the other side of the bar and I became conscious of these two guys, looking over. I found that the blond one was smiling at me. In no time at all, he came over, tapped me on the shoulder and asked me if I'd like to dance.

"That was it. For the rest of the evening we stayed together and then ended up sitting at the bar, talking. Then he told me that his friend, Syd Clegg, had had a bet on whether they were going to be able to get me to dance with them. Syd said: 'Well, she's looking over here, but it's you she's looking at, not me!' And the rest is history! In two years we'd become engaged and married. Syd was Best Man at our wedding and he is my daughter's Godfather.

"I absolutely *adored* Nick's Hungarian accent – voices mean a lot to me; he had a very deep, rich, distinctive voice. He was a doctor… extremely charming and beautifully dressed; I must say that he always did wear beautiful clothes. Later, he became both Eddie and Gordon's family doctor. Nick often made me smile, because in the Hungarian language, there isn't a 'w': it's double v. If he lost his temper he would say: 'Vat do you vant voman?!' – which he often laughed about, I must say. So he was quite a character. Sadly Nick died a few years ago, as I'll explain, in a later chapter.

"Syd and I remain friends; I still see him to this day. That was only my second visit to the *Cedar*. Nick and I returned to the club for special occasions – if there was a big star coming; Edward often had big stars there, like Tom Jones, and all sorts of people. So occasionally we'd go back, to see the stars."

Gordon Fewtrell recalls: "Nick and Rita were very dear friends of mine. When I was forty-two, about twenty-five years ago, when I lived in Handsworth Wood, I lost about three-and-a-half stone, due to pernicious anaemia. I looked as white as a ghost. Rita came by and said: 'I'm going to get hold of Nick and get him to sort you out.' That same night, Nick got me into the Queen Elizabeth Hospital, where I was seen by a haematologist, and found to have just three-and-a-half pints of blood left in my body. If I'd left it until the Monday, I'd have been dead. So Nick and Rita actually saved my life!

"Like Rita and Nick, my wife and I also met at the *Cedar Club*. It was just after the opening of the club, in 1962, when it was new. I met Jane Lisle in there one night, with her brothers. I'd got another young lady with me at the time called Hazel, who lived by Erdington Lakes. I was introduced to Jane, by her brothers. In the old days, it was courtesy. I said: "I'm taking this young lady home first, and then I'm coming back for you!" I drove Jane barmy for a bit.

"She was only sixteen or seventeen at the time. I asked her to give me a kiss. She said: 'I won't let you kiss me. I don't even *like* you!' Anyway, she gave me a kiss and I said: 'I'm going to marry you,' – and I did! We've been married now for forty-two years; we were courting for three years before that, so we've known each other for forty-five years. We've got two grown-up daughters, Sally and Kate. Sally is a chiropodist, with a practice in College Road Erdington; Kate is a receptionist and a facial therapist."

Another of my brothers, Chrissie, met his first wife, Paulette, at the *Cedar* too. Eventually, they parted, and he married his second wife, Lisa Delmain, who was a singer with the *Second City Sounds*. Chrissie was a nice lad; he worked with me for many years. The strangest part is that Chrissie, Roger and Gordon were all lovely kids, who idolised me, because I more or less brought them up, as children. They did everything that I told them, you know? I used to advise them about what to do and what not to do, and they'd listen to my advice. But time moved on – and they met their wives....

Paulette was Johnny Prescott's girlfriend. I used to go out to boxing matches with Paulette and Johnny and with his manager George Biddle. We went to many of his fights. Johnny was up-and-coming and he worked for me on the door, at the *Bermuda Club*. He was quite shy, at that stage, and didn't know about 'power' – the power of *being* somebody; I was trying to steer him in the right direction.

So I'd go to all of his matches. There's actually a film somewhere, in the archives of me, sitting with Paulette, and she's going absolutely ballistic, because he's getting beaten up, in the ring! People seemed to think that she was my girl – but she wasn't. Prescott, as you know, became a big boxer; he fought Henry Cooper and other champions. He was a regular customer at the *Bermuda Club* and my friend, as well.

When he became famous, women started throwing themselves at Johnny, so eventually poor old Paulette was left out. She was an Irish girl with Irish beliefs and what-not. We remained friendly with her. In time, we had her working behind the bar in the *Cedar Club* so that she could meet somebody else. The first one who got involved with her was our Chrissie. He really took to her and they both started going out together; he was falling in love with her. But I noticed that whenever Johnny Prescott came in, she had eyes only for him and would 'fluff' around him. Chrissie used to get annoyed about it: I think she used to play him up, using Chrissie – and so forth. Prescott then tried to get her back and Chrissie was saying that he was going to kill him and so on.

This was while they were courting. I used to say to Johnny: "Don't get hurting him. He's my brother. You aren't with her now – she's free game. They're getting married, so don't be used." Johnny said: "But he keeps having a go at me." Chrissie and Johnny would be full of drink and they'd be firing at one another. So the one night, they got into a big row and I was absolutely sick of it. I said: "Why don't you go into Bond Street and have a fight? Remember, he's a trained fighter!" Chrissie said: "I don't care!"

We went outside and I took Johnny to one side. I said: "Listen John, don't hurt him, because if you do, you've got to fight the other seven brothers – and you won't win!" John was a bit anxious about that; he also knew that I would keep my word – and hit him with an iron bar – and possibly even kill him. So he was frightened – I could tell.

Chrissie seemed to think, from that day, that he got the better of Johnny. But I know for a fact that John was just pulling away. Prescott wasn't hitting him: he was just holding his punches; he could have knocked him out four or five times. Then after a bit, I just stepped in and pulled them apart. I said: "That's it – you've done enough now," and Johnny went home. But Johnny kept away from the *Cedar Club* after that – for quite some time.

Eventually, Chrissie got married to Paulette, but apparently, Paulette was very 'tight', as far as money was concerned: she used to use a teabag about four or five times! It was very difficult to live with; although Chrissie was getting phenomenal wages from me, he never had any money, because, allegedly, she would take the lot – and give him a pound back to spend! It was not as if he needed the pound, because when he was in the club he didn't have to pay for anything; later on, I found that he had other ways of making more money anyway: he was just taking money off the door. When membership fees and so on, were coming in, they'd go in his pocket; I caught him at it two or three times – at one time I had to sack him, because it was getting too much. He was obviously living way beyond his means, although in those days, he was getting at least £400-£500 per week. Allegedly, he couldn't cope with her excessive demands. According to Chrissie, she wanted a house like me; a Rolls Royce car like me and Chrissie was doing his best to keep up with her demands. Eventually I think that her tightness and the fact that he found out that she was seeing Prescott behind his back, when he was working, resulted in his divorcing her. Chrissie also told me that Paulette was seeing Prescott behind his back, when Chrissie was working at the club. He caught her two or three times. Eventually, they parted, and he married his second wife, Lisa Delmain, who was a singer with the *Second City Sounds*. You can read more about Chrissie in Chapter Eighteen, which is dedicated to the four of my brothers who have passed away.

The reason that we included this present chapter in the book is because I used to get lots of letters from people who *had* met at my clubs. Unfortunately, I didn't keep them, so we had nothing much to go on. We therefore set up a box number, via the press and radio and people have since written into us, not only about the dating situation at my clubs, but also about their other memories on the subject.

My brother, John, met his second wife, Carrie, at *Barbarella's*. Carrie, a dancer, was appearing in a Birmingham pantomime, with Jimmy Tarbuck and the *Grumbleweeds*. Carrie's role in the pantomime wasn't exactly a romantic one: she was playing one half of the pantomime cow! She was warned to be careful about dating John, because of the Fewtrell reputation.

In view of the complications arising from some of the romances that began at my clubs, for example Chrissie's, Big Albert's comment about the 'flip' side of the coin, seems a particularly apt one:

"You can imagine the other side: 'She just cost me a fortune. Don't you *ever* introduce me to anyone else like her again!'"

Here are some of those 'Voices from the Past' – people who have recently written to us. Some of the events that our writers mention may be found in more detail, elsewhere in the book.

Andy Cashmore writes:

Dear Shirley,

It was with interest that I saw your proposed book on Eddie Fewtrell. My uncle, Dennis Sullivan, whom you know already, was good friends with him, and could probably help you with some stories; he was mentioned in your Pat Roach book.

I also have good memories of Eddie's clubs – *Rebecca's*, *Barbarella's* and the *Cedar Club*. Because of his friendship with my Uncle Terry, Don's son, Eddie kindly gave my brother and myself a key ring, with the club logos on. These allowed us free entry to all of his venues, which I spent many happy hours in.

Rebecca's and *Barbarella's* had three clubs in one, as they were split into three different types of music. The *Cedar Club* was a place that if you got in before they shut, at two o'clock, you could stay in 'til daylight. *Barbarella's* was turned into a Punk venue, in the late 70s, and I saw many great bands there, including *Blondie*; *Ian Drury and the Blockheads*; Elvis Costello; *Sham 69*; *Siouxie and the Banshees*, to name a few – a far cry from the opening night, when the Top of the Bill was the *Hollies*; and the following week, former Heavyweight Champion, Joe Frazier, and his band the *Knockouts*.

Hope this has been of some interest to you.

*　　*　　*　　*　　*

Kate Cook writes:

Dear Shirley,

Those were halcyon days.

It was lovely to read your article in last night's Evening Mail. I was one of the 'oldies' who used to frequent Eddie's clubs – I still think I'm thirty-something!

I knew Eddie quite well as I was a regular and went in with friends that he knew. He was always the gentleman, but a lot of the men who congregated there were 'Friday night players' and we had to be careful not to be classed as 'good time girls'. We used to spend many an evening with Eddie, laughing our heads off with Jimmy Tarbuck, or dancing with Pat Roach – with the bouncers shouting "Go easy Pat – we haven't reinforced the floor!"

Other wrestlers used to congregate there too, Billy Yukon being one of them. Dave Gouda was the younger generation of bouncer/bodybuilder and he was always very nice.

I used to live in Edgbaston and Pat often called in for a cup of tea with me and my mum on his way for a run around the 'Rez'. In fact, me and my friend even went to Pat's health club on the weekend morning it opened, armed with vacuums and mops – having had a phone call for help at 7 a.m and not having got home the previous night until 3 a.m.! because the builders had run over their time and the place was a mess. We only just managed to get it cleaned up in time for the Mayor to arrive at 12.30 for a champagne reception! Pat thanked us by saying, 'Thanks to the two best scrubbers in town!' We were not THAT amused – but we weren't offended by the double entendre – that was his sense of humour, but because we hardly had our best clothes on! Some of the memories are very bittersweet now – with many people appearing in the obituary columns – and me looking in the mirror and seeing an old lady looking back!

I even stood in one night as a barmaid when Eddie opened the *Sin Bin* in *Boogie's* as someone had phoned in sick. I've never been a barmaid since, but I've never be rude to anyone doing that type of job, as a result of finding out how hard on your feet it is!

Because of being in the city centre and close to the TV studios and the *Night Out*, a lot of singing and comedy acts used to find their way into *Boogie's* – it was very interesting to see famous faces propping the bar up.

You never knew who you would see – Roger DeCourcey, Lenny Henry and Bob Carolgees, although the latter two were mostly in Alan Manning's club, *Maxwell's* on Five Ways, plus many many more…. hilarious fun. I'm sure as I lived most Fridays and Saturdays in nightclubs during the 70s and all through the 80s I would have lots of info for you if I hadn't got 'Old Timer's Disease'! If I can think of anything else of interest to pass on – or names of people who met there, I will be in touch.

Kate

*   *   *   *   *

Pam and Keith Dawes write:

Hi Shirley,

Just a note to say that I met my wife, Pam, at *Rebecca's*, in 1973. We were regular club-goers, usually going twice a week. We saw such acts as Sam and Dave and Junior Walker. We also went to *Barbarella's* as well. We were there on the Opening Night, when we saw Joe Frazier and his Soul backing band. Then it was at least 4am, before *Little & Large* finished. What a great night!

If you want any more info just let me know.

Best wishes with the book.
Keith Dawes.

P.S. Before I met Keith I used to go to *Rebecca's* with my friend. On a Thursday it was free before 10pm, for girls. We used to spend 10p to hang our coats up and 10p for a lemon and lime drink – unless we got bought a drink – then we would have a Babycham! We spent most of the night in the bottom room – the *Sin Bin*, where Sam, the DJ, used to play lots of good sounds – mostly Soul, Motown and Reggae. What great value!

Good Luck
Pam Dawes

*   *   *   *   *

Des Fitzpatrick, of Great Barr, Birmingham writes:

Dear Shirley,

    I read the article in the Birmingham Mail regarding Eddie Fewtrell. I can go back to the mid-sixties, when myself and my friends used to go to the *Cedar Club*, on a regular basis. We also went to the *Carlton Club* in Erdington and became good friends with the likes of *The Move, Carl Wayne & the Vikings*, the *Moody Blues, Denny Laine & the Diplomats*; Steve Winwood – the *Spencer Davis Group* and many more who went on to become world famous.

    I went to quite a few of Eddie's Opening Nights, at the likes of *Edward's No.7, Barbarella's* and *Rebecca's*. Terry Fewtrell, Eddie's nephew, became one of my best friends and I became godfather to his daughter, twenty years ago. Up until two months ago, I have been living in Spain for twenty years, so I have lost touch with Terry. The last time I heard of him was in Leamington, where he has a club and Wine Bar called *Fewtrell's*. Terry is the son of Don, one of Eddie's brothers.

Yours sincerely,
Des Fitzpatrick

*   *   *   *   *

Mary Green writes, from Edgbaston:

Dear Shirley,

    I was so pleased to see, in the Evening Mail, that you are co-writing a book with Eddie.

    My name is Mary Green. Along with my friend, Mary Corbett, I worked at *Barbarella's*. I started working in the cloakroom, on the Opening Night, with a girl named Patsy Remodous. The boxer Joe Frazier opened the club. A few months later, my friend Mary started to work with us in the cloakroom. Patsy then went on to work behind the bar. We became good friends but have now lost touch. Also, there was Patti Bell, Sheila, Anna, Pat, Christine and Bridget, who worked behind the bar. Dave Possall was the bar manager. Alan Chapman was the manager. Chris Fewtrell, who sadly passed away, helped to run the club. Doorman Chris Kelly has also passed away. Tex, John, Richard and Peter worked there too.

My mother, Cathy Walsh, worked at *Barbarella's* as a cleaning supervisor. There are many memories, but this one was a horror – although funny after the event! It was a Saturday night, so we were very busy in the cloakroom. It was raining so everybody had umbrellas. Myself and Mary were taking in coats and umbrellas and two other girls were hanging them up. You would think the umbrellas would be hung up with the coats – not so! When we had finished serving everybody, we found a mountain of umbrellas!

As you can imagine, it was hell at the end of the night. The punters were not happy, and they were all claiming that they had a new umbrella. There were people everywhere. Eddie turned up and said: "Get it sorted, or you're all sacked!" At the end of the night, Mary and myself went to the bar. Eddie said that we could both keep our jobs. It never happened again!

I also worked at *Boogie's* and *Abigail's*. Working at *Boogie's*, the late Jean Broadhurst hired the club for her wedding. The lady members of staff all had to wear white Charleston dresses, with lots of fringes. Everything went well – a good wedding.

Working at *Abigail's* again, with my friends Mary and Patsy, Patsy met Jimmy Lane. They got married and had two children. The last time I saw Jimmy and Patsy was at Chris Fewtrell's funeral. I was hoping to see them at Don's funeral, but they weren't there. It would be nice if Eddie could have a reunion, with all the old staff.

Yours, Mary Green

*   *   *   *   *

Letter from Stevie McCarthy: To protect the identity of some of those mentioned we have deleted some names and made certain editorial changes. Our reasons for doing this will soon become clear!

Hi Shirley,

I worked for Eddie for quite a while in the 70s, at *Barbarella's*, *Boogie's* and the *Cedar Club*. Eddie used to transport us from Barbs to the Cedar, to serve on the Late Bar. He made a fortune, but he didn't pay us ... we did it for the tips.

He had a particular barmaid, who I worked with for as long as I was at *Barbarella's*. I'm sure Eddie will remember this barmaid's mother – she was a mad drunken Scotswoman, known as 'Scotch Nancy'. She was supposed to be banned but the doormen were too scared to stop her coming in.

Eddie had a certain DJ who we'll call 'X'. He worked at *Rebecca's* until it closed, then he came to *Barbarella's*. He was a bit of a ladies' man, despite having a regular girlfriend. One day he took one of the barmaids into a cubicle in the Gents toilets. Unfortunately, Eddie decided that he needed the toilet at the same time. He came into the loo and as the cubicle was locked he enquired: "Who's in there?" "Just me," said the DJ. "What are you doing?" asked Eddie. "Just having a pony," he replied. "I'll show you a trick you hadn't even thought of," said Eddie, and he hoisted himself up, to look over the top of the cubicle! Exit barmaid in tears – to tell us about it!

Barbarella's was a really fantastic place to work. Because it was open seven nights a week, there were a few of us that were there seven nights a week. It was like a family in a lot of ways.

*   *   *   *   *

From Kings Norton, Birmingham, Pam Robinson writes:

Dear Shirley,

I was most interested to read the article, 'Thanks for the Memories', in the Birmingham Mail, on 1st March 2006, regarding your book on Eddie Fewtrell.

During a holiday in Majorca, in 1969, I was fortunate to stay in the same hotel as Eddie and his family. My friend and I spent some time looking after his daughter, Rebecca, who was four years old at that time. In return for this, Eddie, Hazel, and his friends would take us out in the evenings, to some of the Majorca clubs. Following the holiday, we were given permanent free entry to *Rebecca's* and enjoyed many evenings at the club – also at *Barbarella's*; Eddie invited us to a private performance, after the club closed, by Tony Christie!

Going back to the holiday; Eddie had been informed by his travel agent, Doug Ellis, that our flight home would be considerably delayed, due to overseas weather conditions at Birmingham Airport. He offered to *pay for us* to stay a further night at the hotel. We declined – but what a generous person he is.

I just want to add to, I'm sure, the many comments, regarding his generosity, which you will have received from many of his friends and colleagues. What a lovely man – who deserves the title of 'The King of Birmingham's Nightclubs'.

Sincerely,
Pam Robinson (Mrs.)

*   *   *   *   *

Lucy Wallis writes, from Holloway Head, Birmingham:

Hello Shirley,

I go back to approximately 1975. My daughter was nine; I was bored, not getting out. I met a few girls in the same situation, organised our baby sitting services, and away I went. My first 'port of call' was the *Man of War* and Robbo Ash entered my life. We became best buddies. He took me everywhere – I know he was a bit of a lad, as far as the guys were concerned – Paddy Fields, Peter Green, even big Tucker, all treated me with respect and I became one of the lads.

We went to the *Cedar* many times; a club called *Pollyanna's* – Newhall Street – *Barbarella's*, and many more. Robbo knew everyone and we never paid to get in, or had to queue. I was buzzing! We met Eddie a few times, and Pat Roach. When *Edward's* opened, we were there in the first week and went several times. I used to go round helping the staff; bringing the glasses to the bar and emptying ashtrays.

But times moved on; ill health and various problems were taking over. Robbo moved to Ireland – and later died. I moved on, purchased a house, and settled down again. However, now sixty, I still go out fairly often. From where I now live in the city, I could see the recent fire, at *Edward's No.8*. I was devastated… memories came flooding back.

God Bless,
Lucy M/s Wallis
P.S. My name used to be Sheila. I hated it and changed my name to Lucy.

* * * * *

Finally, last but not least, Sheila Williams writes from Nerja, in Spain. Later, at the request of Eddie and Patti Bell, I helped Sheila to re-contact them ... and they were able to catch up on old times:

Hi Shirley,

I live in Nerja, on the Costa del Sol. My family have just sent me a cutting from the Birmingham Mail, saying that you are doing a book about Eddie. I wonder if you would be interested in any of my tales? My friend Anna and I worked for Eddie for many years and he looked after us so much. It was like he took us under his wing, because we were broke and I was in a violent marriage. My friend, Anna, was without family.

I have got some fantastic tales that have been tucked away in my memory; many happy ones. In some ways the Fewtrells were rogues, without a doubt, but Eddie showed us nothing but kindness, for many years.

I don't have anything for the first half of your chapter, about Cupid, as they were all so protective of us. We went out with a couple of people, but the Fewtrells always gave us a talk, beforehand, asking us if we knew what we were doing. They also gave the people concerned a talking to, to look after us. On one occasion I took some pills. When they realised what I had done, they sent my friend and me straight home, with our tails between our legs.

When we went to work the next night, Eddie had got a man in, from the Drug Squad, to give us both a *very severe* talking to, and scared the life out of us. Eddie caught us fiddling, so he put extra money in our wage packet, so we wouldn't need to do it.

I went to work in another club. They sent two bouncers in, who picked me up by my arms and carried me out of there, to go back to work for them.

Eddie bought me my first decent pair of glasses, so that I could see at work, as he knew that I could never afford them. They put a false advert in the Birmingham Mail. We answered, along with other members of staff. We were the only ones not to be sacked, because we said such good things about them – even though we didn't know, at the time, that we were actually writing to the Fewtrells!

One night, Chuck Berry tried to blackmail Eddie, by coming off stage and refusing to go back on, until he had another thousand pounds. So there was a riot in the club. My friend and I had to lie on the floor, whilst bottles came flying over the bar! He must have got his money, or something happened, because he came back on stage. But the bar was a wreck!

I think it will be a fascinating book. I worked at the *Cedar*, *Rebecca's* and then *Barbarella's*, when he opened there.

Look forward to communicating with you.

Many thanks.
Sheila Williams

Chapter Ten

COMEDIANS

Tales from and about: Russ Abbot, Dave Allen, Stan Boardman, Larry Grayson, Dave Ismay, Kenny Lynch, Don Maclean, Bernard Manning, Bob Monkhouse, Jimmy Tarbuck and Mike & Bernie Winters. All of them either performed in Eddie's clubs and/or visited them as customers.

Bernard Manning was born on 13 August 1930 at Ancoats, a district of Manchester, into a working-class Roman Catholic family; he was sometimes referred to as the 'Sage of Ancoats'. Privately, Bernard didn't live up to his racist image: he was on good terms with his black neighbours, sent a local sick Asian child on a no-publicity trip to Disneyland, was a major benefactor of Jewish charities in Manchester and made private donations to anti-racist groups. After his beloved wife Vera aka Veronica, died in 1986, his mother moved in with him; for the past eighteen years Lynn Moran has been his companion.

On Thursday 26 October 2006 I had the great privilege of interviewing him, in the front room of his house in Main Way, Manchester, a home that he occupied for many years. His companion, Lynn, showed me in, and introduced me. Bernard was surrounded by memorabilia, which he referred to, from time to time. It seems likely that the interview he granted me that day was one of his last. During our conversation he was connected up to various monitoring machines. Regardless of this, that kind gentleman made sure that I received a selection of photographs for Eddie's book by First Class Post, the following day.

Just seven months afterwards, on Monday 18 June 2007, Bernard died from kidney failure, at 1510 BST, in North Manchester General Hospital. After his death, his son, Bernard Junior said: "My father was a true gentleman, a people's man and a working class hero." He added that Bernard didn't care what people thought about him: "He was just happy to be himself and spend his life helping people."

'Girding up my loins' before our meeting, I had fully expected to meet the uncouth man that his critics would have us believe that he was; but nothing could have been further from the truth – as you will discover...

Bernard and I first met in 1971, at *Barbarella's*, when the original *Comedians* television show started: approximately three years before the Birmingham Pub Bombings. The *Comedians* series was first televised on Saturday 12 June at 7pm. and every Saturday afterwards, until 24 July, 1971.

"Yes, I met Eddie many years ago. He was a very suave, good-looking young man, with a wonderful family; brothers, and a good wife – a wonderful club, and a lovely office," began Bernard. "The first time I met him I thought: 'What a go-ahead fella.' He had photographs, all over the place – of shaking hands with all of the stars of the day: Tom Jones and some of the Royal Family. He is a real 'man's man', who says what he means, means what he says, and doesn't beat around the bush. He told me that he'd like to book me, and all that carry-on, for future dates, because he fell about laughing. And that cemented our friendship, for a long long time.

"I heard all the stories about Eddie Fewtrell – that he made the Kray Twins look like delinquent choirboys! Well, that wasn't my impression. I knew nothing about any bad side of Eddie. To the best of my knowledge he's always been a gentleman, paid his debts; you always got your money and he always had a wonderful club – with good clients, good food, treated his staff well, and always looked smart. He had a lovely wife, drove the best of cars. I loved the man – he was absolutely marvellous. He was a very good businessman – he could approach people – and *he* was approachable. That's all you can ask of people… and you speak of people as you find them, not how other people *tell* you that they might be.

"Eddie had booked Mike & Bernie Winters, at *Abigail's*; the two brothers were arguing about who was going to top the bill – because that was a big thing in those days – who topped the bill. So because they were arguing over it, he sacked them! Then he phoned me at the *Embassy Club* in Manchester, because I'd just finished an earlier show there. I came down to Birmingham, got a standing ovation, and it was a great night.

The *Drifters* were on the show as well. Mike & Bernie Winters were at a table near the stage. They were friends of mine, for years. I used to watch them in the theatres. At this particular show, they clapped along with everybody else. I had nothing to do with any problems that they had."

Bernie died of stomach cancer at the age of 58, in May 1991; Mike moved to Miami, became a businessman and wrote two books. As I recall,

Bernie's wife, Ziggy, who was a German woman, was digging her heels in, insisting that the brothers wouldn't go on, if they couldn't be Top of the Bill.

"Eddie had already phoned me at the *Embassy Club*," continued Bernard, "so I knew that he needed me, before I even got into my car. My *Embassy Club* act began about eight o'clock and lasted 'til about ten. As Eddie's cabarets finished much later, you'd still got time to get down there. There are occasions in this business, when artistes are ill and they let you down. I was a kind of utility for Eddie! Because he knew I could always pull a crowd and that I was always up-do-date with all the gags. He knew that I could do the job; sing a song and time a good gag – so there was no problem. We became very good friends. It wasn't like doing it for the money. I would probably have done it for nothing, to help a friend out, because I think the world of the man – I think he's absolutely wonderful!

"He's a 'man's man' – a 'good old boy'! You could have a real good night out with him and have a real good time. He always had beautifully tailored shirts on – and a lovely suit. I don't know what he's like now, because I haven't seen him for ages. He turned out well in those days, and he knew everybody – and everybody knew him. You knew where you stood with him, so that's all you can ask from anybody.

"His brothers were very supportive; you cut one and they all bled. I remember Chrissie Fewtrell. He was a nice young man – he really was. His wife, Paulette was a lovely lady.

Shirley Bassey, who he employed later, at the *Metropole*, was a Megastar and the same with Lulu – 'You make me want to shout!' All of these people kept show business going, over the years – and they're still going now – most of them!

"Stan Boardman came on *The Comedians* much later than I did. I was on the first one; he was discovered on the programme in 1974. Stan was a lively comic in the working mens' clubs. He had his first big break off Johnny Hamp, the Executive Producer of *The Comedians*, and he never looked back after that. We were all working for £10, £30, £40 a night in the clubs. Then suddenly when we were on *The Comedians*, it shot up to £2,000. That's when everything really took off."

Stan seems as though he's been with me for forever Bernard. One evening he came to appear at *Rebecca's*, to an audience that were totally black. I was phoned at *Abigail's*: "Stan's here." I said: "Oh – put him on then." (Mimics Stan) – "Eddie, is that you? Are you joking? All I can see out here are eyes! I can't go on here – my jokes are all about coloureds!" I said: "Well, you'd better come over here then. I'll send someone across."

We had all the singers – all the comedians – Charlie Williams, you name them. But Stan is an absolute live wire – he never stops. He's a performer and a friend. I've known him over years and years. He used to say: "Ed – die!"

"There was a club on every corner in those days," Bernard continues. "People used to go out, to see a show; in places like the big *Night Out* in Birmingham. There'd be people like Gene Pitney and so forth – big stars. That's one thing about Eddie – he always picked the best. He had no rubbish – no riff-raff. Gene Pitney, Johnnie Mathis, Tom Jones. He had all the big groups of the day – *Moody Blues*, *The Beatles* – marvellous.

"Eddie Fewtrell's clubs always had the best of everything – wonderful bars, good service, wonderful food; his kitchens were always spick-and-span: you could eat your dinner off the floor – he was that type of a fella. He had a big cabaret – always good lighting; always had a good disc jockey. You'd start off at *Barbarella's*, go on to his other clubs, and then finish up at a club that stayed open very late. I can't remember what that was called, but it was a very late Disco.

"I did shows at each one of them, over the years; sometimes two shows in one night. Stand-up Comedy is really very easy. It's not sweated labour – like playing the drums – or anything like that – it comes easily to me … my driver does all the hard work! Once I get there, I just have people rolling about with laughter – that's my job. I'm seventy-six and I'll be working in Blackpool this weekend. I did a show in Paris and stayed in the *Intercontinental Hotel* – for *DFS* – the furniture people. If you're funny you'll get work – and you'll never starve.

"You'd get nice people in Eddie's clubs. Chris Tarrant was in one night, many years ago, long before he became a Superstar on the telly. There was Jasper Carrott, and a few more. He used to come round to see what was going on. I was in the choir at school – so I was always a good singer at school. Then when I was in the army I sang with the Manchester Regiments Dance Band. We went all over Germany – Düsseldorf, Berlin, Cologne – everywhere. After I came out of the army, I had an audition with Oscar Rabin, at the *Midland Hotel*, in Manchester. Then we went down to West End of London – to the *Lyceum*, near the *Savoy* there, and did a contract with him there. I should have broadcast, the day the king died: that was 6 February 1952.

"Mrs Dale's Diary was on... I'll never forget it. All broadcasting stopped at that point, for the rest of the day, and they played very solemn music. That would have been my first broadcast. I toured with them all over the show. When I came home, the club scene had just started, in the north of England and I started as a compère, at the *Northern Sporting Club*. It went on from there.

"My father was a greengrocer and we opened a club for ourselves, in 1959. The *Embassy*, which is in the Harpurhey district. It was an old billiard hall before I bought it. There's a photograph of me there, taken at the club. In that case over there is a model of the club, which I was presented with. John Charles presented me with that model of myself: flanked on either side by figures of Laurel and Hardy – two of my favourite comedians.

"My mother was ninety-five when she died – there were seven of us. My brother, Frank, died at fifty-three. He was a multi-millionaire. He had a hotel in Truro – his wife still has it. My oldest brother was the company director of a paint firm. My sisters, Alma and Rene, are in Newquay, in Cornwall. They're in their seventies now. They own the *Inn and Out* – a big restaurant there. Every one of us has done well.

"I realised that I wanted to become a comedian at school – I used to tell jokes. I was the class joker – no doubt about that. My teacher used to call me 'Bernard Longtongue' – 'He never stops!' You were supposed to be quiet. But they were lovely teachers in those days – they were always smart, tidy and well-mannered, and when you got the cane, you deserved it – a quick, sharp shock.

"I went to Mount Carmel School – just down the road. I was born and will have lived and died within a five-mile radius. I'll be buried at the Leyton Park Cemetery – just up the road. All my friends live around here – all my school pals. No one else in the family is in show business; they were funny, but they wouldn't get up on the stage. My oldest brother John was very funny, and my son is very comical – he ought to be on the stage. That photo to your left is my son, young Bernard, with his wife, Judith, and their children. I just have the one son, no daughter. Bernard runs the *Embassy Club* now. My wife has been dead fifteen years now. Her name was Veronica.

"I was never away from the Pictures. I knew every comic – Jack Benny, George Burns, Jimmy Durante – I used to love watching them – and Frank

Sinatra, Tony Bennett, Jack Jones – all the popular singers. Most comedians model themselves on other comedians, but I was a pioneer! I bounced lines off people in the audience. If I saw a bald fella I'd say: 'Those see-through wigs are good!' I'd see a gorgeous-looking woman sat at a table and a woman sat opposite her, wearing glasses. I'd say: 'I love women with glasses on. Would you like to put your glasses on her?' That kind of humour came naturally to me. If there's a big fat fella sitting there I'd say: 'They're having a Sponsored Walk. I'll see you later on.'"

It's often the case that comedians, during their act, are actually nothing like they are in real life. Often they're larger than life on stage. Shirley couldn't resist asking Bernard: "When you do your act, which seems, to a large extent, having a go at people, or 'taking the mickey', does it bother you that you're doing it?"

"No, because I can tell a million gags, so when I focus on people for a moment it's just one or two lines, mixed in with many other gags. So it doesn't come across that way. If you're going to do an hour and a quarter, or an hour and a half, you've got to have some material. I've done fifty years at the *Embassy Club*, every night, so you've got to have plenty of new material.

"I used to do the London Scene. That's why I called my club the *Embassy Club*, because that was the name of the first club I worked, in London. It was in Bond Street – very upmarket. Who's the little fella? Davey Kay – he was the compère at the club. One night Bernard Delfonte came in with his mother; these people used to go out to be *seen* in those days. The Cabaret was dancing, a meal and to be seen. I'd be twenty-one – just out of the army. It was the first club that I *ever* worked at.

"If you were a good singer in them days they'd book you. I worked the *Dolce Vita* in Birmingham and the *Big Night Out* in Birmingham. I worked the *Oldham Empire* in 1949 and from there I never looked back. I had several Jewish friends. They took me down to Oscar Rabin and introduced me. David Levi was the conductor and I did an audition for Oscar at the *Midland Hotel* in Manchester. I did shows for him in the West End and all over the country. I had an agent called Danny Vitech for a long time. Elaine Page was just working there. She used to go on first and do the first half and I'd do the second half.

"I used to like Tony Bennett, Jack Jones, Mario Lanza – people like that. The best singer I ever heard was a Manchester lad called Lee Lawrence. He was Jewish. His real name was Leon Saroto. His father was a cantor and he used to do the theatres. A cantor is like a rabbi, who sings in church – in the synagogue; and you've got to be very very good. So Lee Lawrence was my favourite singer. He used to sing all of these beautiful songs, at all of the theatres. I saw him at the *Palace Theatre* in Manchester. I saw Sinatra there too. The *Glasgow Empire* – Lee Lawrence used to do all of the theatres; he was a bit older: about ten years older. I didn't style myself on Lee, but I sang his kind of songs – lovely words and big ballads; a nice orchestra – plenty of strings and flutes... beautiful!

"You'd only have piano, bass and drums, when you went to the clubs. You'd have your own music, which they would play. You just had to get on with it – make the best of a bad job! They're all good clubs – if you're paid! I never walked off to the sound of my own footsteps – I'd always go well: no club could turn around and say: 'We had Bernard Manning, and he was no good.' I always tried to give good value.

"I always had my singing to fall back on, so if I wasn't going down well with the comedy, I wasn't at a loss. Even now I can do a couple of hours and have them rolling in the aisles. That's not being big-headed... it's just knowing my job. So I could sing a good few songs, quieten them all down again, and away I'd go again.

"I liked Laurel & Hardy, but my favourite comedian, apart from them, is a fella called Don Rickells, in America. George Burns, Jack Benny, Groucho Marx – very talented people. George Burns had a very 'laid-back' style, smoked a cigar, and his sense of timing was perfect... that only comes with experience. In my opinion, the essential quality that make a good comedian, is having confidence in what you're doing. Confidence... going out there... not peeping around the curtain and thinking 'What are they like tonight?' Just get out there and do it!

"I went to the *MGM Grand* in Las Vegas, with Johnny Hamp, the producer of *The Comedians*. That was in the lounge of the main room. There were six or seven hundred in the audience. That was when the *Comedians* was all the rage, but I'm the only one of them who went over there – who Johnny Hamp took on a tour of America. We made a video. I was offered a vast amount to stay over there, but I wanted to come back – I'm a family man – it's a big pull.

"In Manchester, the club scene took off about 1956. We had boxing, cabaret and wrestling in the clubs. I compèred at the *Northern Sporting Club*;

we had Dorothy Squires on, David Hughes, Ronnie Hilton – people like that. They were all popular acts in those days. Birmingham followed suit, but the only thing with Birmingham is that you have to have a car to get there! It's full of ring roads, bridges and tunnels; unless you know your way, it's murder! You've only got to miss a turn off, and you've had it. In Manchester it's all on the flat; we've got nothing like that. You can say: 'It's down here, turn left, turn right,' and you've arrived. It's not as big as Birmingham.

"There were loads of earlier Northern clubs. There was a cabaret club called *Kerfoot*. There was Ernie Derbyshire, who had a club. Sid Elgar, who was a Londoner; he opened a club in Stockport, called the *Atherton Palace*. Then there was *Batley Variety Club; Wakefield Theatre Club,* and they used to put all of the stars of the day – Gracie Fields, Satchmo – all the big stars of that time.

"They moved from music halls, to theatres and then to clubs. One of the main things was that, in them days, you could order a meal, at a table with a white tablecloth, be waited on hand-and-foot, with a lovely cabaret, but it didn't cost you the earth, like it would today.

"At Eddie Fewtrell's clubs, although he used to give them all that they wanted, they had to look smart when they went in, even if they were working men. You had to wear a tie, a decent suit, and be well turned out. Word would get around that you couldn't mess around in any of Eddie's clubs or you'd be called to account, then banned," concludes Bernard.

I really used to enjoy working with Bernard, because he was a great character – he used to make me *howl*. The place would always be absolutely packed when he topped the bill. He used to have me with tears rolling down my face. He played in all of my clubs – *Cedar, Barbarella's Abigail's* – he played everywhere. All the fifty years I was in the business, I've had every comedian there is. All the fellas from *The Comedians* show on television, including Charlie Williams. All the people who'd never been heard of – I played them and employed them; I know all of the jokes off by heart!

A lot still make me laugh, but the one who I thought was the greatest comedian ever – and still think he is today – is Bernard Manning. He was funny because he told the truth. Most of the black guys there worked for me, as opposed to being in the audience. He looked people straight in the eyes and they used to *howl*. He used to smile at them – and they'd all scream with laughter.

Bernard was a classic really; he was so professional it's untrue! He'd be there in *Barbarella's*, with three or four thousand people, and he'd be telling these jokes. He always had the lights down low, so that all the emphasis was on stage and the main light was on him. That's the way it's done. The performer is looking into the dark, as opposed to the light; you get a lot more response and the audience get much more involved that way. Then he'd plant a heckler in the audience, who'd suddenly shout out, "What are you doing up there Fattie?" Bernard would stop his joke and say: "Just a minute Eddie. Put the light on that person down there. I've often *felt* one in the dark, but never seen one!" He'd come across with that gag, all the time. I never realised, until he marked my card, some years later. I said: "Oh – I remember that heckler." He said: "I brought him with me you fool! That's all part of the entertainment. They *love* things like that – that's what makes it tick...people involvement. And the laugh is, me making the heckler look silly. They sit down and hide themselves in the dark then – it soon stops them! It puts the others off. No comedian is good without hecklers, because they help to create the atmosphere."

When Bernard came on, at *Abigail's*, he'd been in the kitchen, with Gianni Paladini and some other Italians. So as he came on, he said: "Good evening ladies and gentlemen. I've just come out of the kitchens, and there's hundreds of Italians in there. I had five hundred of them on the end of my bayonet, during the war!"

As he came on, the first thing he saw were Mike and Bernie sitting there, at a table close to the stage. He looked at me and I looked at him and I was going bright red. He said: "Mike and Bernie Winters – comedians? They couldn't find a fart in a colander. They couldn't get a laugh in a brothel!"

There were some coloured people in the audience. Bernard said: "My friend, do you think that it matters that you've got pearly teeth and a black skin? You bet your sweet life it does!" So he was going on in that vein, d'you know what I mean? I've never seen a night when a show went so unbelievably well. That particular night was one of the best nights ever at *Abigail's*.

At the end of the evening, when most of the audience had gone home, Mike and Bernie Winters started to fight. I was in the middle, trying to stop them fighting each other. I broke my gold watch, trying to control the fight, and I finished up with a crack around my left eye, from just trying to help them. Eventually, they broke up... that was the night they broke up. They never appeared on a show together again. That's how Bernie finished up with a dog, as part of his act, instead of his brother.

My son, Daniel, remembers: "I met Bernard quite a number of times, with my dad. One time we'd just come back from the States. Coming back down the motorway, we stopped to have a chat with him; so there were two Rolls Royces, parked together! Bernard told my dad a few jokes, and then we drove off again."

Moving on to Russ Abbot, he began with *The Black Abbots*. They started to work for me at the *Bermuda Club*, would-you-believe? Then after that, they worked for me at the *Cedar Club*. Russ was the Main Man. They worked very well, time after time. Then eventually, Russ worked on his own, and branched out into pantomimes, theatres and TV shows. Wherever he was on, he'd come into the club after he'd finished for the night. The *Black Abbots* were a cross between pop group and comedy impressionists weren't they – and they'd imitate other groups too.

As far as Jimmy Tarbuck's concerned, we've been really good friends for years. I play golf with him when I'm over in Portugal, and he raises a lot of money for the orphanage over there, by doing a few shows at the big golfing hotel that I stay at. There'll be about three or four hundred guests there for these events, including myself. Jimmy organises it. It's a very interesting week-to-ten-days. The photograph with Jimmy's Foreword, at the front of our book, was taken at the most recent tournament. He's mentioned on several occasions, in this book, by various people, so I'm only mentioning him briefly here.

Jimmy Tarbuck's son, Jimmy Junior, has married the daughter of the owners of a big hairdressing company, so he works for them now, promoting their products. His in-laws have companies all over the world – they're multi-billionaires! When I was over in Portugal, they gave me a selection of the products, to bring back for Marleen.

Ron Gray recalls: "I met Jimmy at the *Cedar Club*, during the 1970s. Jimmy was a lovely guy. He had time for everybody and was the most genuine person you could wish to meet. The same today as he was when he started. I saw him at a show in Birmingham, at *Star City*. I had my son with me. Jimmy came running over, kissing me on each cheek. He shouted through the crowd: 'I haven't seen you, Big Fella for years!'

"He and Kenny Lynch were performing together in a show there. Kenny was on the stage too; they were singing a duet together. As Kenny finished his part, Jimmy started his, and Kenny came off the stage, out into the crowd and hugged me; which I thought was quite nice – he hadn't seen me for a while. Eddie tells stories about when he, Hazel, Jimmy and Pauline went to various shows together. They used to go to his house in Weybridge too. They had a great time together. Eddie goes back to Day One with him, doesn't he? You could tell the affection that he had for Eddie, when you were there. It was more than just somebody coming to his club and saying: 'Hello mate – how are you?'"

Singer-comedian Kenny Lynch was born 18 March 1938, in London's East End. Earlier this year, in his rural retreat, which must seem like a million miles away from his childhood environment, Kenny described how, at the age of only seven or eight, he began singing at local pubs, in company with his older sister, Maxine, who was a Carroll Levis discovery.

"The guy said: 'Well, come up and sing at this club too,' remembers Kenny. "It was fine when I got there; there was just a pianist and a bass player. I got up on stage and sang *Mammie* and *April Showers*. The guy said: 'Oh, that will be great tonight – they'll love that.' So I went out to the local pub with my sister; we had something to eat and a glass of lemonade. Next thing I know, it's time to do the show. They opened the curtains and suddenly there were two hundred people sitting there... and I just s**t myself... basically! My sister shouted out from the wings: 'Sing you little bastard – sing!' So I started to sing and after that I was fine. So I did my first gig ever, in the TUC Club in Leightonstowe."

The first band Kenny sang with was Johnny Dalton's band, when he was eleven years old, but he had to stop at 9.30pm, as he was under fourteen.

"Then I started to sing in the *Coach and Horses*, which is a pub in the Mile End Road, London. But I had the same problem; I had to stop at half past nine. That's where I first met all of these villains – these East End gangster people. They used to come in there... for the rest of my life I'm still friends with some of them. They do their thing and I do mine, but I'm still in touch with them. Lately, I've been going to a lot of funerals!

"I met Eddie for the very first time at the *Cedar Club*. *Up on the Roof* came out in 1963; that's why I think it was probably 1964 when I performed as Top of the Bill at the *Cedar* for Eddie. The first night I went there it was good; the second night it wasn't so good. Maybe it was raining, or maybe I didn't go down so well? I only worked the *Cedar Club* two or three times. My first impression, when Eddie came into the dressing room to see me, was that he was very jolly, and I thought: 'Oh, I come from these people'… because he was like an East End tearaway. So I liked him straight away. The first time somebody meets you and they say: 'What would you like to drink?' I know I'm with a friend. He said: 'Hello Kenny. If you want anything, just ask. My brothers are here. Have a good night. I'm going to go back to the other club, *Rebecca's*.'

"He disappeared and came back at one o'clock in the morning. I was still there, because, unlike Jimmy, I go to a club late and stay late; Jimmy goes to a club early and leaves early. So if I go to a place like that, where there would be bands on, I would sit and watch them, because I want to know what they're like and I'm a bit of a 'stayer-upper': I'd stay until two or three o'clock in the morning, listening and talking. Eddie had a great interest in boxing as well, so we had that in common too.

"The *Cedar* was the '*Marquee* of Birmingham' – that's the kind of club it was. The same kind of groups that they had at the *Marquee* – although maybe the *Cedar* didn't have quite such big people as the *Marquee* had; the *Cedar* was pitched at the middle level of performers in some cases, although they had big names like Tom Jones there too. So Eddie had mid-range up-and-coming stars there, at that particular time.

"I remember the *Cedar* as being like a barn; a single storey building. I always thought it was a barn – I don't know why! As you came through the door, the bar was in front of you, on your right. If you came in the side door, the end of the bar was facing you: it came right round like that. There were a few pillars in there. That's where Johnny Prescott first came to see me – at the *Cedar Club*. We'd been friends for a few years, through the boxing and all that. I remember that he and Eddie were very friendly then; it was only afterwards that something occurred.

"As Eddie got his other clubs, he just let the *Cedar Club* kick over; he spent less and less time on it. I don't think it took the same amount of 'dough' as the other clubs did. He started making money somewhere else, no matter how much the *Cedar* had been his 'baby' in the beginning. None of Eddie's other clubs were intimate except that one, because everything was on the same ground floor and in the same room; the only things that were outside of the main room were the stockrooms, the khazis and the bars! His other clubs were on three floors or in three different rooms, and held thousands of people.

"I remember the *Cedar* as being very dark, with bright red bulbs. I worked there two or three times; they were 'one-nighters'. Although the first time I did three nights, and then I did one nights. I'd go in there and see a few people – late at night, when I'd finished performing. Jim Capaldi was involved with a lot of Birmingham bands, before he went with *Traffic*. I think *Traffic* played there as well. If there was somebody like that I'd go and see them. Eddie was more like a friend than the boss; that's why I didn't mind playing his clubs all the time – or going there.

"If you're talking about top celebrities, as opposed to supporting acts, especially in the 60s and 70s, there'd be maybe twenty to thirty artistes, nationwide, who would be Top of the Bill. Because Eddie had several clubs you'd perform at his clubs quite often; whereas with most club owners you'd only perform at their clubs every now and again, countrywide; that applied to most towns, but with some exceptions. Sheffield, for example, was very big for clubs; so were Manchester and Leeds. But in Birmingham they all seemed to belong to the same fella!"

Kenny left the Broadhurst's reception at *Boogie's*, late that afternoon. He had to go back to the *London Palladium*. On the way home he hit a milk float. He phoned me about it, and I phoned Tarby. I told him that I'd told Kenny: "It's no good crying over spilt milk." Later that evening, on stage, Tarby explained to the audience; "Kenny hit a milk wagon on the way here tonight. I told him: "It's no use crying over spilt milk!" So Jimmy used my joke at the *London Palladium*! Kenny has recently been touring with his show, *Swinging*.

"Yes. We do Jersey; we've been to Scotland about four times, these last couple of months; and I'm still doing bits and pieces with Jimmy. Nowadays, what I probably enjoy doing most is the jazz thing, with the *Laurie Holloway Trio*. We do this show at jazz clubs and colleges and corporate things. So I enjoy that most of all, because I can do the songs that I learnt when I started singing – the Sinatra and the Billy Eckstein songs – and the Sarah Vaughan stuff. When I go out with Laurie we call it *Jazz, Jokes and Standards*.

"Jimmy and I still do the *Metropole* occasionally. I do the first twenty or thirty minutes; then Jimmy goes on and does the same length of time; then

I go on and do fifteen minutes with him. Then I come off and he goes on to close the show. Or I go on with him and we do a couple of songs – a bit of Rock n' Roll to liven them up, before they go home. I was working with him up until last year. Jimmy's not to well lately – with his diabetes and things, so we've only worked together twice, in the last nine months, but we're working together next week. We probably did about forty days a year – up until 2006; it's just recently that we haven't been able to. But then I go over for his Golf Week, so we keep in touch all the time.

"Jimmy and I have been working forty-one years together. I met him when he came down to take over from Bruce Forsythe on the *London Palladium*. I was playing in a thing called the Showbiz Eleven – the football team. I remember it as if it was yesterday, funnily enough, which is unusual for me. I walked into the dressing room, at Hampton about half past eleven, twelve o'clock, and as I walked in through the doorway Sean Connery and Tommy Steele were talking. They were directly in front of me so I went and sat with them. They said: 'Have you seen this fella?' I looked over, and there was a fella changing, in a corner. So I said to Sean and Steely: 'Who's that?' Steely said: 'Oh, that's Jimmy Tarbuck. He's just come down to take over from Bruce Forsythe next Sunday, at the *Palladium*.'

"Jimmy has worked all his life – but he shot to fame at that point. I said to Steely: 'What's he like?' 'Well, we don't know. We haven't really spoken to him yet.' I said: 'Well we'll never find out what he's like.' So because we were three and he was one I went over and sat with him and invited him out. He said he was down here and living in Rickmansworth. I invited him out to eat and we got very friendly.

"The one night I was doing a *Bruce Forsyth Special* for ATV. Jimmy had started a week before at the *Talk of the Town*, as a comic. He said: 'Come in and see me.' So me and Bruce finished our rehearsal. I went over to the *Talk of the Town*. I used to know the guy who ran it – George, the manager. Jimmy was on by the time I got there. I walked to the side of the stage and Jimmy was working. He looked over at me and he waved. He said something about me to the audience and he started to sing *Up on the Roof*, without any music. I thought: "What the hell are you doing?" As he started to sing it he had the mike in his hand. I said to George: 'My God, there's a mike on the stand.' As Jimmy started to sing I asked George to switch it on. So I started to sing from the wings. As soon as he heard me Jimmy stopped singing, then he began to mime to my voice, to make it look as if he was singing. Then he suddenly said: 'Ladies and gentlemen, I'd like you to meet a friend of mine,' and I walked on singing. It brought the house down!

"We did a couple of lines of patter between us, on stage – not exactly jokes – then we went up to the dressing room afterwards. Jimmy said: 'That was great. Why don't we do that? Go out and do shows together?' So that's how we started… and we did exactly that *same* thing… we still do. I stand outside and sing and Jimmy mimes. It's tradition to us, but it happened purely by chance! I'll drop dead on the job, whatever happens. I still feel like I'm eighteen!"

When comedian Dave Ismay left school he wanted to become a professional footballer, but due to cartilage problems with his legs, he changed careers:

"I became a police cadet when I was sixteen, which was in 1962," begins Dave. "I was at Tally Ho and at Coventry, but I did nothing but play football. Then I became a policeman but I didn't enjoy it, because I didn't really want to arrest anybody!

"The one thing that really killed it for me was when a drunk came out of a pub, at five o'clock in the morning. I stopped him from falling over really. I found out where he lived and took him to the bus stop, to wait for the next Number Eight bus. But his mates came out of the pub, saw me and thought I was arresting him and gave me a good 'seeing to'.

"I spent five days in the Birmingham Accident Hospital, then left the Force in 1965 and went to work at the *Castaways* – with a fella called 'Mac', who was a bit older than I, and had also been a policeman in a former career. He fancied himself as a singer; I fancied myself as a comedian. Part of our duties was to look after the Band Call for the stars, on a Sunday. Mac used to look after the singers; I looked after the comedians.

"I got very 'pally' with Dave Allen, who had just become a star, but his contract with the *Castaways* was for £200, because he'd signed the contract before he became a star. He and I got on very well together. We used to get drunk together after the show – *before* the show on some nights! A couple of night I slept on the floor of his room at the *Albany*, but by this time he'd done *Sunday Night at the London Palladium* and had become a star, almost overnight; so he was earning big bucks, elsewhere.

"The *Castaways* was a concept. It was on three or four floors, down in Digbeth and was built on the concept of a desert island, as Laurie Hornsby explained, in Chapter Seven. It was previously owned by a guy called Rob Pryke. He always used to wear a bowler hat and a flower in his buttonhole. He was a dapper man. The club was John Reeve's idea: he was very much a 'go-getter'. His girlfriend was a girl called Judy, who was extremely long-suffering. We were under strict orders that the moment she arrived at the club, we were to let him know, because he could have been with any one of his female members of staff or other lady friends – anywhere in the club! So we had to tell him that Judy had arrived – which was quite funny; especially when you forgot – and you forgot on purpose; because she was a highly volatile creature, so sparks would fly!

"Dave Allen and I used to swap gags. He said: 'You can time and deliver a joke – which you can never be taught. If you want to have a go at it you'll do okay, because you have the two vital qualities that you need.' Every comic – until he finds his own style – models himself on somebody else. So for six or eight months, I was virtually doing Dave Allen's act – but with a Birmingham accent; even down to pretending that I'd lost my little finger! It usually worked – and working mens' clubs and audiences in Birmingham would pay me between six to eight quid, depending upon the quality of my act. It didn't always work – they were a bit hard on me," Dave remembers. "You imitate people until you discover who *you* are and what your style is."

According to the BBC Website, sadly, Dave Allen died on Thursday evening 10 March 2005, in his West London home. Dave finished up as a very good *friend*. We knew each other for all the years that I had the clubs, from 1957 until 1989. When I first sold up, he would appear every few months to a year. I'd still see him from time to time, when I started up again too…right up until shortly before he died.

Dave Ismay continues: "I first met Eddie, at the *Cedar* Club, around 1964-65. He knew the majority of the police: he would make sure that you got a drink and that you were looked after. I think I went in three or four times on my warrant card, because it was the 'in' place to be. It was always good 'craic' in there – I think is the word now. It was always very noisy, very brash. There were great-looking girls in there and blokes with flash cars. As I gradually became more established as a comedian I used to go there to soak in the atmosphere – to try to learn and study what was going on in the city. I became a professional comedian in 1967. I left the *Castaways* because I didn't think that the life would suit me and I wasn't earning a lot.

"When people like Bob Monkhouse were performing at the *Night Out*, or any of the clubs in Birmingham, you'd see half-a-dozen comics in there, every night, with notebooks under the table. There was a famous instance in Liverpool, where Bob was working in a place called the *Shakespeare*. He kept gesticulating to me: only I knew what he was doing. I went to the side of the stage behind the curtain and Bob went: 'Guy... Five tables back... tape recorder – get him!' I recognised the comedian. About five minutes before the end, he got up to go. I went to the back of the room and I met him at the door. I said: 'Bob would like the tape please.' He was too embarrassed to do anything but hand it over. It was one of these small cassette recorders; it was the first time I'd ever seen one. And he handed it over; but that used to happen all the time, especially with the good, really clever comics.

"My first wife Lesley, had worked at the *Castaways*, but it just didn't work and we split up. Then I worked as a comic at the *Dolce Vita*; to get on the Bailey circuit was quite an honour in those days: he had about forty clubs around the country. Another Bailey club was the *Cavendish*, out by the Coventry Road. The manageress was Sheila St. Clair – an extremely well-endowed girl... very attractive. We got on really well and we started living together in Stephenson Tower, which is at the back of New Street Station – it's still there.

"Sheila and I got married in Southport. She knew Bob Monkhouse because he worked on the Bailey Circuit. She told him about this penniless comic who she was trying to help – and that's when I met Bob – and started doing the 'warm-ups' for the *Golden Shot*. From that day on we became great pals, until I met Dodie, who was a make-up artist at Elstree. She did the make-up for *Celebrity Squares*, on which I wrote some of the questions and did the 'warm-ups'. We started going out; I fell in love with her and left my wife and two children.

"I was probably his best friend for the last twenty years of his life – and he mine. You could write a book on Bob alone. He's the wittiest, cleverest man. Everybody has said on *Who Wants to Be a Millionaire*, if you had to 'choose a friend', he'd be the ideal person. I still miss him now. He died of Prostate Cancer cancer, because it wasn't discovered quickly enough.

"I knew Larry Grayson when he was Billy Breen and we were both doing the working mens' clubs in Birmingham. He used to do two spots. He was very 'camp' in those days. People never mentioned the words 'homosexual' or 'gay', but they loved Larry; no one ever took issue with him over it. I'm going back thirty-five years to when I first met him. He was discovered very late in life. He went down to do a show at the *Stork Room*, in London, the hostess club. After about a month he was asked to go down and do a huge Gay Review at the *Stratford Theatre* in the East End of London, and he suggested me, to take his place. I stayed with Larry at his Bayswater flat for three nights, as I had nowhere else to stay. There was only one bed, but Larry never made anything of his sexual preferences. He was always a very private person. We slept together for three days. He used to say: 'Just give us a cuddle, and I used to say: 'Not bloody likely – you'll get a smack. You stay on your side of the bed and I'll stay on mine!' But he was an incredible, funny, warm, generous man. From the East End, he went on to do Guest Spots on Saturday night TV shows and, of course, finished up with his own show, *The Generation Game*. I've many other stories to tell you, but they'll have to wait until Eddie and Shirley publish their second book.

"To me, Eddie was the Godfather of the Birmingham Nightclub Scene – he lit the fire for all of us. He took on all the Authority in Birmingham. Eddie had a reputation, which in some respects was probably an unfair one, but it was one that certain members of the police were, allegedly, happy to perpetuate, because it suited them. Eddie spawned all of the clubs that started and it then went on to become the *Cresta Club*, and especially the *Night Out* – in Birmingham. I spent ten happy years, working twice a year at the *Night Out*, because it was two weeks at home for me, compering and doing a Spot and having a wonderful time. But if we're honest, it was all down to Eddie, getting rid of the Red Tape and everything else that was put in his way.

"I suppose I was a big fish in a small pond. There was a little gang of us – Don Maclean and Jasper Carrott, who'd become big stars; there was myself and Malcolm Stent and a few others – like Johnny Carroll, who were lesser lights, but we were well known in Birmingham."

Big Albert remembers: "I saw Bob Monkhouse at *Abigail's*. He was absolutely tremendous – a helluva comedian! Best comedian ever; the cleverest man. He'd get about ten people from the audience to each shout out a subject; he'd remember every subject they'd chosen and he'd tell a joke about each subject. He would socialise too."

Comedian Don Maclean had begun to do well in show business by 1974. He recalls a Hot Pants Competition at *Rebecca's*.

"I'd done a television show with Jimmy Tarbuck; he had his own television show at the time. He said that he was going up to Birmingham and I went along with my wife, Toni.

"In those days all the girls were wearing hot pants – it was *the* fashion – and they all looked sensational. My wife was there in a royal blue and white hot pants suit. They tried, unsuccessfully, to persuade her to enter the competition. Anyway, I was dragged up by Eddie as one of the judges. Eddie and Tarbuck, between them, on this sort of catwalk arrangement, compered the competition, and it was absolutely hysterical! It was all 'ad-lib' but it was very clever and Eddie sort of went along with anything that Tarbuck said, and laughed riotously at him. He always had this wonderful joie de vie did Eddie; he was always a happy-faced bloke.

"Once Eddie started with the clubs, it all seemed to mushroom. My first contact with him was before that. I did a fortnight in *Crossroads*. Deke Arlon was working with me on the programme; he became a record producer and an agent and is now well into being a millionaire, but at that time he was just a young actor. When we were working on *Crossroads* Deke took me down to the *Cedar Club*. From then on we went practically every night. That would be in 1965. Deke knew a bit about the music scene. He said: 'There's a group at the *Cedar Club* who are the best group that I've ever seen.' They were *The Move*. So it was Carl Wayne, Roy Wood, Ace Kefford, Bev Bevan and the others – they were all really good musicians. It was always packed and there were a lot of good-looking girls there.

"That was the first place that I ever met Eddie. By 1967 I started to do a little bit of television and things. He was very keen on promoting local performers or just getting them into his clubs. That was the thing: he wanted people who he felt were well known, although performance-wise, his clubs were more for musicians than comedians. I wouldn't have wanted to stand up and try to do comedy, to his normal audience, but it was different when he'd got a special night on. Bomber was always very much in evidence too."

Don has written an entertainment called *Wait 'til Your Father Gets Home*. He and Malcolm Stent have been performing it this year at Solihull Library Theatre. *The Stage* recently compiled a list of the Top Ten Dames, with Don being voted Number One.

As our *Comedians* chapter draws to a close, Bernard Manning's final comment, in the circumstances, seems particularly poignant:

"I wouldn't like to cross Eddie Fewtrell. If he said it was Christmas, we'd all sing carols! All I can say Eddie, is 'Carry on being the good man you are. It's been a pleasure knowing you. I'm very *proud* to have known you. And I wish you good health and happiness for the rest of your life. Thanks for involving me in your life… thank you.'"

Chapter Eleven

JOHN BRIGHT STREET

Eddie steadily bought up most of John Bright Street, opening clubs such as Abigail's, Boogie's Nightclub, Boogie's Brasserie, Edward's No.7 (a disco bar); Edward's No.8 (a club); Paramount, Goldwyn's and The Hospital; in stages, each becomes an integral part of the John Bright Street complex.

Abigail, Eddie's second daughter, is born in 1971, and his son, Daniel, in 1973. Both are 'Miracle Babies', as doctors had predicted that Hazel couldn't have any more children. Over the years, Eddie enjoys many foreign holidays with his family and friends, together with an assortment of Nannies! Eddie's father, George, dies in the 1970s.

Abigail's, formerly the Savoy Hotel, opens in 1974. It is a sophisticated and luxurious dining and cabaret club, named after Eddie's youngest daughter. The current chairman of QPR Football Club, Gianni Paladini, becomes a close friend of Eddie's and manages Abigail's, for several years. The club was originally intended to cater for customers returning home from events at the NEC. Sadly, Abigail's, in the long term, doesn't fulfil its promise, as people were often too tired to visit a nightclub after an exhausting day at exhibitions and various other shows. Also, the intention to cater for the luxury sector of Birmingham nightlife eventually proves unprofitable.

I remember telling Hazel's gynaecologist, Miss Shotton, the story about Abigail being 'one in a million'. I didn't just do it once – I did it twice. One was a chance in a million; the second was ten million to one! Years later, I made a speech at Abigail's wedding, regarding the tests that they did on me at the *Priory Clinic*, Edgbaston, to see if I could father a child. That was so funny! I said: "Well, you know that ten million to one, Miss Shutton? I've just had a result from a nurse that I know, at the Priory Hospital, who has tested Hazel and confirmed that she's pregnant. So it looks as if whatever I've been drinking must be good stuff. I'd better bottle it and sell it!"

Hazel was absolutely 'over the moon'! She was a lovely girl. As time went on she said: "You'd better get me into hospital, quick!" I rushed her into hospital. I drove on the footpath …everywhere…I just wanted to get her there. It was the Queen Elizabeth Hospital – a private ward. I got her in there at a hundred miles an hour! They said that she'd have to have a Caesarian Section, where they cut the baby out. They did that and the baby was absolutely beautiful – the head shape and everything. We christened her Abigail, so that was seven years after Rebecca.

Rebecca comments: "Obviously technology has moved on: in those days I don't think they had scans. I remember visiting mum in hospital."

When Hazel had the Section, she had a lot of pain, so they put her on a sleeping pill called Moggadon. This was later discovered to be very addictive, if it's taken for long periods of time. For years and years they couldn't get her off them. I had to keep getting her the Moggadon all the time. In the end, my own regular doctor, Nick, who was also my friend, said: "No, she mustn't have them." But she was still getting them off a private doctor all the time, without my knowledge; she was sending one of my workmen to get them.

For Abigail's christening, I hired the *Albany Hotel*; there were about three hundred people there. We were all drinking Dom Perignon champagne. It was a Sunday night. I'd got Ike and Tina Turner on, at *Barbarella's*. Everybody was dying to see Tina Turner – especially. So we all went back. I'd just fitted the first radio mikes to be fitted in any club, so I believe. We'd been drinking all day. It was about ten o'clock at night, so we loaded everybody up, three hundred people, to go through with bottles of Dom Perignon and wine. I said: "Carry it all with you. We'll have a night there."

When I got there, Tina Turner was already on. So I rushed to the toilet, because I was dying for a wee. While I was in there, the manager of *Barbarella's*, Kenny Hatton, came in. He'd left the reception early, to get everything ready for the show. He said: "We've got the new radio mikes," so he gave me one. What I didn't realise was that it was switched on! I started singing and I never gave it a thought. I could hear Tina, and I started singing with her.

All of a sudden, coming out, I could hear her saying: "Who the hell is on this microphone? It's some idiot drunk singing!" And it was me! So I switched the mike off, straightaway, and she carried on with the show. She was on about this crazy drunk, this-that-and-the-other, and I never said a word. But all of a sudden, my missus turned round and said: "It was him!"

She squealed on me. So I can claim to have sung on stage with Ike and Tina Turner… from the loo!

My son, Daniel, was born on 23 November 1973 – a 'Super Miracle Baby', as opposed to simply a 'Miracle Baby'!

Daniel explains: "I came along eighteen months after Abigail. I was also born by Caesarean Section. The physical likeness between my father and myself is amazing – apart from the sideboards!

"Becky used to do my head in – 'munching' my face, and things like that – saying I was chubby! She was a bit older, but Abigail and I were much closer in age. I think she used to do Becky's head in too; she'd have to look after the two of us, when mum and dad had gone out. When we were kids, our parties were different to everyone else's. Ours were like discos for the kids – at the clubs. We'd all play in there – and everyone would run riot.

"We were in Spain quite regularly, because my dad had the boat. I don't remember too much about that; just being with the family and playing on the beach. There was a restaurant called the *Tabu* at Magaluf, which we used to go to. Then we'd go to Tenerife quite often; a short flight to the sun really. Netty and Sue were my Nannies. Sue's husband was Tony Titmarsh – she was really nice. She looked after me on New Years Eve, when Abigail got appendicitis. There was another Nanny called Muriel, who was a really old lady. Dad used to like to get really good-looking barmaid Nannies. He chose them, but Muriel was the exception. I always used to have good-looking women looking after me anyway, which was a good beginning!

"I'm very interested in Sports. The whole family went over to LA, for the 1984 Olympics. That's when Reagan was in power. Me and my mum went to the Opening Ceremony, then the whole family went to all the 'Track and Field' events. We stayed at the *Sheraton Hotel* in Anaheim. We also went to Disneyland while we were there. I was ten. There were fireworks every night. We saw all the swimming events. I wasn't allowed to go to the boxing, but Becky went with dad. We saw basketball as well, which, being in the States, was really good. We were there for about seven weeks.

"I met Daley Thompson, when he won the gold medal, and the javelin-throwers, Tessa Sanderson and Fatima Whitbread. When they'd won the medals I'd go down the tunnel and get their autographs. I was only little, so I could get round everyone! That holiday made a big impression on me;

that's why I did really well at sport, at school – in the 100 and 200 Metres especially; also the High Jump and Long Jump. I was captain of the school rugby team – 'Seven-a-Side'.

"I attended Wycliffe College between the ages of eight to sixteen – from 1981-1989. My mum and dad chose that school, partly because it was quite close to where my dad was evacuated, and also because it was such a good school. As I was going so far away from home it was comforting to think that my dad had stayed near there, when he was a young boy. The cottage where my dad stayed was at Stonehouse, near Gloucester; my school was in the village of Eastington, about five miles from Stonehouse. In a car it doesn't seem very far, but in those days, when you walked everywhere, it would probably seem quite some distance. Wycliffe was one of the most expensive boarding schools. Abigail went to the same school as me – for A-Levels. She teaches English; she's very dramatic – in the nicest possible way!

"I studied Economics and Politics at university. I've always been interested in money – and Politics is quite interesting. Although dad had no formal schooling to speak of, he's always been very astute financially – and there was a lot of 'politicking' going on, behind the scenes, at his clubs – so I followed in his footsteps in that way. When we went to Mauritius, I got up on one ski; dad coached me about how to do it, before we went. You've got to be very fit," Daniel concludes.

"It was difficult when they were born, although I was really excited, to have a sister and a brother," Becky remembers. "I was really excited. I went to school with my news – 'I've had a sister!' But after a while it dawned on me, because I had been on my own for such a long time. I didn't get jealous, as such, because I was quite a lot older, but it took a lot of adjusting to… things were different for me. Abigail and I attended Edgbaston Church of England School. I was a well-behaved pupil. Later, poor old Abigail would have the teachers saying to her: 'You're not like your sister.' She was more extravert than I was. When I was a little girl I had a Fancy Dress Party at the *Cedar Club*, with my school friends.

"I remember going out in the boat – we were in it all the time. Dad taught me to water ski. He was very good at it – my mother was too. Larry Farrington couldn't swim, so he had to have loads of lifejackets on, when he was trying to ski. I wasn't frightened of actual water skiing, but because I was quite young, I was scared of the seaweed underneath – I didn't want to get my legs tangled up in it. I said if they got me a Red Setter dog then I would have a go. I was very young at the time. So I learned to water ski, and they bought me the dog; it was eventually given away to the manager of *Dexies Midnight Runners*, because it was so highly-strung; we couldn't control it.

"The Radvanyis used to come round to the house, after school, and we'd go to their house. They were always there at parties; they lived in Edgbaston too – in Lordswood Road. From a very young age I went to Majorca. We had a very small apartment, in the beginning. Very often, Muriel, who was my Nanny-babysitter, came abroad with us. She wore footless tights. The second apartment was the penthouse, which was much larger, with a view over the sea… a few rocks underneath, but it was beautiful.

"When we went to Los Gigantes I was more interested in boys at that stage, and going to the discos. But I was very shy. There was this boy who wanted to take me to a disco. My mum told me to wear this long dress and I felt really old-fashioned. This boy wanted to take me, and I wouldn't go. In the end they made me go, because they thought I was too shy. I sat there all night, sulking When I came home, I was not happy about it! I didn't do much when I was on holiday. I just sat there on the beach – 'chilling out', while the younger children were playing. We used to spend the whole summer in Majorca; we'd be there for months, but dad used to travel back to work, then fly back again. We were there with mum, for the whole summer really. It was lovely. We'd play on the beach and spend the day there. A lot of my school friends were doing the same, so it didn't seem out of the ordinary, although obviously my father's job was different.

"The singer Elkie Brookes was my Nanny for a time, when we lived in Anstruther Road. She was performing at one of dad's clubs. When I was older I'd baby-sit Abigail and Daniel sometimes too. I hated it, because they would never do as they were told; they would never go to bed! Mum's birthday was on Bonfire Night. I remember Patti Bell coming to my 18th Birthday Party. We had massive marquees in the back garden and my father spent a fortune on fireworks. A lot of them were at Fitzroy Avenue, because it had such a big garden. My mum used to be cooking, all day. She planned it all out; but she enjoyed cooking anyway. She used to make toffee apples for Bonfire

Patti brought her two sons, Dylan and Jake. Poor old Ricky Rickaby was tied to the central pole of the marquee and left there! I remember Dylan climbing up the pole. I haven't seen Patti's sons since they were little. I was very fond of Larry Farrington. I used to run to him when I was very little. He actually taught me to swim, when we were on holiday in Majorca. We went on holiday with him and his wife.

"When I was older and I went out to the clubs, Patti was often there. Mum probably asked her to keep an eye on me; she used to come up and talk to me and that sort of thing, or I would go over to her. To a certain extent, I copied the Punk fashion. Me and my friend Sarah, from school, always used to go to the *Cedar Club*. I dyed my hair bright pink, with Crazy Colours I don't think my dad approved! I didn't have any piercing at all, but I think my dad was really shocked, when I dyed my hair. It was more of a fashion statement really. Some of the bands at the *Cedar Club*, during the Punk days, were terrible – you couldn't really call it music!"

As a schoolgirl, Becky would invite some of her school-friends to the *Cedar*, but the headmaster asked me to put an end to that, as too many girls were taking up the offer!

"Yes, they were all sleeping in school; I think it just reduced down to me and my friend Sarah, in the end. My 18th Birthday Party was a Halloween Party. I remember coming home from college; my father and mother had been setting it up all day. It was a total surprise. I walked into the marquee and I was looking at all of the decorations. My mum had spent ages doing them. I came in and it was all dark; just a few dim lights. My dad was dressed in this Quasimodo costume, but he wasn't moving. I thought he was just a dummy, but then he suddenly came to life, with a roar. I ran screaming out of there… he nearly gave me a heart attack! But it was an absolutely brilliant night. My parents had lots of parties, over the years," Becky concludes.

I bought a place in John Bright Street, called *Abigail's* and spent a fortune converting it into a fantastic nightclub. It opened on 25 February 1974. Brooke Benton was Top of the Bill that night. I flew him from Ireland, paid him a fortune, and he gave a fantastic performance. The trouble was making it pay, because it was too good. We used to park the cars and everything. We finished up selling it back to Ladbroke's. Nowadays it's the *Casino*, at the end of John Bright Street. Ken Hardeman had a similar problem with the old *Celebrity Restaurant*: "I tried to create a little *Theatre Club* upstairs," Ken recalls. "Everybody said: 'Oh, we want one,' but we didn't get the numbers, to make it viable."

Pam Price observes: "In those years, the only person in Birmingham who I consider had the imagination, the where-with-all, the style and the resources, to put something like *Abigail's* together, was Eddie Fewtrell."

Bob Price elaborates: "*Abigail's* was a very good establishment. Their premises were what during the War had been one of the first bombsites: a

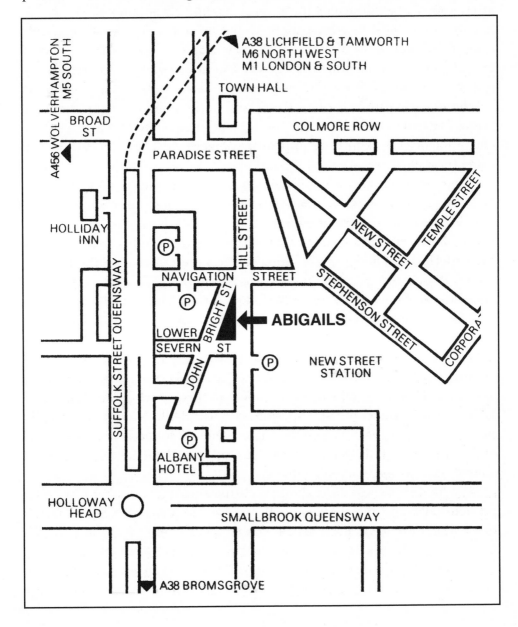

bombed public house, called the *Deer's Leap* (the M & B trademark) which had a moving neon sign of the deer leaping! After the war, Mitchell's & Butlers rebuilt it, in the 1960s, as the *Savoy Banqueting Rooms* and the *Savoy Hotel*. After a few years, this business subsided. Eddie took it over and created this very high-class restaurant, and high-class entertainment – with international acts and bands It was most expensively appointed."

According to Mike Alexander: "After Carl and I had finished, Eddie rang me up and said: 'I'm opening a new club called *Abigail's*. I'd like to put a trio in there.' I said: 'Yes – great!' I went down to have a look and it was just my kind of thing – it was lovely. It was a beautiful dinner-club; no gambling – just dinner. I played and sang in the main room, on the main stage – we had the trio there. We used to get some really nice artistes there and a lot of stars who were appearing somewhere else, who would just come for a meal.

"Tommy Steele was a regular, if he was performing in *Hans Christian Andersen* at the *Birmingham Hippodrome* he would come in for dinner, three, four, five times a week. He used to love *McArthur Park*. He used to get me to play it. It's a very hard piece to sing, with strange lyrics. It was recorded by Richard Harris. The lyrics are 'Someone left the cake out in the rain,' et cetera. It's a classic Jim Web masterpiece, from the 1970s. He wrote *By the Time I Get to Phoenix, Didn't We Almost Make It Girl*? Things like that.

"This one night, Buddy Greco was on – I'd introduced him. He came on and did his performance. Down the road, at the *Night Out*, Jack Jones was appearing and Tommy Steele was at the *Birmingham Hippodrome*. Jack Jones had expressed a wish to come up and see Buddy Greco, at *Abigail's*. Eddie had said: 'Okay. Let him come in – irrespective of what had happened before – yes he can come up.' So we held Buddy Greco's show back so that Jack Jones could come and see him later. The whole place was packed. All of the tables were full. Tommy Steele came up from the theatre and reserved a table; Jack Jones reserved a table.

"Buddy Greco did a fantastic show. At the end of it he pulled Jack Jones up onto the stage and the two of them sang *The More I See You* – and I'll never forget it – it was just great! It was fabulous....and we got him to sing for nothing – he got his dinner free! As they finished, I said: 'Ladies and gentlemen, Buddy Greco and Jack Jones.' Then I said: 'Hey Tommy, do you fancy coming up and singing *Half a Sixpence*?' He said: 'No, leave it out son!'

I was at *Abigail's* for about eighteen months. Then *Peters & Lee* offered me the job and I was with them for four years," explains Mike.

In the early days of *Abigail's* I employed a very tall, good-looking guy as manager. I booked various artistes to appear at Abigail's over a period of weeks. At this time I was over in Spain on holiday. This first manager of *Abigail's* fell in love with Aimee MacDonald. I came back one weekend, with Leamington Jack. Aimee was appearing on the Sunday, so I went in. She didn't know me because I hadn't met her.

I sat there with Leamington Jack; she came on but unfortunately, she was totally unsuitable for the club. I asked my manager how many people she'd been drawing in. He said: "Oh, not many. People doesn't realise how lovely she is!" I asked to speak to her. He said she was too busy to come out and see me, but she was going down to the *Cedar Club*. If she'd got the time, she would have a chat with me! I said, being sarcastic: "Right, tell her thank you very much. I'll look forward to that." I was paying her around £5,000 for the week! Leamington Jack was saying: "Throw her out the door!" According to Gianni, unbeknown to me, this manager didn't pay her the full amount.

Harry Morrall, the owner of the Rainbow had paid this manager for whisky, but he never put the money in the till. When I got to talking to one or two of the waiters, it turned out that all that this guy had done was to sit at one of the tables, being waited on hand-and-foot. After hours, he'd take Aimee down the *Cedar Club* and pile drinks on her for nothing.

To cut a long story short, he had given Aimee the impression that he was the owner of the club. I dispensed with her services, then later visited his flat, to make it doubly clear that, although I wasn't taking legal action against him, he was officially sacked. But he was the biggest BS Merchant you could imagine!

Gianni Paladini, the current owner of Queen's Park Rangers, arrived in England, many years ago, with Naples Youth Football Team, in which he played as a mid-fielder. He had begun playing football at the age of thirteen. He had to stop playing when he was twenty-two, because of an injured kneecap, around the time that he met his future wife, Olga, in a fashion boutique, by the Victoria Law Courts. After returning to Italy and realising that he could no longer play football, he came back over here on holiday. He married Olga when she was sixteen. Around 1967/68 Hazel used to shop at the boutique where Olga worked. Mary Quant was all the fashion then.

"So Olga and Hazel got to know one another well," recalls Gianni. "With that style of fashion and the long white boots, Olga looked quite something!

"At the time people thought our marriage wouldn't last more than a month, but it's lasted all this time. Olga became pregnant with our first child, Stephen, around the time that I first met Eddie. Stephen was born in 1969 and Katie the year afterwards.

"At this time I was working at the *Plough and Harrow Hotel*, on the Hagley Road in Birmingham, as a wine waiter. Eddie and Hazel used to reserve a whole table in the restaurant there, and that's how I first met him. Chris, John and Bomber were there with him too. We had a good rapport between us and as it turned out, he changed my life.

"I went to work for him at his clubs. My wages went up from about £7 a week at the hotel to around £100 a week. We bought a new detached house in Hall Green, and I was able to buy a new car. I was at the opening night at *Abigail's*. You could have a meal there and a cabaret. We were in competition with the *Night Out*, which held about three thousand people. I worked at *Rebecca's Nightclub* afterwards.

"*Abigail's* was near to *Boogie's*. The manager, who Eddie's just been describing, was at the club already, so Eddie made me the restaurant manager – he said: "I like your style." When he found that his first manager was 'on the fiddle' Eddie said: 'I'd like you to be manager of the whole thing.' I said: 'The best thing would be to try me out for a month or two, to see if I can do the job.' As it turned out I could.

"Johnny was manager of *Rebecca's*. Chris was the manager of the *Cedar Club*. Bomber and Gordon worked for him too. So Eddie was the major force. He and I became very close. He looked after me. I could be sure that I was quite safe when I was working for him. Nobody messed with Eddie, although there were many times when I witnessed unpleasant scenes.

"He was careful about the stock, the machines, the equipment; everything was well controlled – that's why he was very successful," continues Gianni. "As the manager, I never had to 'smack' anyone. I'm a great believer that it's always best to talk to people in a reasonable way, to sort problems out. Eddie was the same – that way your customers would always come back. People in his clubs came there to enjoy themselves, to meet the girls and have a good time.

"I remember one particular businessman, who took his employees out to *Abigail's* for a special night out. But when I handed him the bill at the end, he was shocked. He said: 'Tell that effing Eddie Fewtrell that I'm not going to pay the bill!' He didn't realise that Eddie was standing behind him. You can imagine it, can't you? There was a massive punch-up and I had to call the police, to sort it out. When they walked in they asked Eddie what happened. He said: 'I don't know. Arrest everybody here' – and he'd been involved in the fight! His answer was always the same if there was any trouble – 'Arrest everybody – they've been drinking my booze!' That's classic Eddie!

"Every Sunday Eddie would treat myself, my wife and my children to Sunday Lunch, at the *Chateau Impney*, or somewhere like that. We worked all week, so the only time we could go out like that was on Sunday. We used to go out very much together."

Becky confirms: "That was a big family event – it was lovely. As children we would play outside in the grounds. It was a really happy time."

Gianni recalls: "The only thing that I knew about the Queen in those days was that she was the queen! Being the manager of *Abigail's* at the time, we used to have a lot of famous people coming to the club: all the famous singers and stars and sports people. This one particular day I was told: 'The Queen is coming tonight!' So obviously I wanted to make sure that myself and all of the staff were smartly dressed. I bought myself a suit from one of the most expensive tailors in town – you know – with an expensive evening jacket … and we all waited for the Queen.

"Then I saw these people coming in and I thought to myself: 'Maybe these are the people who are doing the acoustics – for the Queen?' But they all looked like 'Pufftas': that is a word that Eddie used to use. They were in concert at the *NEC*. It turned out that they were the pop group *Queen*. Everybody thought that was very funny at the time!

"Tom Jones would come to *Abigail's* after he'd finished his show. Russ Abbot was there almost every time, because he used to work with his group the *Black Abbots*. But he was so funny! The best time of all would be after most of the other people had gone. The people who did these acts would all enjoy themselves. Bryan Ferry was very pleasant. When he'd been performing at the *NEC*, Bryan would come back to relax after the show, because Eddie used to provide people with a special room, in which they could relax. Although he was such a big star, he was quite reserved and shy. I really liked his style as well – he used to dress very smart.

"Bernard Manning would take the Mickey out of the Italians, especially as I was there. In the middle of the show, he would say: 'I remember your tanks, during the war; they had one forward gear and four reverse gears!' Eartha Kitt was a strong woman; she used to pull my hair – I had long, curly hair – you know? Bernard Manning would go into the kitchen before the show and have a meal.

"Stan Boardman was always comical and laughing. Jimmy Tarbuck, for me, was especially comical, because he was laughing, most the time, so I used to laugh too. We had a lot of very prestigious cabaret stars at *Abigail's*. Eddie used to give a red rose, dyed blue, to the customer's wives. They'd have a glass of champagne; there'd be cooking on the table. It was the most sophisticated club in town, really. We used to have French and Italian waiters; all of the waiters were foreign. So was the chef.

"Although I'd worked with Eddie for a long time, I always kept my contacts with football. At the time Italian football could not have any foreign players, playing for Italy. But the rule then changed. Italian football clubs could have foreign players, in Italy. While I was still working for Eddie, I helped to arrange various deals between English players and Italian clubs – that's how I got involved. Dennis Roache was the top agent in England. When Aston Villa played Juventus in the European Championship, Gordon Cowans played for Aston Villa, scored a fantastic goal, and the Italian people loved it. So when Giuseppe Bonetto, the general manager of Juventus, went to work for Naples, he asked me if I could contact Gordon Cowans. I knew him before through the nightclubs. When I finished working for Eddie, I returned to football, which I'd kept my interest in. Eddie wasn't very pleased when I stopped working for him. He didn't want to lose me, because we had a very good relationship as well. I left there in 1983," concludes Gianni.

I had a big apartment in Palma Nova, Majorca. I went there quite a lot, with the boat – to relax. As soon as ever I got there, my arrival would be announced – in the newspapers. Majorca, at that time, was saturated with thousands of Birmingham people: it was a Birmingham place. This was during the 1960s and 70s.

Doug Ellis, who's just resigned as Chairman of Aston Villa, had a place over there. He had his own travel agency in town. He used to fly me out for ten pounds. It was just a return ticket. I suppose that was the equivalent of fifty or sixty pounds now. I'd have all my clothes waiting for me there when

I arrived, so I'd only got to get the plane. The family would stay there for about six weeks at a time, during the school holidays. I'd go out there with my boat and stay Sunday to Tuesday; fly back Wednesday; stay Thursday, Friday and Saturday, to put all of the clubs together. Hazel would remain in Spain with the children; she'd have two or three Nannies. Then I'd fly Nannies out.

I had my boat over there, during the 1960s and 70s. Leamington Jack used one of my flats – because it was across from one of his kids. One day he came to me and said: "I've been over there and all of those wives over there, they're all having affairs with different geezers. They're having the time of their life there! I was watching from a distance." Strange as it may seem, four or five different women broke with their husbands, a few years later, and went off with Americans. They and their husbands had all been childhood friends of mine, but they all broke up and went over there – they're still in America today.

A lot of things were going on that I didn't know about. I went back with baby-sitters, to look after my children, because my wife was there as well, for weeks at a time. But all the Nannies kept running off with waiters, and this-that-and-the-other. I was going backwards between Spain and England, getting new nannies all the time, without actually realizing what was going on!

To put a stop to it I chose a big, tall Nanny, called the White Tornado, who wrapped herself up, wore a big hat, scarves all around her and wouldn't take her clothes off. But within two or three days, she'd run off with a waiter as well! The Spanish men were absolutely mad about Englishwomen, because they were all supposed to be 'hot under the collar'; it was absolutely barmy.

Then I hired another Nanny called Muriel, who was about sixty and built just like a pencil. She used to wear Long John tights. I'd walk on the beach with the kids and her; you could see all the waiters, hiding behind the parasols, laughing, because of this suit that she'd got on. I used to be really embarrassed, because I was normally seen with some of the most beautiful girls in the world. Then all of a sudden, here I am walking with Muriel! As I walked on the Spanish beach, with my two red-headed kids, Daniel and Abigail, you could hear people say, "He must have strong genes!" There was also a lovely looking black girl, called Nina.

I got a telegram from Hazel, to say that yet another Nanny had run off again, so I asked a girl called Anna, one of the most beautiful girls you've ever seen. She was an employee of mine, who worked on Reception at *Abigail's*. Anna is the friend whom Sheila Williams talks about in Chapter Nine. Anna was absolutely striking. I put her on Reception, because she was such a darling.

Eventually I asked her if she would you like to go to Spain, to look after my kids. She agreed, so I put her on the plane and took her back to Spain. Hazel was 'over the moon', although she was a bit concerned when she saw how beautiful she was. It was hard enough keeping the ugly ones there; we'd got no chance of keeping this one! So I trusted Anna. Things seemed alright at first, but eventually, she decided to stay over there, with a wealthy guy named Klaus.

I would stay abroad for a while, especially in the summer; the managers ran the clubs themselves. I'd fly back at weekends – to clear all the tills. Do the Friday and Saturday night in Birmingham, then fly back abroad on Sunday. That's what I was doing all the time. I'd also go to Los Gigantes, around December and January, but not actually at Christmas, because that was a particularly busy time at the clubs. It was just a two-hour flight and we'd spend time around the pool, in the lovely hot sun. This was the early days... so was Torremolinos. I got the apartment when the children were young, so Torremolinos was the best place to go. The children were young in the 1970s and 80s, but we took family holidays from the mid 1960s all the way through to 1989 – a period of about twenty-four years. I sold the Palma Nova apartment to Mike Millard, the jeweller in 1989, which is also the year when I sold my first group of clubs to Ansells.

After a few years Hazel didn't want to go to the flat in Torremolinos any more, so, as Daniel explained, I took the family to the Olympics, in LA. We went to Hawaii and took a tour of Pearl Harbour with Rebecca... which was very eerie. We did a lot of American tours in the 1960s – Disneyland and so forth. We went everywhere. Hazel's favourite place was St. Lucia. She was there quite a lot. All the little islands: Bermuda, Barbados. I think she went everywhere. I took her all over the world.

I also took Nikki Radvanyi with us, Rita's daughter, who was a friend of Rebecca and Abigail's. Nick and Rita often came with us on holiday. Chrissie's first wife, Paulette, came with us too, because I felt sorry for her after she and Chris had parted. I paid for her. I'd take her to America – and all the way round – because she'd help us with the children. If I didn't take them, because they had Nannies, she'd have a complete holiday.

I had a club in Majorca, which was also called *Barbarella's*, and I had a penthouse there. It was in Palma. I had another club in Torremolinos, called *London Town*. This was in the 1960s. I had this 'boole' boat, which was a very light yellow: on the water, it looked absolutely magic. The name of the boat was *Rebecca's*. It was a big, speedboat, holding about eight to nine people. You could ski four people at a time.

There was a guy there called Johnny Hart. He had a reputation for all kinds of water skiing…that's all he did. Now Majorca was saturated with beautiful girls of all nationalities: Swedish girls, Danish, German – absolute film stars. There was a place there called the *Ski Club*. So I got back and I had big fat Larry with me and my brothers, Johnny and Chrissie. I'd never been on a boat before in my life. So we took this boat back to Palma, got it off its trailer and floated it. Then we all got on to it and I put my captain's hat on. I started the engine up. It had a big car motor inside it, so it was powerful.

We all jumped on board. I then discovered that if I pulled the stick back, that made it stop, but I never realised that if you pulled it all the way back, it would go into reverse and stop immediately. They said: "Where are we going now?" I said: "We're going now to do a 'pose', in the *Ski Club*, where all these film star types and boat owners hang out."

To cut a long story short, I came in to the bank, pulled the lever back, without realising that I was putting it into reverse, rather than putting the brake on. The boat hit the landing jetty; I came straight over the top, and crashed the boat. Being made of fibreglass, it sank and we all got thrown out by the force of the impact – straight onto the beach!

Luckily, no one was injured. Someone ran up to me and said: "Can I have your autograph?" I asked him why and he said: "Because you're Danger Man – you know you are!" I'd already learned that in that kind of situation it's best to humour people, because they're so convinced that you're that person. So I just signed 'Danger Man'.

Everybody gathered round: "Where's your boat gone?" Everybody was screaming and laughing – because we looked like a right load of 'prairie 'ats' (prats). But nothing used to bother me in those days – money was not a problem. I said: "Alright, I'll have another boat." Just a week later, I had a brand new boat back in Palma. But this time I went out when there was nobody about, from seven o'clock in the morning, until well into the evening, learning to drive it properly.

Within a week, I could ski on one ski. I could get up out of the water and onto one ski. Jack Parsons, a friend of ours, helped me to do it. We set ourselves targets. I said to Jack: "Now come on, what we've got to do is to beat that Johnny Hart." He could even ski on a chair! Eventually I managed it too. Johnny came past, skiing on a chair – showing off. I said: "Hey John – how long did it take you to do that?" He said: "Seven years!" So I said: "I'll be on that chair next week." I had a bet on with him... he didn't think I could do it that quickly.

Then I went back to the *Barracca Bar*, where Johnny Hart relaxed and entertained. I went past on the chair, shouting: "How's that John? I'm coming past on a settee next week!" Everybody clapped, because they knew I'd only taken a week to do it. The other thing we used to do was to ski bare-footed, which I learned to do, just another week later. I said: "Look John, within a fortnight, we've done what it took you seven years to do – and we've done the no skis as well! So that's not bad is it?" The Press came to me and asked me how long I'd taken to do it. I can swim now, but I did all of that without being a swimmer, although I had a safety ring on.

My brother, John, took a photo at *Abigail's* in 1975 – the 'Sheik' photo. We all dressed up as sheiks – I remember it ever so well. I decided to go and get Bill Cutler – he was the one who bought the *Wheel Club*. He wanted to buy the *Cedar Club* off me, but I finished up selling him the *Wheel Club*. I told him that there were loads of sheiks coming to *Abigail's*. So me and Leamington Jack went in, with a sheik driving my Brabus, or the Rolls. We walked into *Abigail's* and Bill never realised that we weren't real sheiks. He was running around looking for us and I asked him for £50,000. He went to get it for me, but I said: "I won't have it now – I'll come back later."

I bought the advertising space on the back of half a dozen buses. They'd travel all over Birmingham advertising items like: 'Eddie Fewtrell presents a good night at *Barbarella's, Rebecca's Abigail's, Club Cedar* – the clubs were on there, and the name Eddie Fewtrell was going out – all over Birmingham! I kept it like that for years.

Becky remembers seeing the *Drifters* at *Abigail's*, one night. "The three of us had a table at the front – dad, my mum and me. It was an amazing club; very plush, and the food was very up-market... and the shows".

As you'll know, from Chapter Nine, I first met Rita Radvanyi over forty years ago. My sister-in-law, Paulette, who was married to Chrissie, introduced us.

"Hazel and Edward and Nick and I knew each other extremely well, through the children and even spent holidays together," explains Rita. We had a wonderful few years. We went to Los Gigantes in Tenerife. Fortunately Edward and Nick got on well, so the whole family became Nick's patients.

"I can remember an instance around 1980, when Edward was really worried about Hazel; she'd been in so much pain, while we were on holiday. When we got back, Hazel was rushed as an emergency to the Nuffield Hospital. She was operated on, because she'd got lots of gall stones. After that we formed a bond, and we became extremely close; that's when Edward asked Nick to take on the whole family as patients. We had holidays in Majorca. Edward and Hazel had an apartment there and my parents enjoyed themselves so much that they bought an apartment there too. So we had one or two holidays there.

"Edward, as you know, had more clubs than anybody I've *ever* known. I think he was operating eight clubs, all at one time. *Abigail's* was the most beautiful club; I think probably the nicest that Birmingham had ever had. You entered through the Main Reception area, which was beautiful. Then you had to go up into the lift. There was a massive nightclub on the first floor, with a beautiful stage and big silver drapes; a little bit like Las Vegas style, I suppose – very plush; very glamorous. You could have dinner and watch a floorshow. I should think that half of Birmingham must have been to *Abigail's*, at one time.

"A funny thing happened once, when we were in Los Gigantes on holiday together. There was a car dealer sitting by the swimming pool; dripping with gold, which must have been burnt him in that heat: it was about eighty degrees plus; he'd got so much gold on! He was saying: 'I know all of the Fewtrell Family you know? And Edward, I suppose, I know better than anybody. In fact I sold Eddie his first Rolls Royce.' Edward said: 'Well that's funny, because I bought it off Tom Jones!' He said: 'Oh, are *you* Eddie?' I think he was in such shock, because he'd made such a fool of himself, but as you can imagine, we were all hysterical!

"So our two families had so much fun together. For the children's birthdays and for Hazel's we always used to have the marquee; for a special Bonfire Night we all used to go in fancy dress. We had the most incredible parties ever. It's part of my life that I'm sad now has gone. But life changes and we all get older. But Edward and Hazel were the most fantastic host and hostess, and they were *always* giving parties. It gave us the chance to meet so many people, from so many different walks of life.

"I can't say that I met many celebrities at Edward's house, because he did tend to keep his private life separate from his club life. The side of Eddie that involves the 'gangster' element was something that Eddie was happy to let continue. He did have trouble with the Krays, but it suited him to let people think that, because after that period he had no further trouble from gangster elements making threats.

"He'd even got a phone in the toilet – because I got locked in there at a party one evening. They couldn't hear me calling for help because of the music. There was no inside door handle, so I was locked in there for ages! I phoned my husband, Nick, at Lordswood Road, asking him if he would phone Edward on his mobile phone, because he always answered that, to tell him that I was locked in the loo! But Edward was never *not* working," observes Rita.

"He always found time for the children. Sometimes he would take them to school; many times he would pick them up from school; he always found the time to be at their parties. Then of course, he'd got to go back to work, until the early hours of the morning."

Rita was involved in the *Gangsters* film, when Pat Roach was the Stunt Director.

When I was selling *Abigail's* to Ladbroke's, Harry Morrall, Bill Cutler, Alan Manning and the *Rum Runner* all objected to me having a new licence. All three of them already had one. What they didn't realise was that I had been in this before any of them, with the exception of the *Rainbow*, which had a very small card school. So Ladbroke's gave me a top solicitor and said money was no problem – I'd got to get the licence. I remembered that there used to be a club on the Bailey Circuit, called the *Cavendish*, by the *Swan*, Yardley. The *Dolce Vita* belonged to the Bailey's as well. I knew that they'd had a Gaming Licence there at one time, but all of a sudden the club was closed down and not used for years and years. The Gaming Board had turned *Abigail's* down, saying that there was no way that they were issuing any more Gaming Licences.

There was a big dispute in court. Ladbroke's were prepared to pay anything, for me to get a licence. So I negotiated a licence deal with the Bailey Circuit and I got them to pay; I couldn't do it myself, so the Baileys did the negotiations and they bought the licence for the Bailey Organisation. I don't know what they paid for it. When we returned to court, I knew that I'd got a licence under my belt, but I said nothing about it; it was kept very secret.

On the night before we went to court, who came in to *Abigail's* to see me, but the owner of the *Rainbow Casino*, Harry Morrall, who sadly died recently. Harry was supposed to be a very good friend of mine. With him was a guy called Frank. He whispered in my ear, trying to find out what was going to happen the next day. Well, I wouldn't let on exactly what was happening, but I said: "Well you'll see tomorrow that you're gonna lose!"

Alan Manning was someone who I'd put in the business and looked after, all my life, but he was frightened that I was going to take the business away from them. We went to court the next day. Alan went into the box first of all, to make his objections. He turned round and said different things. So I stood up and requested the right to question those who were objecting, which was granted. So I asked Alan: "According to what you said at the last meeting, the only objection that you've got to my having a licence is that you think that there are enough gaming licences in Birmingham and you don't think any more should be granted. Is that right?" He said: "Yes." I said: "Is that your only objection?" He said: "Yes." Then they put Harry Morrall in the box and I asked him the same question and he said yes.

I looked at my solicitor and said: "Is it alright for me to tell the judge what's happening?" He said: "Yes Mr. Fewtrell. You're doing very well!" I said: "Well sir, we have bought an existing licence, which has been here for many, many years." When the judge realised that we'd actually got the licence he said: "Well in that case, it's granted!"

Chapter Twelve

BOOGIE'S, EDWARD'S AND GOLDWYN'S

Boogie's, formerly Rebecca's, is managed, in turn, by Peter Jones, Gianni Paladini Roger Fewtrell, and Norman 'Nobby' Nobbs. Although less sophisticated than Goldwyn's, Boogie's will eventually emerge as the second most successful of his clubs. Eddie purchases a substantial building opposite – a former exhibition centre. He needs to have the building open for Christmas, as the first of his two 'Edward's' clubs, so the builders work nightshifts, and Eddie helps with labouring, carpentry and laying carpets. Whilst Eddie is still laying the floor, at the new Edward's No.7, Bob and Pam Price arrive, with the committee. Eddie rushes back home, gets bathed and changed and throws on a dinner suit! Edward's No.8 opens later, then becomes a rock venue, from 1987 to 1989 inclusive. Paramount and Goldwyn's open in 1988 and 1989 respectively, followed by The Hospital.

The following passage, by Stephen Hands, provides a great opening for this section of our book. You'll meet Stephen again, later in the chapter.

*   *   *   *   *

'Eddie Fewtrell must have been a man with laser like vision, to tempt us out of the friendly joviality of our much loved in-the-sticks pub, on a Friday night: smoked filled locals, where there's a lingering taste of Cape Hill brewed Carling Black Label supped at a galloping pace; lightly malted and slightly spinning heads, mixed with a left over unsold Cheese Cob. Well there had to be more to life on a Friday night!

There was a magnetic spell, which grabbed me and a group of friends, to a cool corner of Brum. Here is the party, *Club Tropicana*, whatever the weather. We're the Young Guns the new in-crowd… we're going for it; we were hip and being promised a good time, like never before. The tunes are pumping and booming, the smoke in the dark room, highlighted only by streams of direct light, danced to the beat. My soul is charged here, my happiness guaranteed, if only till chucking out time. This place is the coolest and chicest area of Brum, this is where it's at and I'm in here!

Another large Jack Daniels and Coke.... it may be only 5.30 in the evening but in *Boogie's Brasserie* and *Edwards No.7* it's Happy Hour, and we're loving every minute of every alcohol soaked hour. Some of the lads are in the *Casino* next door, but not me. I want my cash to last, as there is a long night in store. If I can last the pace, there's *Boogie's Nightclub*, if I can get in... wonder if Nobby's on the door tonight?

Eddie's pubs were great, I remember seeing his Roller one night outside *Boogie's*, and saying to my mate, "Whose is that then?" – EF1 or something like that. "Oh, that's Eddie Fewtrell's motor, he owns this end of town. Well fair play to you Eddy, because you started something good in Brum. The man with the Laser Vision. Who needs Specsavers eh?'

*   *   *   *   *

Tony Brook, of Halesowen began working for me in 1981, as a car valet, at my used car place, Daniel Edward Motors, in Halesowen. He also helped to repair and repaint the *Cedar Club*. Eventually, he transferred to *Boogie's Nightclub*, when he was in his early twenties.

"*Boogie's* was a marvellous place to work," recalls Tony. "Although the pay was low, there were beautiful girls everywhere and I was given free admission. I would march to the front of the queue, where Head Doorman Nobby would be shouting his market-type spiel: 'Three floors, three pounds admission – a pound a floor!' Eddie would be sat at the end of the bar, checking everything; he would often chat to me and buy me a pint. He had a house built from scratch in Farquhar Road, only for his wife Hazel to declare that she didn't like it and would not live there. 7 Norfolk Road, however, was a beautiful house."

The Farquhar Road house flooded, while I was in Vegas: ice burst the water tanks in the loft; it took months to dry out!

"Although *Boogie's Brasserie* was a roaring success, it was too small to really pack the customers in," continues Tony, "so Eddie acquired a lovely big building opposite, which became *Edward's No.7*. The focal point for *Edward's No.7*, two ornate mirrored archways on the balcony, were found behind a false wall in the old building and restored to their former glory. When it opened on time, a lovely Italian man, called Gigi, (Pier Luigi Netti), was installed as the manager, and was hugely popular with customers, from the outset."

Gigi's situation was a rather sad one. His wife had left him and he was in a little flat in Edgbaston. I found him sitting outside *XL's* in the daytime. Nick Radvanyi couldn't treat him as he wasn't his GP. His regular GP refused to see me, so I phoned for an ambulance, saying that I had found Gigi in the street. I went with him to Dudley Road Hospital, where they found that he had throat cancer, which they then treated.

He was an alcoholic. His wife, Gianni Paladini's sister-in-law, wouldn't have him in the house. I allowed him into *XL's* for a while, until he started drinking the spirits. His wife objected and so did the manager, so I asked Gigi to stop going there. He managed *Edward's No.7* for some years, but when I became ill myself, I lost contact with him. He used to sleep overnight in his van, either outside the club, or parked in my drive! I understand from Tony that Gigi died recently, from throat cancer.

Tony Brook continues: "Eddie was very much a 'hands-on' boss and used to come into *Edward's No.7* most weekdays, to have his lunch, and have an informal meeting with management, behind the scenes. When *Edward's No.8* finally opened, behind schedule the punters failed to materialise in great numbers. The competition had caught up, with the opening, nearby, of the *Dome* and *Pagoda Park* nightclubs. In typical never-say-die attitude, Eddie eventually reinvented *No.8* as a rock venue, with live bands, and soon packed the place out.

"As the 1980s progressed and prosperity improved, people came in greater numbers to Birmingham, where the number of licensed premises was expanding. Eddie was determined to take advantage of this and opened *Paramount*, then *Goldwyn's Nightclub*. *Paramount* was the subject of a legal challenge by the film company of the same name, who insisted that their logo was not replicated in the pub. Don Fewtrell was introduced as manager of the club, along with his partner, Nina.

"The pedestrianisation of John Bright Street and Lower Severn Street was a good idea, but actually resulted in a drop in customers, because buses never went past any more. One night, Eddie was on the door at *Goldwyn's* when there was a horrifying attack. The doorman had refused entry to two scruffily-dressed men. They came back with a petrol bomb and threw it at the door, resulting in the foyer of the club erupting into a fireball."

My youngest daughter, Abigail, recalls: "Sometimes Dad would ring up people who were appearing at the *Alex* or the *Hippodrome* and ask them to give him a 'plug' on the telly. For example Ben E. King rang up the house. He'd just re-released the hit record *Stand By Me*; it had come into the charts again with the film. I answered the phone and he said: 'Can I speak to your father? It's Ben E. King.' I said: 'Stop messing about. It can't be Ben E. King. Who is it really?' But it *was* him. Dad spoke to him. He was going on the telly that night and dad said: 'Give us a plug.' And they always did; whether they were going on the telly or the radio. They'd say something like: 'While I'm in Birmingham I'm going to visit my old friend Eddie Fewtrell. He's got a good night on at *Abigail's*' – or wherever."

By 1985, we'd moved to Norfolk Road. Becky remembers: "When mother and father bought the home at 7 Norfolk Road it was a complete wreck. They did it up, but mum sent us to stay in the *Holiday Inn* hotel, in Birmingham, for weeks on end, during the summer holidays, while all the house alterations were being done. It was just the three of us, Abigail, Daniel and me. Dad used to leave us in the hotel. I was older at the time, so I was looking after them, but it was very stressful being stuck in this room – just the three of us."

Radio presenter Phil Upton and I first met at *Boogie's Nightclub*, in 1985. He walked into the club, with the intention of getting a DJ gig, having just started DJing.

"The first guy I met was his manager of the club, who was described to me at the time as Johnny Paladini, but who we all know now as Gianni Paladini, remembers Phil. "I asked him if I could DJ at the club. He said (Italian accent): 'Alright – you come in and you do a-Monday and a-Tuesday and a-Wednesday. I'll pay you forty pounds.' I thought: 'Right – this is great; I'm getting forty pounds, cash.' It was unbelievable. Only subsequently did I find out that I was supposed to be getting forty pounds a night – not forty pounds for three nights! Eddie was actually the person who made sure that I got paid the right amount.

"The first time I spoke to Eddie, he walked up to me while I was in the middle of a DJ set. He said: 'Great night, great night. The crowd are loving it!

Get Johnny to give you a pay rise.' Once he found out what I was on he said: 'Oh no – he should be giving you that every night!' I said: 'Ah – alright,' but he straightened that out. So my first impression was of someone who looked after me, but was a *huge* character. He wasn't imposing – there's a difference. You knew who he was, whether you knew him or not. If you went into the bar of *Edward's No.8*, or any of his clubs, he'd have his position, in the corner of the bar, surrounded by an assorted collection of colourful characters.

"I remember being scared s**tless! The legends of him were about; every DJ knew all the stories about him. They'd go: 'Oh, you don't know about that? Oh well, when the Kray twins came… he did this and he did that', so you'd immediately build up this persona of the guy – before you'd even spoken to him."

In fact, most of the Kray business happened in the late 1950s, when I had the *Bermuda Club* – although some of the characters and problems followed me into the *Cedar Club* era.

"But this was Birmingham Nightclub legend," continues Phil. "So I actually started at *Boogie's Brasserie*, which is now the *Orleans Nightclub*. Then I progressed into *Boogie's Nightclub*, around the corner, on Lower Severn Street. Then he opened *Edward's No.7* and *No.8*. I was actually at the opening night of *Edward's No.8*. I worked at *Edward's No.7* quite regularly. Afterwards, I worked at the *Paramount* and the club that was above it – *Goldwyns*. *Edward's No.8* opened around the mid-1980s, judging by the records that I was playing on the opening night – *Miami Sound Machine*, *Doctor Beat*, *Sister Sledge*, *Frankie*.

"Having started in the *Brasserie*, which was the Wine Bar on John Bright Street, I was very much the junior member of the DJ team. You knew you'd made it, when you made the main room of *Edward's No.8*; you were then regarded as the Number One DJ. There was a huge cross-section of clientele – proper Brummies. Everybody from Robert Hopkins of Birmingham City Football Club; that was in the days when footballers went out drinking most nights, before we got the healthy diet and all the rest of it. 'Hoppo' would spend pretty much every night of the week at *Boogie's Brasserie*. Robert still is a Blues legend, but he would be there, at the end of the night, when you'd have an assortment of, as-it-were, 'hangers-on'.

"Meanwhile, I was at Matthew Boulton College, doing my A Levels. I was on the Students Union; my job, as Communications Secretary, was to arrange all the parties. I'd go to *Boogie's Nightclub*, buy the tickets and distribute them all back at Matthew Boulton. I was leading quite a hectic lifestyle at that point: studying, organising social events and DJing...I couldn't do it now! So that was my first insight into nightclub life, organising these parties.

"That's when I met Bomber Fewtrell for the first time. Obviously he was the Number Two brother. He actually fired me once, on New Years' Eve 1986 or '87, but I got reinstated the following night – Eddie put the fire out!"

I didn't want to lose him – Phil was a brilliant DJ!

"When I started there Roger Davies more or less organised the DJs – told them which venue they were working at and so on," continues Phil. "But Roger's time came and off he went. Everybody said: 'Eddie will get you to do it.' I said: 'I'm at college, I haven't got time.' By that time I was studying at City of Birmingham Polytechnic, taking a degree in Communication Studies, so it was like – 'How do I turn down Eddie Fewtrell?' I don't *know* anyone who goes and says no to Eddie Fewtrell! I was scared s**tless – I'd got to go to him and say: 'I don't want to do it.' I sounded out a few managers, including Dave Wagstaffe and Richard Walker, who was manager of *Edward's No.8*. He said: 'Well as long as you go and tell him and you've got a good reason, then he'll be fine,' and he was; but for an eighteen or nineteen-year-old kid...

"By the time we got to 1996, and he opened *Club Millennium*, we had a lot of respect for each other. Soon after that experience of having to turn the job down, ironically, we seemed to become closer; whether it was because I turned the job down and he had more respect for me, I don't know."

In 1987 Phil started working for BRMB, presenting the lunchtime show and a Friday evening Dance show, which was also heard on Mercia and Leicester Sound. Then he took over the *Drivetime* show, followed by the afternoon show. Phil can now be heard on BBC WM, as the Breakfast Show presenter, every Monday to Friday, from 7-10am. I was a guest on his show, on Friday 13 July 2007, as part of a 'phone-in' about my clubs.

"I visited Eddie at his house at 7 Norfolk Road, just after I'd said no to him about the job, so this would be around 1985-86. I met Hazel there briefly. Danny was there too; he was about thirteen. Even at that age he was already the heir apparent – a 'chip-off-the-old-block'. It was obvious that he was going to follow in his father's footsteps, into that line of work."

In fact, Phil, Hazel wanted Daniel to become a solicitor, doctor or banker; she didn't want him to go into the nightclub world!

"Back then, Eddie did a lot of his business at home," continues Phil, "so I'd go round to Norfolk Road. I remember walking to his house, in the up-market end of town, Norfolk Road, Edgbaston. He was the first guy I knew who had portable tellies in his house.

"When I helped launch *Edward's No.8*, I turned up with my boxes and they were still tacking down the carpet. One night, the roof leaked at the top of *Edward's No.8*. I remember grabbing the keys off Gianni.... 'I'll get up there and do it!' Eddie bought the buildings around the back of *Edward's No.7*, opposite the *Alexandra Theatre* and turned them into *Paramount* and *Goldwyns*.

"*Goldwyns* was above the *Paramount* disco bar, which opened in 1988, before *Goldwyns*.

I DJd at the *Paramount*; which was designed as a much more laid-back, classier Wine Bar sort of atmosphere. *Edward's* had incredible music a lot of soul and a lot of 'angst'

I was into black music in a big way: Soul and Hip-hop; that was why I DJd in the *Sin Bin*, in the basement at *Boogie's*."

Although I gave most of my DJs a reasonably 'free hand', I also asked them to avoid a certain kind of music, as it tended to encourage the taking of drugs. Patti Bell was very much Birmingham's Queen of Punk, so-to-speak, in terms of fashion design, but she'd rather dance to James Brown, music-wise. The Punk Movement had its heyday in the 1970s. In contrast, as a DJ of the 80s, Phil was very much Post-Punk.

"We wanted to create more of a Wine Bar atmosphere in *Paramount*," Phil explains, "so the music I played there was all *Sade*, pronounced *Sharday*, Grover Washington, laid-back sort of music. Miami Vice... that was the fashion; I can remember wearing a white jacket, rolled up to my elbows, with a low-cut white T-shirt underneath. Leather trousers were quite popular, but it wasn't like a Rocker – it was quite smart. Remember, these were the days when you still sometimes had to wear a tie to get into a nightclub. That's all gone now."

"Having read into a bit of DJ history and about Northern Soul, they talk about how these early clubs were actually a bed-rock for the Soul Nights. At *Rebecca's*, for example, they played a lot of Northern Soul," Phil comments. "You let your DJs establish what should be played."

That's true. Hazel was more 'on the ball' as far as pop music was concerned and about the various bands. My expertise was building up a club empire and choosing the décor, to create a particular atmosphere.

"Although you disliked the Punk Scene Eddie, it was good business. Ironically though, and Dave Juste will probably confirm this, on the Rock Nights you had less trouble off the Rock crowd than you did from the regular Saturday night customers."

Yes, the Rock crowd were so grateful for having their own club (*Edward's No.8*) that they made a point of avoiding trouble. They had a vested interest in keeping it as a thriving club.

"Eddie began to look at his Rock crowd as a fail-safe night really," continues Phil. "No one would trash your venue, they would spend money and it meant good business. It appealed to a wide audience and he didn't fell threatened. But there was something about these Soul Nights that I know he felt a bit threatened by… the black Afro-Caribbean audiences that came to them. As a naïve seventeen-eighteen-year-old, I wasn't aware of drug-related problems.

"*Paramount* opened in 1988; *Goldwyns* opened a year afterwards; just before he sold the clubs to Ansells. Only after *Paramount* was a roaring success did they decide, 'We could do a lot more with this.' The upstairs was nothing but a warehouse; they gutted that, and turned it into another room, which became *Goldwyns*," explains Phil.

"Back then, with London being the capital city, it was a lot more cosmopolitan, so the audience would be a lot more mixed. In Birmingham, we didn't have people who would travel far and wide, to the nightclubs. Certainly in *Edward's* and *Boogie's* they were Birmingham clubs, full of Birmingham people and that was it; you wouldn't have people from London, Leeds, Liverpool or Manchester travelling down to them. With a few famous exceptions, most London venues were pubs with a DJ. You have to bear in mind what was happening culturally, around these times. In 1985-86 there was the birth of what we now know as Underground Clubs. These were very simplistic. In contrast, Eddie's clubs were all-singing, all-dancing. He spent a lot of money on installation: the right lights, the right sound, the right effects and fittings. It was all about looking classy and creating that kind of ambience.

"In Eddie's clubs you had to work the lights yourself; this was before the age of having a lighting jockey. Nowadays you have a DJ and somebody else who is just responsible for working the lights. In those days you had to do it all. I was very clumsy – still am, as a person. I can remember several times DJing, walking across to the bar, to get a drink and falling arse-over-tip on the dance floor. There was some kind of polish or shine that made it absolutely impossible to walk sensibly! This was downstairs at *Boogie's* and I'd go 'wa-hey'… arse-over-tip! I'd get comments like: 'Oi, 'andsome – try walking for a living!'

"Most of my memories are about the personalities that were around at the time. Nobby Nobbs was like a *legend* on the front door. Knowing him as I do now – hard man boxing trade – you get a completely different picture, but he would play up the lads something rotten on the front door – making out that he was gay or bi-sexual: 'Come on lads – give us a kiss!' Pat your bum – all the rest of it. But if you even remotely suggested that yourself, he'd have knocked your block off! He just played you up, and you got in – no problem. He'd sit there, in his 'tux', with a bow tie and a flat cap on. That was kind of how you'd recognise him. It was mad, because when I saw him five or six years later, in a boxing ring I thought: 'S**t – that's Nobby Nobbs, the doorman at the time!'

"Steve Gibbons was the star of the first live rock show that I compered, at *Edward's No.8*. Up until then I'd just DJd, so I was pretty nervous when Eddie came up with the idea of bringing live music into the club. He was always looking for another attraction. He booked three Radio One DJs in a row. I was the first time that I'd ever seen DJs or radio, live, in Birmingham. He had Mike Reid, Gary Davis and Simon Bates, one after the other, at *Edward's No.8*. They did about an hour each, on stage, and we played the records. He did *that* one-off, then we got some live bands in – it was always 'What's the next thing?' So, first-off, Eddie decided to feature the *Steve Gibbons Band*. I didn't know who they were. I was a nineteen-year-old kid whose musical knowledge was limited to house and funk and soul. I was very nervous, because I'd got no idea what they were going to do. This guy comes out and he's like Mick Jagger – this is 1986-87.

"I said: 'How would you like me to introduce you?' 'Just say we're the *Steve Gibbons Band* – that's our name.' For a nervous nineteen-year-old my primary concern was getting the name right. I might have called them the *Steve Gabbons Band*, or the *Dave Gibbons Band* – or whatever. When you think about their position now, in Birmingham's nightlife culture, it seems

Turning Point *Charity Function: Princess Diana, a patron of the charity, with Pam Price. Photograph by Simon Livingstone Studios. By kind permission of Bob and Pam Price.*

Abigail and Eddie meet Princess Diana at the International Convention Centre, *Birmingham. It's no wonder she's smiling, because the recently divorced Eddie is asking: "How's your love life?"… then invites her to dance at* **Boogie's!**

Dinner Dance and Cabaret

Chris Fewtrell
proudly presents

A Night of
Entertainment

Dinner Dance
~ and Cabaret ~

Friday 3rd September 1999
at the
Albany Banqueting Suite

Includes:
- Four Course Meal
- Well-known impressionist Paul Melba
- The Ivy League
- Pedro - Rock & Roll Dj inclusive Karaoke
- Vocalist compare Tony Rome

A Night of Entertainment

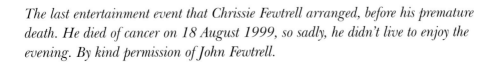

The last entertainment event that Chrissie Fewtrell arranged, before his premature death. He died of cancer on 18 August 1999, so sadly, he didn't live to enjoy the evening. By kind permission of John Fewtrell.

Hazel and Eddie at the Poppy Ball. *Photograph by Alan Johnson. By kind permission of Rebecca Fewtrell.*

Bob and Pam Price, attending the annual Poppy Ball *at the* Metropole Hotel. *Photograph by Simon Livingstone Studios. By kind permission of Pam and Bob Price.*

Wishing you

every success

on the night

from

Eddie Fewtrell's

Group of

Companies

ZIG ZAG CLUB
34 AUCHINLECK SQ., FIVEWAYS, BIRMINGHAM B15 1DV
XL's NIGHT CLUB
34 AUCHINLECK SQ., BIRMINGHAM B15 1DV
XPOSURE CAFE
FLETCHERS WALK, PARADISE PLACE, BIRMINGHAM B3 3HJ
CLUB MILLENNIUM
LEVEL ST., BRIERLEY HILL, WEST MIDLANDS DY5 1TY
HEALTHSTONE VENDING LTD.
34 AUCHINLECK SQ., FIVEWAYS, BIRMINGHAM B15 1DV
GENERALVIEW PLC.
34 AUCHINLECK SQ., BIRMINGHAM B15 1DV
HEALTHSTONE PLC.
34 AUCHINLECK SQ., BIRMINGHAM B15 1DV

A page from the Poppy Ball *Brochure for 1999, advertising Eddie's 'Second Wave' of clubs and businesses; advertising was a means of sponsoring the charity. By kind permission of Bob and Pam Price.*

Eddie and Hazel in Hong Kong. By kind permission of Rebecca Fewtrell.

Daniel meets Isaac Hayes, in New York. By kind permission of Daniel Fewtrell.

Becky's wedding to John Moon, September, 2002. L-R: Daniel, Becky (Rebecca), and Abigail. By kind permission of John and Rebecca Moon.

Kate Fewtrell's wedding reception, at the Eaton Hotel, *Hagley Road, Birmingham, on the 23 May, 2004: Back row, L-R: Gordon (bride's father); Sally (sister); Steve Parker (bridegroom); John Joannou (Sally's husband); Front row, L-R: Luka (Sally's son); Jane (bride's mother); Kate (bride) and Ellie (Sally's daughter). By kind permission of Gordon Fewtrell.*

Marleen and Eddie celebrate their marriage, in March 2005. They have known each other for just over seventeen years, having met in June 1990.

Eddie and Marleen have run a successful business together, the Singing Stud, *for over twelve years. Marleen's mother put her on a horse, over in Denmark, when she was just four years of age… and that was it!*

The Jimmy Tarbuck Classic, *January 1993: This annual event is held at the* Meridian Hotel, *Don Felipe, Portugal. Performing, from L-R: Kenny Lynch, Jasper Carrott, Jimmy Tarbuck and John Lodge, of the* Moody Blues.

Eddie with Ian Saint John, at a reception for Jimmy's charity golf tournament in Portugal, 2006. Russ Abbot, Stan Boardman, Jasper Carrott, Robert Powell, Alan Hanson and Tim Brooke-Taylor are also regulars at the tournament.

Eddie with Pauline Tarbuck, Jimmy's wife, at the Jimmy Tarbuck Classic, 2006, *hosted by the* Meridian Hotel, Portugal. *The money raised each year helps to support a local children's orphanage, plus the* Variety Club.

Eddie with 'The Two Kennys' – Hatton and Lynch – at the Jimmy Tarbuck
Classic, 2006, *in Portugal. The event has been running for twenty-six years.
Kenny Lynch first talked Eddie's good friend, Kenny Hatton, into going, as he was
"quite a good golfer." Kenny Lynch and 'Tarby' have attended all twenty-six!*

Dylan is the oldest of Steve Gibbons and Patti Bell's two sons. This photo was taken at the Ceole Castle *in Moseley, where Dylan is a DJ. 'Boogie', on the right of the picture, shares the same name as one of Eddie's nightclubs. Patti and Steve's younger son, Jake, has his own band, and plays as a pianist, with other bands. Jake promotes bands at the* Ceole Castle; *Steve sometimes participates in these events. By kind permission of Patti Bell.*

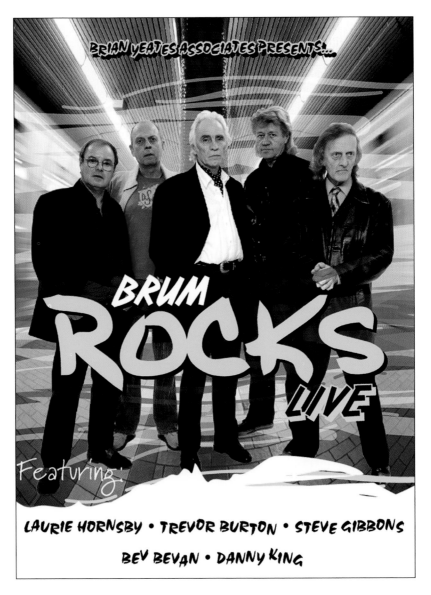

The Brum Rocks Live *concerts, from an idea by Brian and Ashley Yeates, continue to delight audiences across the West Midlands. They hope to extend their performances around the UK, next year. From L-R: Narrator – musician Laurie Hornsby, Trevor Burton, Steve Gibbons – (Dylan's father) Bev Bevan and Danny King. Poster by kind permission of Brian Yeates Associates. Four of the celebrities involved, including Brian, feature in our book.*

Marleen, Finlay, Eddie and Connor enjoy a visit to Birmingham's National Sealife Centre. *Finlay and Connor are Abigail and musician David Keogh's two sons. Eddie has five grandchildren altogether.*

Connor and Eddie take a rest.

George and Florence (Flo) are Daniel and Leslie's children. George is named after Eddie's father; Flo, after Hazel's mother. By kind permission of Daniel and Leslie Fewtrell.

Becky and John Moon's daughter, and Eddie's 'little bundle of fun'..........
granddaughter, Isabella.

ridiculous. But to a kid who'd never heard of them before, just getting the name right was a big deal. They really rocked it. They sang *Tulane*.

"Eddie had a lot of things going for him. At the time, he was the only gig in town. We didn't have the plethora of venues that we have now. You've all round, from the Mailbox, to Broad Street to the Arcadians at Summer Row. He didn't have a lot of competition. I heard that several people would have to go to call Eddie, to get his blessing, before they opened a venue. Eddie was brought up under the old tradition of cabaret nightclubs, but he wasn't so inflexible that he couldn't move with the times. When we got to the Eighties, he realised that the cabaret clubs were on their way out; when the *Night Out* had to close, you *knew* there was a problem in Cabaret.

"I know DJs who pilfered from the bar; DJs who'd try to walk out with a bag, and when they opened it up there'd be twenty bottles of beer in the middle of it all. I know managers who'd pilfer from him," recalls Phil.

Tony Brook explains: "Dave Juste was the man who helped Eddie to re-invent *No.8s* as a rock venue, by booking the bands and organising DJs. This was so successful that on weekends, the top floor of *No.7s* was used as an overflow for *No.8s*, via a disused staircase."

When *Abigail's* eventually closed down Gianni Paladini transferred to the *Brasserie*. My good friend Pat Roach used to visit quite a few of my clubs – and help me out from time to time.

"Yes, I used to see him – especially at the *Cedar Club*," confirms Gianni. "When he was making a film he'd come in there to relax. He was a wonderful man – very modest. Although he was a big man, sometimes I used to think that he was shy. All of the Villa players used to come to *Boogie's Brasserie*."

In 1982 we celebrated the deal that Gordon Cowans and Paul Ridout of Aston Villa, had just done, with all the fellow managers. I broke open some bottles of Dom Perignon, at Boogie's, which was selling at £100 a bottle. I said: "Cheers!" and gave them all a glass of champagne. Just as I said "Cheers!" the manager of Naples took the glasses off Gordon Cowans and Ridout and said: "You're not allowed to drink now." They looked at me and I said: "Well, you've just sold yourself!"

"This was in 1982," continues Gianni, "and I was making money in this way, as an agent. So then I decided to leave. Eddie wasn't happy about it, but he had to accept it. So that changed my life and I became involved with football again."

Norman 'Nobby' Nobbs was the final manager at *Boogie's* and made a great success of it, turning it into my second most successful club ever.

"You had to be one step ahead: you had to suss out what people were thinking," recalls Nobby. "The idea of 'security' was all bollocks in those days: there were no contracts signed – you just did your job. There were none of these security badges and all that game! You just had to use your brains. If you let the 'aggravation' in, you've got to get them out again!

"As you know ,Eddie, I've always been an independent and very self-controlled person…I reckon that's why you and I are on the same wavelength! I remember how a group of us used to collect the money from the John Bright Street clubs and pubs, and take it to the bank. The routine would be regularly changed and we also changed the reinforced vehicle, each time.

"Eddie knew that. *Boogie's*, which wasn't so luxurious, did much better than some of the clubs that were. It was catering largely for the working class. Ron Gray and myself helped Chrissie to arrange special fight events. Around 1983/84, we had a Heavyweight Title Fight. Billy Aird, from London, fought this Liverpool guy, Gordon Ferris. I was working for BRMB, with Simon Smith, who was well known in the club circuit: he was a celebrity, for ITV Sport. So we brought a few guys back to the club. We had about two staff on – it was a quiet night.

"Anyway, we had about ten coaches to watch this fight, so they all came back to *Boogie's* afterwards; the club was packed – because you were such a popular guy. I phoned you and said: 'I think you'd better come down here!' We had to scramble around for barmaids – everybody seemed to descend on *Boogie's*. It was unbelievable. We used to bring people in after the boxing. We'd get all of the local villains back to *Boogie's,* after the match. They all had a good time – they'd bring their girlfriends. So we used to be very popular.

"When Eddie started *Goldwyn's* he couldn't get his breath, because *Boogie's* was still taking more money than *Goldwyn's*. Eddie asked me: 'What are you doing?' I said: 'Well I'm bringing everybody – that's what I'm doing!' On the club scene, somewhere like *Boogie's*, the more people you got in the less trouble you had. It was when you didn't have many people in that you got trouble. I used to love it when it was packed. It had a nice little restaurant.

"In the 1980s, it was the most popular club, because they knew we didn't take liberties and nine times out of ten we catered for what they wanted to hear. Eddie always had good DJs – he treated them well. You can't just shut a club at two o'clock. Eddie knew I'd never just say: 'Everybody out!' – and start grabbing hold of customers – asking them to leave at closing time. If you do that you're asking for a load of trouble. If I had people that I couldn't get out, I'd turn the music off, turn the lights down; sometimes I'd turn all of the lights off – just for a few seconds; they'd be sitting there in the dark! They'd look at me and I'd say: 'I think it's time to go, isn't it?' Then they'd go: no fuss; no panic. I stopped working for him in 1989, when he sold up. We had a strict code; an unwritten code," Nobby concludes. "When Eddie was talking to somebody, I could tell whether he was just talking to them 'willy-nilly', or whether he meant it."

Big Albert put a big charity do on at *Edward's No.8*. Eventually that charity became Heartbeat. At the first charity show at *No.8* they had Jim Davidson on, *Cannon & Ball*, Marti Caine and Tony Christie... they were all pals of his.

"We raised £8,600 for the Children's Hospital, in Birmingham," explains Albert. "It was Keith Smart and myself who organised that. We put the charity events on at Eddie's clubs and at mine; but we did this one at Edward's and he was really supportive. It was about 1985. I've got loads of memorabilia like that and I've been in lots of books too.

"I started Nobby in the boxing game. They built a gym in the *Rum Runner Club*, for Dave Roden and myself – and Nobby started training there. Dave Roden, is now on the Boxing Board of Control; he and I actually built that gym ourselves. The Berrows paid for it. It was an old Victorian building. We borrowed a truck and had to carry the breeze blocks up four floors, to block all the windows. I still do boxing shows now," Albert concludes.

Tony Christie was there when I opened *Boogie's*; he was one of the first that I put up there. He was quite young at the time and he came there with his wife. So the *Cabasa* was where we started putting on cabaret, for the older person. Downstairs were rock bands and shows and things like that. We had the *Tony Richardson Trio* up in the *Cabasa*. Tony had his own little plane and he took me flying; his backing group backed Tony Christie. 'Tiny Tony', Tony Hallam, was also one of the managers; he married a barmaid.

Later on in the evening, at the clubs, we used to have a tap dancing record. The DJ had to put it on at a certain time. He'd look to me for a signal – that the place and the mood were right. It was usually when everybody had quite a lot to drink… early in the morning. Everybody was under instructions that when the record came on, everyone, including the barmaids, had to stop what they were doing and start tap dancing – even the DJ himself and the doorman! They all thought it was their shoes that were making the tapping sound, but it was actually on the record.

Dave Juste recalls: "The first time I met Eddie was in late 1986 when John Nevin and me went to approach all of the clubs in Birmingham about doing a Rock Night. Most of them said no. Eddie was the only one who would give us a chance. We opened the Rock Night on 18 April 1987. *Edward's No.7* was hugely popular. If you didn't get there by half past seven, on a weekend night, you were struggling to get in, because by eight o'clock, there were queues all the way down the road. Inside was already full and usually it was a 'one out, one in' system. Basically, it was a four-floor building. *Edward's No.7* was on the ground floor and the first floor and *Edward's No.8*, which was above that, was on what would be the second and third floors. So the nightclub was above the pub. Then *Boogie's Brasserie* was across the road. Again, it was a similar set-up where *Boogie's Brasserie* was on the bottom two floors and *Boogie's Nightclub* was on the top two floors.

"When I was 18-25 there were very few places for people to go," Dave elaborates. "That would be between the years 1981-1988. On John Bright Street you had *Edward's No.7* and *8*, *Boogie's*, *Sam Weller's* and the *Kaleidoscope* as well, just across the road. But, twenty-six years ago, there wasn't really any of the Broad Street development that they've got now; it was a very limited number of good venues to go to. On Broad Street now, there are more bars and clubs on one road that there were in the whole of Birmingham, twenty-five years ago! The mid 1990s was when it all started to kick-off on Broad Street, which was the time that the Licensing Laws changed in Birmingham.

"In late 1986, I walked round to all of the nightclubs in Birmingham, asking if they could they give us a weekend night – a Friday or a Saturday. We got knocked back by everybody, apart from Mr. Edward Fewtrell. Richard Walker was the first person I met when I walked into *Edward's No.7*. Eddie was actually in there that day and Richard took me round to meet him. He gave us a crack at doing it in *Edward's No.8*, in April 1987, giving us one floor of *Edward's No.8*, and one floor of *Edward's No.7*. We opened on 18 April 1987. At about 25 to 9 we had a look outside the front doors; there were about twenty or thirty people there. But then literally, within twenty minutes, about thirteen hundred people turned up. There was a queue all the way down the road, across the road, before it was pedestrianised; past *Boogie's*, past all the Burger Bars and round the corner, up to the entrance of the NCP, by *Goldwyn's*.

"We did that for three or four weeks, but we had to turn people away, because it was so full. So Eddie scrapped the other floor of *Edward's No.8*; stopped all the 'trendies' coming in – the Kevs, Sharons, et cetera. He gave us all three floors. That filled up again. So now, all of *Edward's No.8*, became a Rock Club, plus the top floor of *Edward's No.7*, and it was still full, every week. Then John dropped out; he's now a design engineer, in Canada. Eventually Eddie asked me to work there full time. *Edward's No.8*, as it was then called, was basically a Rock Club, from then onwards. There were club nights there nearly seven nights a week," remembers Dave.

The Rockers were very grateful to me for giving them an exclusive club. So they wouldn't make any trouble because of that. That ran from 1987 to 1989 inclusive.

"At one point we actually used *Goldwyn's*, while Eddie still owned it; between 1987 and 1989, because *Edward's* maximum capacity was 375. We needed a bigger venue and Eddie had *Goldwyn's*, which later became the *Bier Keller*. *Goldwyn's*, ironically, had a capacity of only 350, which was less than *Edward's*, but it was about four times the size; there were shows there where we put a thousand people in! We don't use Cover Bands, or Tribute Bands. We work only with the original artistes. Some of the bands that we had playing at *Edward's* were people like *Faith No More*, *Nirvana*, *Rage Against the Machine*, the *Proclaimers*, *Trans-Vision Vamps*, *Pearl Jam*, Maria McKee was another one. The list was quite amazing. Within a year of starting I was booking bands, promoting; putting shows on. Before long, I was dealing with a lot of the big London agents, for major acts."

Our Golden Handcuffs chapter describes how I sold up all of my clubs to Ansells Leisure. At that point they made Dave the Licensee-manager. He worked for them for two years and did so well there that it became the biggest profit-maker in the UK.

"Yes, out of all their pubs and clubs in the UK, *Edward's No.8* was the biggest profit-maker of the lot," recalls Dave. "I wouldn't go to the presentation, because it was a bit too corporate for me, but in my absence they presented an award for the amount of money it was making, because we were so busy, six or seven nights a week. They had a venue in Hanley, called *The Place*, where they spent two-and-a-half million quid; it held a thousand people more than *Edward's* did... and it still couldn't get close to the amount we made," concludes Dave.

Shirley interviewed two younger generation customers of *Boogie's* – Stacey Barnfield and Stephen Hands. Stacey works for the Birmingham Mail and contributed to an article dated Saturday 18 November 2006, about the recent fire at *Edward's*. Stacey's piece ran alongside the main article, entitled 'Memories go up in smoke', written by Lisa Smith. Stacey studied to be a graphic designer at Solihull College. Now in his early thirties, he left Solihull College, in 1992, subsequently took a Media course, and was then offered a placement on the Solihull News newspaper, as an editorial assistant.

"I left the Solihull News in 1997, to work on the Sunday Mercury," explains Stacey, "then spent a few years there as a sub-editor. In 2000 I joined the Magazine Department, with the Birmingham Post & Mail, to go back more into a design background. My wife, Catherine, has been a journalist on the Birmingham Mail, for eight years. I took over the running of the Magazine Department, when my editor left. We launched a magazine called *City Living*, which was all about the flats and the apartments that were being built around that time – giving a new lease of life to the bars and restaurants – like Brindley Place and the canal side developments.

"The period we're looking at with regard to Eddie's clubs is from 1990-2000: a ten-year period. When I was in the middle of my college year, myself and a few friends would go out to Birmingham. We'd study at Solihull Technical College, on Blossomfield Road, Solihull, but then we'd come into Birmingham, for a drink – pretty much every weekend; mixing with other students and people of our own age.

"There were six or seven of us; we're still close friends now. Also, I had a couple of friends who played in a band, called *Where* who were a great band to go and watch. They played 70s music; we were all interested in a similar kind of music. We bought our clothes down the Rag Market, because we didn't have much money.

"There were two main venues of Eddie's that we used to go to: *Edward's No.8* and *Goldwyn's*. *Edward's No.8* was a fantastic place – a dark place, with nightclub lights. You'd go in through the front door and upstairs onto the first floor. There was a floor up above that. The first floor was our kind of music: 60s, independent bands; a typical nightclub atmosphere in there… noisy. There were padded chairs and a couple of alcoves. To the right you'd go on to the dance floor with a DJ; on the other side was a seating area. It was all quite open space. Up on the second floor was more of a Rock Music scene – Heavy Metal music; but it was the first floor that we were really interested in.

"*Edward's No.7* was a disco bar; *Edward's No.8* was where we saw all the bands, before Broad Street took off as an entertainment street; when John Bright Street was the main place to go, with all the bars: *Busy Lizzie's, Rosie O'Brien's*; there was the *Futurist Cinema* and the *Ikon Gallery*, which is now in Brindley Place. The John Bright Street area was an entertainment hub, before it all spread out down Broad Street and the Mailbox; those places weren't there then, they were just normal streets.

"You knew that you were going to have a really good night," continues Stacey. "We saw quite a few local bands, some of which are probably no longer in existence. Of the two most famous bands we saw at *Edward's No.8* one was a band called *Suede*; this was about 1992-93. They went on to achieve Chart success, but they've split up since. *Oasis* was the other group; they're one of the biggest bands in the world now. We saw them play at *Edward's No.8* in 1994. The two brothers, Liam and Noel Gallagher had a quite cocky, arrogant personality; they had a reputation for fighting and hitting each other. Noel Gallagher writes the songs and he's very influenced by the *Beatles*. And they were identical in the way they looked. They were a fantastic live band; really good musicians. You knew that you'd seen something special that night and that they were going on to do great things. I saw them in other Birmingham clubs, but only in *Edward's No.8* once.

"*Goldwyn's* was just on the one floor. It was a long room, above the *Paramount* pub, with a stage down the far end. The interior was a bit more lavish – it was mirrored! Again it was a good atmosphere, and the music was similar to what was being played at *Edward's No.8*. I would guess that the people, who were going there when we were there, weren't the kind of people that it was created for."

Mike Alexander worked for me on and off at different times in his career. Later on he worked for me at *Goldwyn's*.

"*Goldwyn's* was on Suffolk Street, adjacent to the *Alexandra Theatre*," explains Mike. If you came out of the front door of the *Alex*, turn right, cross over the road, it would be the next building. It was a lovely place. I don't remember being there much, but we had Bernard Manning there and Joe Longthorne. When *Goldwyn's* finished that was it – I didn't work for Eddie again after that."

Stacey went to my clubs in the ten-year period from 1990 onwards, by which time I had already sold them all to Ansells, so it would be under different ownership. But I was still *officially* acting as a consultant to the brewery.

"It was a good atmosphere in the early hours, when we left the club," recalls Stacey. "Nowadays you hear all these cautionary news items about drugs and stabbings, but a decade or two ago, it was quite safe. I hope I'm not thinking back through rose-tinted spectacles, but I really don't remember any problems like that.

"We used to hang around outside the front of *Edward's No.8*, at the junction of John Bright Street where the bars I mentioned were and the fish and chip shop. We'd have something to eat before we took a taxi home and there'd be crowds of people milling around; they'd all come out from different areas. So you'd have the Rockers, coming out of the top floor of *Edward's No.8*; you'd have us with our long hair, from the lower floor. Then you'd have the people who went more for Chart Music coming out of places like *Rosie O'Brien's*."

Sadly, the situation in the early hours of the morning had deteriorated by the late 1980s; that's one of the reasons I eventually sold up. You'd have gangs of youths coming in from Handsworth and similar areas, bringing in their own cans of beer and hanging around outside the chip shop, trying to chat the girls up, as they came out of the shop.

"We used to go to other clubs beforehand," continues Stacey. "If you were going for a really good night out, it would be Thursday, Friday and Saturday.

"*Edward's No.8* was a really good club, a really great atmosphere, and I was genuinely upset when I heard that it had burned down. *Oasis* went from playing places like *Edward's* with two or three hundred people – and now they hold the record for the biggest gig in the world – when they played at Knebworth, in 1997 – there were 125,000 people there. It's amazing to see how they've progressed! The times change, the trends change," concludes Stacey.

Stephen Hands was born in Kings Heath; when he was fairly young, he moved to Hall Green. His first job, around 1983-88 was working as a chef at the *Robin Hood* pub, Hall Green.

"I eventually managed a pub, from 1995-98, in Cornwall Street – the *Cathedral Tavern* – in the financial part of Birmingham City centre," explains Stephen. "I'd previously been a Relief Manager at pubs around the city. The *Cathedral Tavern* is more of a Wine Bar now; the *Hotel de Vin* was nearby, which used to be the Eye Hospital."

Stephen described a range of other pubs that he'd managed. In 2005 he and his brother-in-law ran a Financial Control company. He currently advises clients about Inheritance Tax and does research work for a Birmingham accountancy firm. The 1983-84 period, when he was working at the *Robin Hood*, was the time when he first began to visit the city centre clubs.

Stephen recalls: "In the 1980s, myself and a number of friends were drawn to the city centre clubs. There were two areas where it was mainly all happening. You had New Street, round from the *Yard of Ale*, by St Martin's, to the pub, *Cagney's*. Then you had the Fewtrell Company's operations, which were centred on John Bright Street. Eddie was an independent concern, whereas the *Yard of Ale* and *Cagney's* were more managed operations, for national breweries.

"Eddie was taking over derelict buildings and totally refurbishing them, which he did very well, because his style of operation was ahead of its time. He was a very good marketer, because not only did he have great facilities, but he also had great marketing skills; things like tapping into the 'Happy Hour' market. Conventional thinking is that on Friday evening at five o'clock, you don't discount, because those fall under the main hours… but *he* did."

I introduced one particular offer, where I doubled up on whatever drinks customers bought. At the end of only one week I received a call from the Licensing Inspector, while I was on holiday in Spain. He asked me to knock that scheme on the head, as people were collapsing in the streets, drunk out of their minds! The railway stations were half empty – the commuters were flocking to my clubs instead. It was total chaos!

"I was eighteen, when I first went to *Boogie's Brasserie*," Stephen continues. "You'd be drinking things that you don't *normally* drink, because of the offers. If I just had a sniff of Jack Daniels and coke now, it would transport me back to that time! You bought one of those and got a 'shot' free. We'd stand up at *Boogie's*. The music's loud at those sorts of places anyway, so you wouldn't really be able to talk much. You're half drunk and the lighting's very subdued, so you just tend to look round or go and have a dance. *Boogie's* and the *Brasserie* had fantastic up-to-date lighting, linked to the sound system and the music. You'd come out of *Boogie's Brasserie*, do a right, then the nightclub was behind."

Boogie's was the first club in Birmingham to have a synchronised sound and lighting system, which changed automatically, according to the record that the DJ was playing. The combined system cost me £150,000. We had to adjust the strobes, however, as people were falling over on the dance floor!

"I remember seeing Nobby on the door," continues Stephen. "Someone pointed him out to me; he trained boxers at the *Shakespeare* on the Stratford Road. I never spoke to him, because my main goal was getting past him. What was great about *Boogie's* was that they had different types of music there; before you knew it you'd all be split up, heading for the floor that played the music that you were into. You'd wander up and down the stairs, having a look at the place; maybe have a dance.

"There were places on the corner, at the top end, for taxis, with a very powerful woman, calling out from a block of flats, controlling as many as two hundred and fifty people below her. She used to shout out of the window: 'Oi, your taxi's over here!' That was there for many years, until very recently, when John Rocher, the glass designer, designed all the new apartments round there. The old taxi ranks, chip shops et cetera, have all gone now. That was before it was all sold out and you had M & B trying to get into the market, with *Kaleidoscope* and *Sam Weller's*.

"*Edward's No.7* was ahead of its time: you walked in there and it was like 'Wow!' That was the first time I'd ever seen MTV. I'd heard of it, but the screen was there and there was MTV on it. This was almost the start of the music video. *Edward's No.7* was opposite the *Brasserie*. *Edward's No.8* was the Rockers place. They were all very close to each other, almost across from the *Paramount*, which was also way ahead of its time. It was very well designed; well managed – similar to the others; it had a good feel about it. The *Paramount* was similar to *Edward's No.7*; although maybe, to begin with, it attracted the in-crowd, because they were curious to see what the new club was about. They eventually move on and you're hoping that, by that stage, everybody else is there as well. It was just the one room, at street level.

"Years later, in 1993, I was Assistant Manager at the *Crown*, in Corporation Street, which is opposite the Victoria Law Courts. Some guys came in and said: 'Have you heard of the Fewtrells?' I said: 'Yeah.' They said: 'Well, they just need to come into the pub. We'd appreciate it if they could just have a corner of the pub for a while.' Nothing actually came of it," concludes Stephen, "but it was just that I got the feeling: 'Well, I'd better not say no anyway' ...because Eddie's name was still known so well – across the city!"

Rebecca comments: "In a way it was quite a status symbol, having a dad who owned a chain of nightclubs. I was very proud of him. The downside of it was that when you were out at one of his clubs you were very protected; you could never be chatted up by anybody. One of the doormen or one of my uncles would approach anyone who tried to, and have a quiet word with them. I was chaperoned all the time."

Daniel had a slightly different problem. People would sometimes chat to him at the bar, simply because he was my son, and they were trying to capitalise on that; so he could never really be sure whether someone liked him for himself, or for what they could get out of him. Eventually he developed a stock response, when people asked him if he was Eddie's son. He'd reply: 'He's the guy who invented the lighthouse, isn't he?' Although that didn't always work, because as Danny explained, some of them weren't educated enough to appreciate the joke! Rebecca has lived constantly with the social complications of our family name too.

"People would ask me a lot: 'Are you Eddie's daughter?' They used to tell me stories about my dad... even when I got into a taxi, the driver would do the same. At one time I worked on Reception, at nearly all of dad's clubs. I used to work at the rock club – *Edward's* and I worked at *Goldwyns* too. The funny thing was that people used to say to me: 'I know Eddie Fewtrell. I know his family and his daughter.' I was sitting there thinking: "Well, I don't know you!" "

Chapter Thirteen

SUNSHINE AND RAIN

Our cabaret takes a dramatic turn, ladies and gentlemen, with laughter, plus chilling moments in Clubland, as Eddie, friends and family reveal a range of scams, raids and 'ducking and diving'. These include police operations, cabarets from Hell and keeping the Krays, Richardsons and Lambrianous at bay. Humorous tales contrast with more sinister happenings, by way of light relief!

In Chapter Seven Chris Lewthwaite mentioned the warning light system that he was asked to use in the *Cedar Club*. On the front door there were buttons and a series of lights: red, yellow and green. Behind the bar there was a switch, which, when pressed, flashed a yellow light at the front door, so we knew that assistance was needed at the bar. If it was a button on the side of the stage, which is probably what Chris remembers, a red light flashed at the door, indicating trouble on the dance floor. All the doormen would rush in there, to get hold of the people who were causing trouble – and get them out; leaving one man on the door. The secret was, to get them out as fast as possible. They would then be put out of the door by the stage, if it was the dance floor; or the door by the bar, and if necessary bring them back to Reception; but it was best not to do so, because they'd meet the people coming in!

I was quite a capable driver, with a PSV Licence – I've still got it. The police rugby and football teams used to come to the *Cedar Club*. I shall never forget one occasion, when the rugby team, over forty police officers from the Tally Ho, came to the club for a booze-up – a 'play-up'. The bus was parked outside. I looked into the *Cedar*, at about four o'clock in the morning, and everybody was absolutely legless, including the driver. I was quite sober so I said: "Alright Inspector, get them all back on board and I'll drive you back." They were absolutely 'over the moon' afterwards, because I'd delivered them safely back to Duke Street!

Dave Ismay recalls: "I was out with a colleague late one night, when we came across a hole in the pavement – the cellar entrance to where they used to roll the barrels down to the *Rum Runner*. It had obviously been broken into, so we got the manager out. He opened up and said: 'Would you gentlemen like to take some more of the stuff – to make my insurance claim worthwhile?' So my colleague went to fetch his car and we loaded quite a few bottles into the back, which we split up later. But of course, in those days, we were always looked after!"

Thanks Dave. Switching to the *Cresta Club*, I got a phone call at night, from Kenny Hatton. He said that Jimmy Tarbuck had been on the phone to him. Could I get a full Concert Grand piano and radio mikes to the *Cresta Club*, for Bruce Forsythe, as he was playing there on the Sunday evening? This was Sunday afternoon. I said: "How can I lift that Grand Piano; it weighs two or three tons! If you can find someone to move and do it, you can borrow it." So they moved it to the *Cresta*, in the back of a lorry. I'd bought the piano for *Abigail's*; the one that Mike Alexander used to play.

All the microphones worked without chords. They put the piano on stage, at the *Cresta*, but the stage was only made of chipboard, so the piano went through it. We had to look around for some block-board, to put under each leg. I said: "I hope when Bruce Forsythe plays tonight he doesn't completely disappear through the stage, with the piano!" Then I added: "Whatever you do, I'm not responsible for what happens."

I formed a club for night club owners, where everybody paid so much into it, to finance Martin Hone going to Westminster, in order to try to get the law changed – for Late Night Licences and so forth. That first came about because of Geoffrey Allen; he was an MP, but he was also my accountant at the time. He lived in Spain, in Alicante. As I explained in a previous chapter, Geoffrey found a way for me to get a Two o'clock Licence.

I must tell you about Iron Arm Ted. His real name was Teddy Crigland. He was one of my customers at the *Bermuda Club*. He had no arm – it was made of iron. He was a hard guy. Frankie Warwood was one of the Warwoods who made jewellery in the Jewellery Quarter. He was often in the clubs and he witnessed the shootings.

Dave Ismay was in town, when one particular incident happened, and tells the story: "There were two gangs in London at that time: the Krays, who we all know about and the Richardson brothers, who were the lesser known ones, but just as evil. As I understand it, the Richardson Mob arrived at Snow Hill Station, on one platform and were met by a deputation of various Birmingham nightclub owners, their families; their foot-soldiers, and persuaded that they should move across to the opposite platform and catch the next train back to London," recalls Dave. "That's a story that became famous amongst people in the Birmingham entertainment business and the Underworld. Entertainment became part of that culture, because when you're a comedian or an entertainer, you tend to stay out until three o'clock in the morning; you spent most of your time in some club or establishment.

"I remember a man cleaning his pistol in London's *Stork Club*! That was a chilling moment. It wasn't so much that I thought he was ever going to *shoot* me – it was just the sheer incongruity of that. You know – "What are we doing here?!"

"When Bob Monkhouse and I were in Barbados, we had a lot of fun with the natives. The one guy, it's in Bob's book actually; Neville, his name was. He had a little shanty, next to this beautiful house of Bob's, because it was his land in Barbados and he wouldn't sell it. Some days he was fine but when he'd had half a bottle of rum he decided he would hammer and bang all day. This racket was going on one day and we knew that he was altering his house again. Bob said to me: 'That bloody racket. What do you think he's doing now?' I said: 'I think he's painting this time!' It was just one of those moments and we both dissolved in laughter. There were loads of wonderful things with Bob.

"With Larry Grayson, we had quite a lot of time on our hands, so we'd often go to the Pictures. One day we decided to go on the Thames River Boat with all the 'plebs'. Suddenly, we saw in the distance a Royal Navy launch, hurtling towards us, at top speed; it went past us with a huge wave of spray. The guide informed us: 'Obviously, something important is taking place at Admiralty House.' Larry said: 'Not at all. They've run out of fags at Portsmouth!' That was the sort of thing he used to do all the time," concludes Dave.

Within three weeks or so of opening, I had the Casino running, downstairs at the *Cedar*. The bell rang downstairs. I had a guy called Norman, a lovely guy, who was a gambler. He finished up as a good friend of mine. We used to go to Vegas a lot. When the bell rang, this particular night, I went to the door. Chrissie was usually on the door. He said: "We've got a problem outside." Once again there were five guys outside and another guy who was the doorman from Bob Pryke's place – down in the Fruit Market – the *Castaways*. I said: "You're not coming in here." They said: "Are you going to keep us out?" I said: "Yes, I am." These were the same people who I'd injured or put in hospital, when they tried to attack me in the *Bermuda Club*. However, they all finished up in hospital again. The ambulance came to take them away. This was now the third time that this had happened. Trouble like this continued all the time, so I turned round and said: "If you come back again, I'm going to kill you!" The way I felt at the time I would have done, but of course, as time went by, I just forgot about it.

I heard no more about that for a while, but then it got about that all the Fewtrells had done them, whereas, once again, it was just me and Chrissie who'd sorted them out between us. A few days afterwards, I was driving up the road in my van, to David Hill's, a warehouse, to get some glasses for the club. As I drove back down towards the club, I saw this big fella, from London, with two other fellas. Stanley Kay, who is a big fella, was driving my van. I asked him to stop the van. Everybody thought he was a Fewtrell! He had a broken nose and he looked like a great big boxer. I said: "Come with me." What people didn't realise was that Stanley Kay couldn't fight his way out of a paper bag! So I've gone charging across the road and dived at this big fella and at the two others. I whacked them, then the three of them got up, and ran down the road as fast as could be – I couldn't catch them! So I let them go.

We nearly always paid performers by cheque. This went on for years; all of the agents knew that this was the method, and there was never any trouble. But apparently, some groups had been given cheques that bounced – by other club owners. I got a phone call from John Tully, on one occasion, at four o'clock in the morning. He said: "They won't let me go. They're holding me captive!" He put one of the group on the phone. He said: "We don't take cheques and we're holding John Tully captive until you get here!" I said: "Well, you'll have a long wait, because there's no way I'm coming all the way over there, at this time in the morning. You either take the cheque – or you can keep him for ever. But I've got to warn you – he don't 'alf eat a lot; he drinks too… and he snores! So if you don't want to take the cheque, you can get stuffed!"

I finally got another call from Tully at five o'clock in the morning. He said; "You so-and-so – you left me with that lot… you told them to keep me!"

I said: "Yes, but they took the cheque, didn't they? They've let you go!" But that was John – he was a worrier. And that kind of situation would worry him to death. It wouldn't have bothered me… but there you are.

Chris Lewthwaite remembers: "At the bottom of the hill by the Blues Ground, in Small Heath, there was a real dive. It was an old converted wooden church. We used to play there occasionally, although we had a little spell when we were playing there every other week. It was a really hard, tough place – there were all sorts of people in there! You'd read in the Mail, nearly every Monday morning, about some knife fight outside – someone being stabbed or whatever.

"Some of the customers were, allegedly, lesbians and homosexuals, which at the time was not as open as it is now. You'd see blokes dancing around and kissing each other – it was a surprising sight, to say the least! There were also some quite nasty characters in there. If *they* requested a number you immediately stopped playing, and switched to their request, or there could be trouble. It was a frightening place – so much so that we used to hide in the dressing room and lock ourselves in there, when we weren't on stage!

"The one night we weren't playing on the Saturday night, I believe that somebody who was thrown out of the club threw a petrol bomb in there. The whole place was burnt to cinders, because it was a wooden structure. There were all mixtures of races and creeds; there was always trouble, at some stage of the evening.

"Before it was rebuilt, it held a couple of hundred people. We were playing in there one night, when a huge-looking Irishman came up to the stage and shouted at Roger, who was playing the organ, which is a very heavy instrument: 'Play some f***ing Blues!' Roger said, 'Yes, okay… in a minute.' At which point this guy used an expletive and punched the side of the organ so hard that it moved a foot across the stage! So we had to stop what we were playing, immediately, and play some Blues. He then gave us a big "thumbs up" and said: 'That's better!' So it was very tough, trying to please everybody, at that place. Although I've said that it was firebombed, that's hearsay, but it was definitely raised to the ground. As the organist, Roger would be the one approached with requests. He was threatened with a knife on at least two occasions!"

Ron Gray used to work on the doors at the *Gary Owen*, which was about a mile away from the club just described. "Me and Brendan Joyce, the owner, were pals you know; Brendan used to box. Funnily enough I spoke to him a couple of days ago. The Indians have got it now. I think they use it for weddings and various functions like that. He owned a lot of property, in that area. There was a big page, a couple of weeks ago, in Post People. It burnt to the ground and then they rebuilt it, just like the club that Chris is describing.

"The second building was twice as big as the first," Ron continues. "The new building had a roof like Tesco's! It was a beautiful place inside. The steaks were the best in the country, let alone the West Midlands. That applies to the original club too. Entertainers, coming down the motorway, would turn off to the *Gary Owen*, for their breakfast."

We were recently advised by the former owner of the club, my good friend Brendan Joyce, that he sold the *Gary Owen* in January 2006 to a Hindu owner. It's just off the Coventry Road.

"Gigging musicians at that time didn't earn a lot of money," recalls Chris Lewthwaite. "I worked for a small advertising agency at one time. Rose was a secretarial typist there. She was engaged to a friend of Eddie's. She was a stunning, beautiful girl, of normal height, but with a beautiful figure and jet-black hair: very sexy – and she knew it! She was very friendly with me, but I wasn't interested in the other side of it, because I was very recently married. Rose was always on about Stan, her fiancé. While the *Cedar Club* was being built, she often referred to it, and about some of the difficulties that they were encountering.

"She was watching the rehearsals too, with Carl Wayne and going on about what a smashing band it was. I was talking to someone about two years ago and discovered that Rose had been brutally murdered. I'd love to know what actually happened, but I believe that Stan was one of the main people involved in the club, along with Eddie."

Rose was actually one of two adopted twins, a boy and girl, who were separated at birth. Stanley Kay eventually married her and they had a home in Snitterfield. Her brother came over from Australia. One particular evening the brother returned to Snitterfield, whilst Stanley remained at the club with me. That evening, Rose's brother killed her with a ball and chain, but we don't know why. He was subsequently jailed for her murder – that's a matter of public record. Her husband, Stanley, was heartbroken.

For obvious reasons, we've been obliged to be careful, throughout the book, about the Underworld side of events. However, there are books that cover that period, including *Inside the Firm*, by Tony Lambrianou.

"I'm in every one of those books," observes Big Albert. "I carried Charlie Kray's coffin.

"That's how I first met the Krays. I arranged Charlie Kray's funeral and carried his coffin.

"I was at a major funeral last week – Joe Pyle's funeral. Quite a few of them have died, over the last few years. I've known them ever since I was a kid, so I'm associated with them still, to this day.

"The thing is that there are a lot of my stories about the Krays and Birmingham," explains Albert. "Funnily enough, Johnny Lambrianou was at the funeral, last week. Tony Lambrianou died three years ago, this month. Tony was allegedly jailed for getting rid of Jack the Hat's body. There were a lot of good 'operators', meaning villains, in Birmingham. Some of the villains from Birmingham went to London. They used to go to the *Hundred Club*."

The Bermuda Club period was the main time that the Krays were involved. They came to see me when I first opened it. At least two of their main henchmen then continued over into the *Cedar Club* days. At the time when all of that was happening, Albert, with all due respect, would have been too young to realise what was actually going on.

Being saddled with all of that responsibility, from a very early age had a profound effect on me so that when I finally got somewhere, my attitude was 'nobody is going to take this off me'! I always ran my businesses as good businesses: I always paid my debts. I didn't owe anyone anything.

All the tough guys in the world were coming after me. In the beginning, I had no reputation; all of my brothers were younger than me; there were two older ones, but they were in the army. So I had to deal with everything on my own. When people came to the club to demand various things – people coming out of pubs drunk, especially cockneys – as soon as they opened their mouths you could tell that they were country yokels. They used to demand that I let them into the club; but there was no way that I would stand them coming in, if I didn't want them to. The police actually had a lot of respect for me, because I stopped a situation where people were coming to me for Protection Money. I was the person who kept it out of Birmingham.

My childhood definitely toughened me up. I couldn't get any credit – because my father never used to pay anybody! George used to come home drunk every night and there'd be fighting in the house. He was really miserable and aggressive, when he drank whisky – which would make him like a madman. I always knew, from the time that I was a very young boy, that you had to *watch* a whisky drinker, because it does turn a lot of people nasty. So I was always wary of them.

I never forgot my early days as a young lad, with no money, so no one was going to get the money off me that I made later. I didn't want to do it illegally, but I thought it was ridiculous that, in those days, you couldn't get a drink after ten o'clock at night – so did the police and the magistrates – because they were amongst my customers!

I learned from my very first club, that you had to show them who was the boss – because if you do, people want to come to *your* club; they know there's going to be no trouble there. That's why I became successful, plus the fact that my brothers grew up, and I also had plenty of men. I spent the money on security guys. I would tell my doormen that if they beat anybody up, they'd get beaten up by me! They were not to hurt anybody; they were just to escort them through the door, unless of course, they were violent, and we had to fight back.

Security Guards go on special training courses nowadays. I set all of those up. When I was invited to become Chairman of *Clubwatch*, by the Chief of Police, I got rid of all doormen with 'form'. I set up the rule that under no circumstances could they get a job on the door, if they hurt anybody. They had to have a Police Licence, and so forth.

What people often don't realise is that I didn't want any trouble – I *hated* trouble. I just wanted an easy life. But I'm afraid, when you've got a club, which holds two to three thousand people, you've always got 'n' amount of people who want to fight. It was inevitable. The *Cedar Club* only held 400-500 people, but *Rebecca's,* in Severn Street, held nearly 3,000! However, after about six months, people *knew* that if they were involved in a fight, they wouldn't be allowed in there again – and there were only about four or five clubs to go to. We were having all the best stars, the best bands; they *wanted* to come there – they *loved* it. The atmosphere was fantastic. There were three lots of different music – three floors; the most up-to-date strobe lighting. I'd spent a lot of money making it that way.

There were loads of girls there – more girls than men, you know what I mean? Everybody would say: "There's ten girls to every one man!" Many a time the customers would say: "Oh, please don't give me the sack!" because they were petrified of not being allowed in again. But I was so strong – if they were involved in a fight, they would go.

The other thing was that we had a *powerful* door: we had Nobby Nobbs, who you've already heard about, on the door; everyone helping him was physically fit, which was vital, especially as we also had boxers as clients – they had been physically trained to use their hands as weapons. As Nobby used to train them, he also used to control them. I wouldn't stand for anyone taking liberties. I think I got known as a very fair man. I never took any liberties with anybody.

As a matter of fact, I'll tell you something about me. I would be in the club after 'time', with one or two friends. I would have so-called villains who would insult me. Rather than just throw them out, I used to do something ever so good. I'd have all my doormen around me, all of my friends, and everybody else, then all of a sudden I'd stop the music and say: "Who are you?" They'd say so-and-so. "How many are there of you?" Then I'd say: "Who's the best fighter amongst you?" They'd say: "He is." I'd say: "None of my men will interfere. Come into the middle of the dance floor and I'll fight you now." Many of them were much taller than me, but it didn't matter – the bigger the better! I loved the big ones. I've fought men who were as big as a tower – even slaughterers.

I'd boxed up until I was eighteen – I was very useful actually. So I'd stand in the middle of the dance floor; I always wore rubber-bottomed shoes, as opposed to those with leather soles, so that I wouldn't slip on the dance floor. I'd be doing a straight left and a right cross – and the fact that most of these were well drunk as well... I would just watch their eyes. You *know* when they're going to throw a punch. It's like the shotgun: you watch the eyes – and the eyes tell you what they're going to do. So when you knew what he was going to do, you'd send out a straight left, so I could put him out within about three seconds. Then it would be all over... and the word would get around, that I was absolutely fast: it was all over in seconds. I don't think, to be fair, that I ever lost, because I was determined *not* to lose.

I wouldn't have to do that every night; it would be approximately every three months. Actually Seamus Dunleavy, whose biography, *Finally Meeting Princess Maud*, Shirley co-wrote with him, came into this, at one stage.

On one occasion, at four o'clock in the morning, these three guys were giving me some stick. I wouldn't take action straight away; I'd laugh it off. You'd take so much and then you'd say: "Well, would you mind leaving now?" They'd say: "No, let's have that fight then!" The one guy, this particular night, when I'd put him down, as he got up and the other two were helping him, they used Seamus' name to say that he would come and get me. So I said: "That's okay. I shall be seeing him tomorrow." The next day, I phoned Seamus and told him what had happened. He said: "Who was it?" So we told him and he sorted them out, straight away. The next day they came to me and pleaded with me to take him off their back. This sort of thing used to happen all the time.

So I didn't care who it was, or what they said. I was saying to someone the other week, "What you have to understand is that in 1957/58, the Krays were well known in London, but in Birmingham I'd never heard of them. So when they told me who they were, it didn't mean a thing, I just said: "Piss off!" They were on my turf, so my attitude was: how could they think of taking me on, in Birmingham? A little while later, the Lambrianous came down, throwing their weight around – and I did the same with them. I beat them up and threw them out – it's as simple as that.

Some years later, the Lambrianous wrote a book, *Inside the Firm*, in which they said that they took Eddie Fewtrell's girlfriend, June McDonald, to the *Beggar's Bush* and that Eddie Fewtrell got really upset about it and beat them up or something. But it wasn't *my* girlfriend, it was Donald's girlfriend. So June McDonald must have said that she was going out with me! I suppose she said that to protect herself, but I knew nothing about it.

At the time the book came out, I'd rented a flat for Marleen, in Stratford-upon-Avon. My car was parked outside, with 'EF 2' on the licence plate. About nine o'clock on the night, a knock came at the door. I answered it and there were two people there. They said: "Are you Eddie Fewtrell, because your car's outside?" I said "Yes." They said: "Would you autograph our copy of the Lambrianou's book?" So I said: "What do you want me to autograph that for?" They said: "Well, you're in it!" They showed me and I signed the book for them, but that was the first that I'd heard about it! When it came out, everybody was asking me to sign this book, but actually I don't know why, because I'd had nothing to do with them really.

According to the book Reggie Kray allegedly slayed Jack 'The Hat' McVitie in a London basement flat on 28 October 1967. Tony was there throughout the night. He helped, allegedly, by disposing of the body. Tony began a life sentence in 1969, following a show trial. He also led the Gartree Prison Riots of 1972.

Sir Geoffrey Dear disbanded the *Serious Crime Squad*, in Birmingham, because, if you remember, it was so bad: corruption was so widespread amongst some of the officers. Situations of this nature are, of course, a matter of public record.

There was one senior officer in the CID, so he didn't wear uniform. We'll call him 'X'. In the days of the *Bermuda Club* there were two guys. One of them had who'd been robbing post offices: he was a builder, and used gelignite from the building sites to blow the post offices up. This other guy had the same car as the builder, but he hadn't done the job. X followed this innocent guy home, and planted gelignite in his front garden. But they got the wrong guy, and he was sentenced to seven years. They came to see me and said that this guy had done this that and the other. I said that I wanted to remain neutral. But eventually they put X back into uniform.

The only time that the *Cedar Club* got raided, it was by X. I was at home one Sunday night, when Stanley Kay, who was the licensee, phoned me and said: "I've got someone here who wants to talk to you." It was two minutes past ten at night. They never raided you at eleven o'clock or twelve o'clock, because they had to pay their officers overtime. As far as they were concerned, they normally finished working at around ten o'clock, although I was open until two o'clock in the morning.

X said: "Is that you Eddie?" I said: "Yes." He said: "Well, you can eff off!" I said: "Thank you very much, X. You've got your own back then?" He said: "I just thought I'd let you know." I said: "Thank you very much. Make sure you lock up. There's plenty of people in there, being served after Time. I owe you one."

But he was so against his fellow officers as well; he was against everybody! There was another guy there who was an officer – top man – elderly. I can't remember his name, but he was a total alcoholic. He used to drive us mad all the while, coming in to booze. He was on the Drugs Squad as well. X was always trying to get me to turn this officer in. He was always saying: "Report him, report him!"

Apparently, X was doing this all over town. In those days certain police officers like him, allegedly used to stitch a lot of people up – plant evidence on them, all the while. The same thing happened with my father. If you went to a pub and parked your car outside, and you actually had the keys on you, you could be arrested for being drunk in charge of a vehicle. If you left the keys with the licensee of the pub, you had no intention of driving. The one day, my father gave his keys to the landlord, but one of these police officers, I'm not sure which one it was, took the keys off the landlord, threatening to revoke his licence if he said anything. Then he planted them in my father's pocket, arrested him for being 'drunk in charge', and got him three months in prison.

Les Hemming remembers: "We were performing our first set of the evening, on stage at the *Cedar*. From the stage, which was set quite high up, you could look right through the club, to the front door, where Eddie would be standing – front of house. To the left was the Casino, just behind the bar. Don would usually be running that.

"We announced that we were just about to finish our usual first set. Then Don came up to us, at this very high stage; we were still singing and playing away there. I bent over to hear him and Don famously said: 'Keep playing lads, keep making a noise. We've got a bit of trouble at the door!' We had no idea what a profound statement that was, until the next day, when we heard that allegedly, the Krays' henchmen had paid the club a visit and apparently Eddie had told them all to go away."

Roger Shropshall comments: "Eddie was the Guv'nor of Birmingham Clubland. There were all sorts of people in London. There was Freddie Mills, the boxer, who mysteriously died, although the official verdict was suicide. There have been programmes about it. The whole episode remains shrouded in mystery. The *Pickwick*, in Fleet Street, London, was where Simon Dee and all the stars at the time would go, to watch the *Peddlers* and also there were lots of other people doing things – which we're not going to talk about! We played *Peddlers* music too, so in certain respects, there was a similar atmosphere in the *Cedar* and the *Pickwick*."

"One night I'd been at a booking," remembers Brian Yeates. "I went up to the *Cedar* afterwards and Frank Fewtrell said: 'Oh, you're just in time!' So I went to do a 'snatch-back' with him. He just wanted me to keep watch while he got in the car and they drove it back. He explained what he was doing and said: 'You don't have to worry about it.' Then when he got back he phoned the police and told them that he'd taken it back; in case the guy he'd reclaimed it from phoned the police. The guy had stopped making the payments.

Eddie and Frank were really close. There was a nice warmth about Frank. It was very sad when he died, especially with him being so young… that was the thing."

A lot of people, because I was such a powerful man in the nightclub scene, with lots of people under my control, thought that I *was* a gangster or a villain. I wasn't. I was just a normal person, who believed in fairness. There was no way that I'd ever take a liberty with anybody. In fact, if I had a fight with anybody, all of my doormen were under strict instructions not to interfere. If I was getting the wrong end of the stick and I turned round and said: "That's enough," I would have shaken his hand after. As it turned out, that never actually happened to me; but there was no way that I'd batter a person first; normally I only had to hit him once, and it would be all over. I'd be concerned about bringing him round and making sure that he was alright. If there was anything wrong with him, I'd be the first one to take him to the hospital.

But people just get a thing about night clubs. They think of the old days of Speakeasies, with guns and everything else. It's not like that at all. It's not like James Cagney – "I'm on the top of the world ma!" That's a lot of nonsense. I would do everything in my power to make sure that everyone who came in my club – nuisance or normal – they would go home exactly as they came; apart from the fact that they might be the worse for drink. My policy was to send people who were drunk home in a taxi – especially girls; send them home, away from town; away from the other people, where they were safe.

We'll ask Don Maclean to end the chapter on a humorous note:

"There was a famous story about a fella at a club, trying to keep the crowd quiet. He said: 'Now order, order. We've paid good money for this next lass… and we want you to listen to her. And whilst on the subject of money, we've had new gentlemen's urinals erected in the car park, so from now on, there'll be no more peeing on the car wheels… Ladies and gentlemen – Dusty Springfield!' I was there the week after, and everybody was talking about that! It became part of club folklore."

Chapter Fourteen

POPPY BALLS AND BROKEN HEARTS

Bob and Pam Price recall the famous Poppy Balls, the drug addiction Charity, 'Turning Point', supported by Princess Diana, and various charities that Eddie and his contemporaries have been associated with. Martin Hone describes the 'movers and shakers' on the Birmingham scene, from the 1960s onwards. Hazel and Eddie continue to have marital problems. Phyllis and Bill remember various shows and the contribution that Eddie's brothers have made to his success.

Pam Price recalls: "I got involved with lots of charities, over the years, but I suppose the main one was the *Poppy Ball*, which I was involved with for over thirty years. I was Chairman. We must have raised about a million-and-a-half in total, during that period of time. It was usually held at the *Metropole*, although the event is finished now. Our financial system was quite unique, because we used to hold the money in Birmingham. The money from the *Poppy Appeal* goes to London normally, but Birmingham actually started it, before the *Earl Haig Fund* began.

"It was started by a group of Birmingham businessmen, to raise money for the soldiers who were coming back from the First World War. So we held the money at the Birmingham Council House – the Lord Mayor's Committee – and we spent it on doing up houses in Birmingham, for war veterans. One of the old soldiers, or his wife, might have a stroke, so in all likelihood he would have to be parted from his wife and go into an old folks' home. If we spent the money on doing up the old soldier's house, putting in a bathroom and a chairlift, Social Services would then go in to help them every day. In that way, the old couple could stay together in the family home. So the money stayed in Birmingham and during the entire period of thirty-three years, not a penny of the money raised each year was taken out for expenses. Everyone involved worked on a voluntary basis. I organised these events and we had a special committee."

Bob Price, Pam's husband interjects: "The money was passed on to the Birmingham Committee to dispense it as they saw fit."

"It was also used to pay for veterans' funerals, or to provide them with food if they'd fallen on hard times and needed more nourishment," continues Pam. "But I was also involved with so many charities, including *Turning Point*. We had a house in Church Road Edgbaston, where we looked after young people. Unfortunately, this later had to close, due to lack of funds. These young people were recovering from drug addiction. The name, 'Turning Point', signified that they were turning away from their drug addiction."

"Princess Diana was a patron of *Turning Point* and came to Church Road in Birmingham on several occasions, to support the charity," Bob recalls. "We've also been involved with the *Birmingham Mail Christmas Tree Fund* – for Christmas presents for the needy of Birmingham. We'd arrange a dinner dance or whatever; then on alternative years we'd raise money at Christmas for the *Sunday Mercury – Give a Girl Health*, another part of the *Birmingham Mail* Group, which was the welfare of girls and young women. They used to send them on trips to Switzerland, if they had chest problems and so forth. It was run in conjunction with the old Christian *Kunzle's Charity* – Kunzle's the chocolate manufacturers, who were at Five Ways, years ago. Kunzle was a chocolate entrepreneur, who used to send boys with chest problems – and there were a lot of them in those days, in the twenties and thirties, to Switzerland, for the mountain air," explains Bob.

Pam also recalled that at the height of its popularity, each year she'd have a waiting list of around four hundred people, all wanting to go to the *Poppy Ball*. According to Bob, such was the prestige of having a permanent table booked for it, that one chap left his table to a friend – in his will – because it was such a special thing to have!

A Score of Honour was there because you took tables and hotel tickets and donated to the *Poppy Ball*'s Fund for that year. They were held annually, for around thirty years. I attended and supported them throughout that time. Everybody who was at the *Poppy Ball* was *somebody*, so everybody wanted to be in the hall, but there weren't enough tables. I had my table for years and years. It was a very prestigious place to be seen. If anybody should have been given an award, it should have been Pam Price and Bob – for the work that they did for the *Poppy Ball*.

Hazel would come out with me to charity functions, such as the *Poppy Ball*, to look the part, if you understand what I mean? But there was nothing left of our marriage – everybody could see that she wasn't interested in me; when we were out, if we were sitting at a table, she'd be at the opposite end of it, and I'd be talking to somebody else.

Hazel was very involved with Jewish people – she should have married a Jewish guy – that's how she was. I don't think it was her fault. She was up in the morning, to get the kids off to school early: seven or eight am. I'd be picking them up at four and staying with them until ten, because those were my hours. Most of the time I'd be at home with the children; Hazel got home at about four or five o'clock in the afternoon.

The tablets that Hazel was taking proved to be very addictive. Then she was in a bit of a motor accident, where a car ran into the back of her, so she had back trouble as a result too. Then she fell down a ditch and put her back out a bit more. After that she was on distelgesics. So consequently, over many years, she was taking a cocktail of Moggadon, distelgesics, and also Valium, in addition to that. She was *eating* paracetamol tablets.

Understandably, this cocktail of drugs gradually changed her personality. I think that's what it was. But they weren't like drugs that addicts take; she used to smoke a lot too. She was on these drugs for years without me knowing, because I was very busy. She was sending one of my workmen up to the private doctor, to get drugs on prescription, every week. She was more or less storing these drugs.

One day, Ricky Rickaby came to me and said: "Eddie, I don't know whether I should tell you this, but the doctor's told me that Hazel's been having two or three hundred pills a month – she must have hundreds in the house!" Apparently, this is the way that people who are hooked on drugs become; they can't get enough. I went to this other doctor, who was supplying them and said: "All of these drugs are in my name. You're not to give her any more. She'll have to have them in her own name." Then I went down to the house and found hundreds of pills everywhere; in the fridge, in the cupboards. I collected them all up and just left her a bottle of each type, in the fridge. There was Valium, Distelgesics and Moggadon. I locked all the other bottles of these three drugs, in a massive safe, which she had no access to.

Well, she went absolutely ballistic when she found out. You'd have thought that I'd robbed her of everything. She wouldn't speak to me at all. It got to the stage where I was the enemy, although I was only trying to do good, and really, I was the one who was being victimised. So her personality changed terribly. She was about thirty-five by that time – five years younger than I was. She began to get really hooked on drugs in 1972, at the age of thirty-five and this continued for at least another eighteen years, up until the time of the divorce. So it was gradually building up and up ...which changed her whole attitude. She would hardly ever come out with me.

She'd come occasionally to the *Poppy Ball* and things like that, but she'd become a nervous wreck. Before she went out she would have two or three large vodkas, to give her confidence to face people, although normally she didn't drink much at all. Consequently, we'd only be out about ten minutes, before she'd collapse. Or she might make it through the night, but that was it. I knew we wouldn't be out long, because I'd have to bring her back. When we had to go out, she'd be completely out of control and the 'life and soul of the party', while she lasted; but in reality she was far too much 'over the top'. Then I'd find, as we only just got there, that I'd have to get my driver to take her home again; that would either be Kenny Hatton or Ricky Rickaby. Sadly, Ricky died about two years ago. He was found dead in bed. He was thirty-six stone – a very large guy!

Ron Gray comments: "Bob Price was everywhere you went around the town, at one time, because with his job he was a very popular man. He was at all the dos, and he supported me later when I was promoting. I went to the *Poppy Balls*. Bob and his wife, Pam ran them for many years. It was so hard to get tickets for it, but I think me and the wife made three of the balls. Wonderful dos; they were packed out every year, and they made a fortune for charity. He spent a lot of time on that. I always used to kid him that, as he was always in the paper, I could recognise him by his face!"

Martin Hone observes: "We always reckoned that during the 1960s and 70s, there were approximately three hundred families, who made Birmingham 'tick'. It was a view that came about through entertaining people... and eventually with the very substantial charity work that went on; with the balls that took place and the major dinners. You'd got the Jewish community that had their J N F Dinners, what they called the 'Gentlemen's Night Out', which were out-and-out Stag Dinners, where they raised the most remarkable sums of money. These were the Jewish Brummies – who helped make the city tick. There were several families from the community: the Glasses, the Blumenthals and the Zissmans, who were high-profile player on the Birmingham scene. They were in business and in politics.

"But in the main, I've estimated that the big circle around Birmingham, of the commuters that lived around Sutton Coldfield, Solihull and Barnt Green – those who'd made money, invariably came into the centre. If you had a ball or a dinner you knew that you'd sell tickets to those people – and they were the 'movers and shakers' of the town; they were the ones who'd been successful; they were the captains of industry. Don't forget that in those days we still had major industries in the city, like Lucas; Dunlop; Rubery Owen, Neville Industries; Accles & Pollock; Austin; Jaguar – and whatever. And those captains of industry supported the beginning of the leisure growth in Birmingham, as it changed from a very heavy industrial city to the city that we have today.

"Most certainly Roundy Rudell, the jeweller from Harborne, was a strong supporter of charities, and the Johnsons: these were charity-hearted people. They'd take one table or more and then they would entertain. This is where I began to also note the continuing corruption, and seeing who was entertaining whom on the city scene.

"You were a great charity supporter Eddie. The egos of the men who ran the clubs in those days used to come to the fore, because if there was an auction they'd be on their feet, almost *throwing* money at the auctioneer, to make sure that their name got mentioned! I was as guilty as we all were of that. If you wanted to raise money at an auction, then frankly, you didn't go beyond Harry Ruben – he could get 'blood out of a stone'. He was one of the most outstanding auctioneers," concludes Martin. "Do you remember him?"

Whilst we're on that subject, I was in the *International Convention Centre*, on another occasion, at a *Turning Point* Lunch. Princess Di was coming round with Pam Price, who was introducing her to various people. But I'll tell you more about that in the next chapter, as it happened after I'd sold my clubs.

Carlos, the chef, because he was such a good friend, wouldn't take money off me. He was a homosexual. Because I knew so many jewellers, I had a little gold chain made for him with his name engraved on it and 'thank you very much, from Eddie' on the back. I gave it to him and after that I think he must have thought that I fancied him, because every time that I looked at him he'd flash his eyes at me! He came to me one day, around the late 1980s and told me that he'd got an invitation for me. "The Mayor of Solihull has heard so much about you, that he's invited us to tea. He's asked me to bring you, because he's heard so much about your charity work, he's asked to meet you. We've got a big tea at three thirty on Wednesday afternoon."

The time came, to take tea with the mayor, but I was busy – because I was always busy doing something. To me the business was more important than going to tea somewhere. Carlos came to collect me, but I said: "I'm sorry Carlos, I can't come – I've got to do this." Some months later I was at a dance at Solihull Council House. We were going round and being introduced to certain people, one of whom happened to be the Mayor. The Mayor said: "Eddie Fewtrell? You're the only one who's ever refused to have tea in the Mayor's Parlour. They're usually queuing for it. Nobody would miss it – they'd fight for it!"

On another occasion, I was in the *Albany*. It was a very special event and Princess Anne was there, with her husband. I was standing there with my wife and John Kemp, who was in haulage work. All of a sudden I saw Councillor Freda Cox go by; she later became Mayor. I shouted; "Hey, Freda!" She turned away, but what I hadn't seen, was that she was in front of Princess Anne. They came over to me. Freda said: "Oh Your Highness, this is Eddie Fewtrell. He does a lot for charity. Princess Anne said: "Oh hello – nice to meet you." I introduced John to her.

She said: "I understand that you do this and that," (referring to some of the causes that I supported). I said: "Oh yes, I collect a few pounds together – to put into the kitty, to help people." Then she said: "Very nice to have met you," and off she went. I introduced Hazel to Royalty on three occasions, but every time I did she got really 'stumped' – she didn't know what to say.

When Princess Anne had gone, Hazel said: "What did you shake her hand for?" I said: "What do you think I'm going to do to her?" "You're not supposed to do that!" She was telling me off for shaking her hand. It wasn't protocol, in those days, but it is nowadays, because I made it so! I've always shaken people's hands when I meet them, no matter who they are. But here's the joke. Gregory, who was the Greek owner of *Liberty's*, was standing at the side of me, so I introduced her to him. The funny thing about him was that if you introduced him to Royalty, or other important people, he'd click his heels then bow. But when he tried to do that to Princess Anne, it was nearly disastrous. I said: "Be careful – you nearly 'nutted' her!" She started to laugh and all of the press came running up to us; they wanted to know what we'd done, to make Princess Anne laugh, because she was normally so serious.

Hazel had this 'thing' about not wanting to put on weight, especially as I was constantly mixing with really attractive women at my clubs. Becky confirms: "She was always worried about her weight. I don't think I ever had a weight problem until I left home!"

Daniel recalls a Canadian Rockies holiday in 1986, with Hazel.

"Mum's Aunt Olga lived in Port Moody, near Vancouver, British Columbia. Mum was a pen-friend of hers for years. Then mum and I eventually went over to meet her there, in Vancouver. We spent a few days there with my mum's auntie, then toured the Rockies, visiting Jasper, Banff and so on. That was a big thing for me. We were going to emigrate there as a family, after my dad sold out, but that never materialised."

According to my sister Phyllis and her husband, Bill Wheeler: "We were always invited to the 'dos' that Edward used to have; he very rarely left us out of any social situation." Remembering the *Poppy Balls*, Bill comments, "There were that many in the family, you'd want more than one table – and then there were the friends. Friends and family would be mixed in together on each table, but all of the tables would be close to each other. There was a dance and a show."

Phyllis comments: "My claim-to-fame with Eddie is that I used to change his nappies! His personality is such, that no matter where he's been, he's always got on well – and he'd got that little laugh – it was infectious. I love him to bits!"

"He's also got a wonderful foresight," continues Bill. "You could bet your life he would be a big success – no matter what he went into. The fella was so full of flair… and charisma. And he also has a wonderful sense of humour. He loves to tease me. Every one of the brothers has that same sense of humour."

"Eddie was always a strong supporter of charities, but our John's a nice person too," adds Phyllis. "Gordon is very caring – and he's more sentimental. He always calls me sweetheart. In my opinion, the fact that Eddie had his brothers to help him, for all those years, is a key factor in his success. I think it's very important that you emphasise that."

Chapter Fifteen

GOLDEN HANDCUFFS

In 1989, Eddie sells his flourishing empire to Ansell's Brewery, for over £10 million. Under a 'Golden Handcuffs' agreement, he is forced to retreat from the city for three years, although at the time he thinks it will be considerably longer. Hazel and Eddie have an acrimonious divorce, soon after the sale goes through.

Eddie takes a QE2 cruise and plays golf, but boredom soon sets in. Musical Director Mike Alexander and Eddie stage a spectacular show at the Metropole, in 1990, which is intended to be the first of many. Eddie has problems with medication, followed by a nervous breakdown. He enters the Woodbourne Clinic on the first of two occasions, but eventually recovers. This is, without doubt, one of the lowest points in Eddie's life. However, as soon as the three year agreement with Ansells expires, he searches for new clubs. Daniel Fewtrell recalls the traumas of 1989 and his subsequent travels. He reflects on the traits that he shares with his father and those where they differ.

Dave Juste explains: "In 1989, Eddie sold up to Ansells Leisure. They bought all of his clubs off him. Ansells then installed me as the Licensee-manager of *Edward's No.8*, and I worked for them for two years – up until 1991, when I left there to go to *XL's Night Club*. It was in receivership at the time. We were there for nearly two years, doing the Rock Nights, before Eddie bought it, in 1992."

Tony Brook elaborates: "When Ansell's took over, for a reported ten million, things were not the same and most of the old staff, loyal to Eddie, began to drift away; some with redundancy payments, and some sacked. It was the end of an era. In my opinion, Ansells failed to make a success of the empire. We all hoped Eddie would have a happy retirement; little did we know that he would eventually start up again, and a new chapter would begin."

When Ansells took over, I was employed by them as a consultant. There was the same amount of customers in the pubs and clubs, but insufficient bar staff, so people couldn't get served quickly enough. In fulfilment of my contract, I tried to alert the managers to various shortcomings, but was accused of interfering. I was also used as a scapegoat in terms of the drinks stock ordered by management and discrepancies. After six months of trying to advise them, I was told not to bother, although my contract remained secure. However, when *Abigail's* was sold to Ladbrokes for a lot of money, they kept me on as a consultant, for three years, at sixty grand a year.

Daniel remembers: "1989 was a particularly traumatic year for our family, for several reasons. John Bailey was a friend from boarding school. He was a good long distance runner. We met him while the family and myself were on holiday in Tenerife. It was a coincidence that he just happened to be there too. We all had a really good time, but then his luck changed the night before New Years Eve. We were sitting on a rock, on New Years Eve, during the day, planning what we were going to do that evening. By the rocks was a blowhole, with a hundred-foot drop. As the waves came in, a freak wave came right over the top. We'd never seen the waves actually reach so far up. The sea just dragged John under. We hadn't realised that he was sitting in a danger spot – it was a freak accident. They didn't find his body for a while. That was very traumatic. He was a bit older than me, but we were friends; we were in the same rugby team and in the athletics team as well. Dad had just sold the clubs. He and mum were already going through a stressful period, so when that happened to John, things became even more traumatic… everything went pear-shaped!"

According to a close family friend, "Hazel was afraid, around that time, that Edward wasn't his normal self and he wasn't behaving rationally. They went out to Thailand. I think it was to celebrate a wedding anniversary – or something like that. Hazel booked it, rather quickly, as a surprise, but Edward hadn't had all of the injections that he needed. So he went to a doctor and had loads of injections quickly, although he should have had them over a longer period of time. Once he'd had this great big cocktail of drugs injected into him, he started to behave in a peculiar way. He returned from Thailand and had his breakdown."

In fact, Hazel and I went to Thailand, to try to get ourselves together. But we had loads of problems with the accommodation that Hazel had booked, so at her request, I was continually upgrading them, to First Class hotels, as we travelled around. Luckily, money wasn't a problem. Meanwhile, we got a telephone message from Rebecca, in Norfolk Road. Daniel was supposed to be at his boarding school, but Rebecca told me that he had been having major problems there. He was now at home and she couldn't handle him. Hazel then suggested that I should buy Daniel an aeroplane ticket, then he flew out to join us.

Soon afterwards Hazel suggested that I take Abigail to Spain, on a ridiculous errand, although the reasons behind her request would eventually become abundantly clear! Eventually I gave in, and returned with Abigail to Spain, taking Ricky with us too. As true as God made little apples, we arrived at the restaurant, only to find that a waiter, whom Abigail had become infatuated with, had other girlfriends. So Abigail wanted to come back home, straight away. I managed to get her on a plane, that night. Ricky and I were unable to get a return ticket until two days afterwards. Abigail said: "I've got a letter for you dad, from mum, but I don't want to give it to you!" I didn't know what it was, so I didn't press her about it. Ricky and I played golf for a couple of days, then returned home.

Shortly afterwards, Hazel and I separated – although it came as a tremendous shock to me. Having returned from that Spanish holiday, to my home at 7 Norfolk Road, Edgbaston, I found that the locks wouldn't work. So I went back to the café, where Ricky and the taxi driver were waiting. I said: "Give us my case out. You really won't believe what she's done now!" I opened it and it was full of lady's clothes! It was a Samsonite case, but at the airport Rickie had picked up a case that looked like mine. I found a name and address inside and arranged for a motor to go down, to swap cases; the owner lived in Devon, or Cornwall!

Meanwhile, it looked like I might have to spend the night in the *Albany Hotel*. I went back to my house in Norfolk Road, and saw Hazel's window open. This is in *Blythe Court*; it's three storeys high – a massive house. So I looked up, saw the open window and thought: 'Oh – I can get in there.' I went down to the side of the house, where we kept a ladder, got up there, went to the top and began to open the window. But it was just like something out of a *Psycho* film, because as I did it, this mad woman pushed me and the ladder away from the window, with all her might, and threw a piece of paper at me.

It was actually Hazel, but the fear in her face was unbelievable; it was just as if something had happened to her – like *Psycho* – you know? I was going backwards, but I managed to turn – how I did it I don't know! I realised that I'd got to jump off the ladder quickly. In front of the window was a piece of grass, so I jumped off the ladder, hit the grass and rolled over. I broke my glasses, grazed all me arm. I could have ended up with a broken neck if I hadn't done something. The ladder came down, but never hit me. I managed to get up and just by the window there was my little study. I could see Hazel in there, on the phone, just like a mad woman. As I've explained, she was heavily on drugs: Moggadon, Valium, and some others. She was supposed to be under a doctor's supervision.

She didn't open the door and the next thing was that a Panda Car pulled up on the drive. Some police officers got out and said: "Eddie, you're not supposed to be within three miles of the place." I said: "I'm afraid that I don't know what this is all about. I've just come back from Spain." That was obviously what the paper was about – it was a Court Order of some kind. So I said: "Look, this is my house. I haven't been served with this paper." At that, a police officer jumped on me and forced me into the back of the car. I'm absolutely gasping for breath, because of my asthma. They didn't realise that I'd just been pushed off a ladder! They whisked me round to the police station in Harborne.

The Chief Inspector said: "Hello Eddie, what are you doing here?" I said: "I've just been beaten up by your two officers." He said: "Oh, don't come that!" I said: "I'm not." He said: "If you're going to be like that, I'm not going to bother with you." I said: "You've soon changed your tune!" I asked them to give me the phone and I phoned Doctor Y, who'd been my private doctor for about twenty years. Unfortunately, his secretary told me that Doctor Y had had a nervous breakdown – his wife had cleared all of his bank accounts out – and he's run back to Ireland. I said: "Are you joking? I'm in a police station!" I couldn't believe it. Anyway, I got in touch with Nick Radvanyi, who lived just around the corner from me. As you know, he'd been my pal all my life – and he was my doctor too. Shortly before all of this happened, Nick had also been going through a difficult time in his life, but fortunately, I'd been able to help him. Now, all of a sudden, the situation was reversed: I had to phone Nick up and ask him to bring his camera, because I'd been beaten up by the police, on top of the injuries I had from falling off the ladder. Nick took all the photographs and the copper said: "You can go now Eddie, if you want to." I said: "I was quite within my rights, in going back to my house, because I'd had no idea previously that I wasn't supposed to."

Hazel was born on 5 November 1937. Our divorce eventually went through in 1990, when she was fifty-three and I was fifty-eight. We went to court and she wanted £500,000 for each kid; she wanted all the money; she wanted the house, the furniture, the lot. I was let down badly. My accountant went with me and the court asked for the cheques there and then, from the company. They demanded the money straight away and the house – and they got it. It was torture.

Hazel told everybody that I'd already been having an affair with Marleen. Hazel wanted £500,000 for each kid; she wanted all the money; she wanted the house, the furniture, the lot. She'd made herself appear in court like a little old lady, who hadn't got a penny. I never even recognised her myself! She cried and got the court completely on her side – she was so bitter. Hazel got *everything* that she asked for – bang, bang, bang! My solicitor, who was also a woman, looked at me and said: "I cannot believe this. All I can say is that it's because of your notorious name."

Hazel said that she was petrified of me, the nightclub situation, the magistrates – the lot. They must have believed her. She had police from Manchester come down, to testify, because she didn't trust the Birmingham police to be impartial – which in a way was true. So consequently, they wrote the cheques then and there, for Daniel and for Abigail; they had to have a new house and car a-piece, fifty grand here, five thousand grand there.

I turned round and said: "Well, I've paid out all this money. Let her have a million pound for the house and let me have the rest," to which they agreed.

But then she sold the house, and nobody ever disclosed how much she got for it. Believe me – that's what happened! All I got was her bill, for forty grand, and mine for the same. I just turned round in the end and said: "I'm not going to fight this case any more – I'm not paying out any more money." They said: "Oh no, we've still got this and that to discuss." I went up there, stayed there for two hours, but in the end I just got fed up, because she was going to get my money and property anyway, so I just walked out of the meeting. The next day I got a bill for six grand! So that was me finished – I didn't want to know any more about it.

Becky comments: "My childhood was very happy. My brother and sister came along – that was fine. I began to notice arguments and things like that, when we moved into Norfolk Road, around the time when I was fifteen or sixteen, in 1980. As my parents were finally divorced in 1990, we're talking about the last ten years of their marriage, when it became really noticeable.

Before that, as far as I knew, everything was fine. I never thought that my parents would divorce. At school a lot of my friends' parents were divorcing, but I always thought that my mine never would. It was a real shock when I realised what was happening."

In 1990 Mike Alexander came to me. He was devastated because Shirley Bassey, like all the other top artistes, had just decided not to use live musicians – because the policy of television and the media was to use tapes, as it was easier. I said: "Come and work for me. Go and get hold of Shirley and we'll put one-night shows on, once a month, at the *Metropole*." I'd already been arranging annual shows there and put boxing matches on there too.

Bob Price has said that I should have been an impresario, because that's what I was doing really in so many ways – arranging and organising events... I loved doing that. I asked Mike Alexander to contact Shirley secretly, tell her that she was going to be singing with an orchestra, which he would arrange. He would be the Musical Director of what would be a live show. We'd put a comedian on with her and a dinner. It would be just like the *Poppy Ball*, in that respect and we could start to sell tickets, once we knew what it was going to cost us, to make a profit.

We worked it out that the tickets had got to be £150 each. We printed them. Mike costed it, then we worked out the price together, but I ended up selling most of the seats, because I knew the people. I sold about four tables of tickets, with ten people to a table. I knew the Broadhursts, Paddy Lynch, who did all of the scaffolding; all sorts of people.

Kenny Lynch remembers: "Eddie had invited me – and I was in Cardiff. He knows Eddie Avoff, who also knows Shirley as well. I used to be managed by Shirley's agent. We were together with the same agent, for seven years – a guy called Maurice King – and his partner, Clive. We went down there – myself and Eddie Avoff – and we shared a table with Eddie. Our table was over in a corner. They've got giant rooms that they can split into sections. The tickets were very expensive, and they didn't sell as well as Mike Alexander and Eddie had hoped. I remember him telling me... he said that for the money he was paying, he was doing it without profit – that's the last thing I remember him telling me. I said: 'But it's packed!' He said: 'I know – but she wants too much!' He definitely told me that he 'did his orchestras' over that one! I think he gave her thirty-eight grand. If you do that, and you hire that hall, you've got to charge something like three hundred quid a ticket, but you can't do that, because not many people will turn up. So he did it as a prestige type of thing."

That's exactly what happened, Kenny. The plan was to follow that one show with a series of top celebrity shows, at the *Metropole*. Mike and I were going to have other top artistes and combine it again with a first-rate dinner. But unfortunately, the timing was such, that it became impossible. My brother Bomber staged a similar, but more financially viable show with Shirley Bassey, at the *Metropole*, a year or two later.

Mike Alexander observes: "The thing that makes you a *great* Musical Director – and I think I am – is that you have to have sympathy for people on the front of the stage. Because if anything goes wrong, it's their name – at the end of the day, people aren't going to say that the Musical Director came in on the wrong note; they're going to say that he or she (the artiste) came in on the wrong key. It was the Salena Jones Show or the Shirley Bassey Show. From a good MD's perspective, it could never be their fault, so you have to be sympathetic. Personally, I couldn't do that. If somebody said to me; 'You're crap – get off!' I'd say: 'Okay. Goodbye.' So you try to help them if they've got stage fright. Nearly every artiste has 'nerves' or 'stage fright' before they go on.

"I'd worked for *Peters & Lee* for four years, finished with them, worked for Freddie Starr for about ten days, left Freddie, and then got offered the job with Shirley Bassey, while I was with Freddie. I worked with Shirley Bassey through the early 1980s up 'til about 1987. Actually it was when I had this break with her that I went to work for *Goldwyn's* again.

"The pair of us formed a company called *Fame International*. Eddie financed it and I did the donkey work, with the help of Eddie's staff. Because I'd worked with Shirley Bassey I knew her manager and I knew how to make contact with her, which was otherwise very difficult to do. Her manager, a man called Oscar Cohen, in New York, said: 'Yes, it's going to cost you this. We want 25% now and we want the other 25%, a month before she appears.'

"Shirley lived in Monte Carlo and had a flat in Marbella; her son was there too," Mike continues. "So I had all of the phone numbers and if I was over there on holiday I'd call her and we'd meet up. I'd always used British orchestras with Shirley, since the 1980s, so I knew all the guys; the sound companies, the lighting companies. I knew all of the people involved with putting a show like that on. I had meetings at the *Metropole*, organised menus – things like that.

"Two suites were booked: the *King's Ballroom* and the *Queen's Ballroom*, at the *Metropole Hotel*. We had hotel rooms too. The show was an *amazing* success. Eddie and his family were at the front; all of the brothers were up there. I didn't sell all of the tickets. The cost was horrendous! There was a thirty-piece orchestra for Shirley; another ten-piece band on the dance music. I had a Quartet playing dinner music. We had dancers on; Roy Walker, the comedian. We had a five-course meal, it was absolutely fantastic! The *Metropole* staff still speak about it now.

"The actual concept of this type of entertainment was a really good idea, but sadly, just at that point, Eddie became ill, so he was unable to extend the idea into a series of shows. This meant that although I had organised the whole thing, it just wasn't possible, from a practical point of view for me to be involved any further with *Fame International*, the company that Eddie had formed with me. So the whole thing petered out," explains Mike.

Whilst we're on that subject, I was in the *International Convention Centre*, on another occasion, at a *Turning Point* function. Princess Di was coming round with Pam Price. I said: "Hi, how are you Princess Di? How's your love life then?" She said: "Not very good." I said: "Well I'm available – I've just got divorced!" I said: "Where have you been all day, because I seem to be in front of you? When I was fetching the children from Edgbaston School, you were in front of me. You went into that building, just down by the Botanical Gardens." She said: "That's where we had lunch." I said: "Well you were there earlier on and now you're here. Are you following me about?" She said: "No." I said: "Well, if you're available tomorrow, you can come with me for a dance at my club – *Boogie's*." She said: "That would be nice." I also introduced her to Abigail, who had just done a play for *BBC2*, in which she played her.

I went to the *Albany Hotel* and I stayed there for about a month, then I moved to the *Royal Angus*, around the corner, because that was nearer the *Cedar Club*. When I came out of the *Royal Angus* I was ill – I was pretty bad. Because I shouldn't have been on my own so much; I was thinking about things all the time – dwelling on things – and getting into a depressed state. I wasn't working, because I'd sold all I had. So I went and saw Doctor Z – (here we go again – another alias!) at the Woodbourne Clinic, which is a clinic for alcoholics and for nervous breakdowns. I actually knew him quite well, because he used the club. He was going out with a Lap-top Dancer. His wife had left him and he was now very serious about this dancer.

So I went in – and I became very ill in there. This was in 1990, shortly after my divorce.

When I disappeared, and nobody knew where I was, Nobby Nobbs found me at the Woodbourne Clinic. Rita Radvanyi then came to see me, and so did some of my brothers, this first time that I was ill.

Rita elaborates: "He said: 'Rita, get me out of here. I'm absolutely fine. The more normal I become the next thing I know I'm having an injection and then I'm asleep again, probably for a couple of days. I want to get off all of the drugs that they're giving to me. I want to get out of here and find a house.' So Eddie and I went house hunting; I was working for an Estate Agent at the time. We found a house in Rodman Close, Edgbaston, which was also just around the corner from Blythe Court and from me.

"I had a phone call one Sunday morning, about ten. He said: 'Rita, I like that house. Can you come and pick me up and we'll go round and I'll do a deal.' I said: 'Edward, we can't just turn up at the doctor's house, on a Sunday morning!' He said: 'We can. Come on – come and pick me up, and I'll do a deal.' So that's what I did. I apologised profusely, as the doctor opened the door, in his dressing gown. Edward offered him the money that he wanted. They shook hands and the deal was done. That's how he did business: I want that, so I'll get it. Even though it's ten o'clock on a Sunday morning, let's go and knock the door and get it sorted out."

So within a few months of my divorce, I moved into Rodman Close. You've never seen a house in such a filthy state in all your life. They wanted £220,000 for it. I said: "I'll have it, but I want to go in now." As Rita says, the doctor wanted a month to move out now, but for an extra five grand he agreed to move out the next day.

I moved into the dining room then had the house totally refurbished. I met Marleen, as she'll explain in the next chapter, and she came down to stay with me. Lo and behold, Hazel came sailing round in the new Mercedes that I'd bought her. Then I paid another £100,000 for another, four-door version for her. I kept buying her things – don't ask me why. Maybe I thought we could get back together. It seemed so ridiculous – we'd had all those years at the club and all the money – and then to be parted. But she didn't want to know. She was going out with this other guy – that's what it was all about. She'd been having affairs, for several years, and she wanted to be free.

I suppose it was a difficult lifestyle that we'd both been living for years; rather surreal, in a way? It could be argued that with me being busy, running the clubs, she may have felt lonely, although, from what I heard afterwards, she wasn't! In reality, although I was seen by everybody, with loads of women, they never saw me at half past four in the morning, on my own, being taken home by big fat Rickie Rickaby, my driver and bodyguard. I wouldn't drive, because I'd have a drink after everybody had gone – and there'd be just a couple of good friends there. We'd sit and have a talk. Most of them were divorced – Rickie and my manager were.

For the record, I've never been an alcoholic and I never took drugs. I hadn't been drinking – I never was a big drinker. I saw Doctor Z and he said: "You'd better come in; you're in a bad way." He examined me and said: "This mixture you've been taking, you've got Valium, Cannabis in it – and a cocktail of drugs – all sorts of drugs." I said: "Let me tell you, I never take drugs." The only thing I could think of was that I'd been 'fed' them somehow. He kept me in the clinic for six weeks until I was reasonably alright. My brother Chrissie and my other brothers came to see me at Woodbourne, while I was there, but not their wives. I'd go for walks and maybe go and see my sister, the one day. Woodbourne is just down the road from 7 Norfolk Road – in the same road.

Daniel did his A-Levels after school, around 1990, then took a year out in between that; did a little bit of travelling in between, then did his A-Levels in a year.

"Then I went to Italy for two summers back-to-back; that was language training," recalls Daniel. "After I finished that, I went to university in 1992. When I finished university I went travelling, around Central and South America. Basically I did a journey from Mexico, all the way down through Central America to Belize. It's called 'trekking'. I used every type of public transport that you can think of. I also used buses – you know those buses where the cattle are on board too?

"We travelled all the way down from Mexico, to Tierra del Fuego in Argentina. Essentially I travelled solo, although I'd meet people along the way. I went through the Amazon, then all the way down to the southernmost point; then came back up again, through Chile. That was in 1994.

"I did a Spanish language course before I set out. When I was out there I was speaking Spanish all the time. From South America I travelled back through the States, then back up to Canada. I travelled around the States by the Auto Drive-aways, so you picked up a car, which you could then deliver to another State. I did a journey from Toronto to LA. I drove about three-and-a-half-thousand miles in about three-and-a-half days. I saw nearly every State in America – really fast. All that travelling gave me a great opportunity to mull over various ideas; giving me a greater perspective about what I wanted to do with my life. It was also a way of 'finding myself'.

"Then I worked in Granada, in the Caribbean and took my Scuba Diving Instructor's Certificate. It was beautiful, but I got Island Fever after a while, so I got out of there. When I got back I did my pilot's training; that took me to America and South Africa – I was over there for quite some time. So I flew light aircraft over there. I still do about ten hours a year, to keep my pilot's licence.

"I met Isaac Hayes over in New York. He was doing a free Charity Concert. Isaac is the singer with the deep voice, who did the theme music for *Shaft*. I spoke to him briefly. Then when I was travelling through the States I ended up in St Louis. There was a Rock Festival there and I met a rock group called *Skunk Anansi*. I got talking to their lead singer and ended up in the backstage area at the concert.

"I picked up the phone once at home and there was a deep American voice: 'Can I speak to Eddie please?' I couldn't believe that it was Ben E. King calling! I'd got his albums upstairs – I'd got into those. He did the song for the 501 Jeans adverts too. Abigail answered the door and the phone to him, on other occasions.

"When I was at boarding school, I didn't have much to do with the clubs, during term time – not during the early years anyway. The similarities that my dad and I share are that we are very people-orientated: we enjoy talking to people. He can also be very funny – sometimes without even realising it! When he believes in something, he will do it to the best that it can be done.

"He doesn't 'suffer fools' at all. I probably 'suffered fools' before – in the past; when I was growing up, but then as I've got older, I think I've probably become more like him. One of the disadvantages of being Eddie's son was that in the clubs and elsewhere, people would frequently approach me, because they thought that your dad had influence – money and stuff. So I had the wrong kind of friends – sometimes. You have to find out who likes you for yourself – or whatever. Naturally, that put me on my guard with people, but I'm over it now.

"Mum loved the stars; she thought it was great, because she'd get my dad to book the people that she liked. She told me that she sat there, talking to

Jimi Hendrix, Marc Bolan and people like that. Dad could see the potential for making money by hiring various artistes; mum was more on the artistic-musical side, so they worked well as a team, in that respect," Daniel observes.

Despite all that's happened, I'd do exactly the same again. I've enjoyed every moment. I've got my sorrows; it broke my family up and I can understand how it did. But in life, whatever you do, you grow apart. It's not like when you're young. I believed Hazel married me very quick, because the basic truth is that she had a very strict father. She hated living there with him. I think, with hindsight, that Hazel only married me because she wanted to get out of that house and away from him. Having said that, I loved Hazel – she was the most beautiful girl in the world. I think the actual cause of our break-up was a combination of two things: firstly, the legal drugs, given to her by hospitals and doctors, which proved, in time, to be very addictive; secondly, my obsession with money, which I saw as a means of giving my family the best of everything – in stark contrast to my own, poverty-stricken childhood. The following letter was written by Hazel, then hidden in a secret tin, together with some of her most precious photographs. Until Becky showed it to Shirley, recently, I had no idea that it existed.

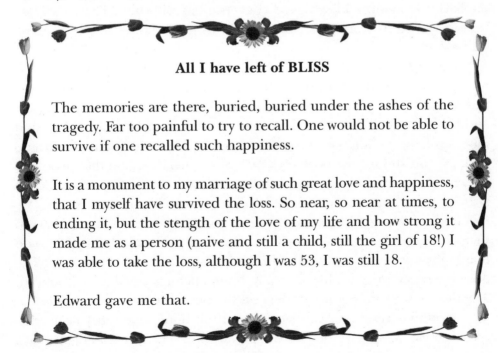

All I have left of BLISS

The memories are there, buried, buried under the ashes of the tragedy. Far too painful to try to recall. One would not be able to survive if one recalled such happiness.

It is a monument to my marriage of such great love and happiness, that I myself have survived the loss. So near, so near at times, to ending it, but the stength of the love of my life and how strong it made me as a person (naive and still a child, still the girl of 18!) I was able to take the loss, although I was 53, I was still 18.

Edward gave me that.

I think that Hazel really loved me, in the beginning. I *was* a workaholic, but for our children – and what she wanted. She wanted the best education for our children. That's why I worked so hard – to get the best for all of them. In all fairness, I neglected myself. At the end of the day, when I'd done all that, I looked around me and I'd lost everything personal to me. I'd lost all the love… and my wife; the marriage had been broken up for years and years. I did everything to keep Hazel happy, but I finished up on my own.

Daniel comments: "One of the differences between dad and myself is that he had a really hard upbringing as a child – I don't think he saw much love, while he was growing up. I think he finds it difficult to convey his feelings – having grown up during the war period… and being one of ten children. I've learnt to understand that, but I think I've been more fortunate, because I've had a lot of love from my parents.

"The best times that I had with dad were when he used to drive me back to boarding school. I used to love that. I think it was a refreshing thing for him as well. There was a period when I weekly boarded, for a year or two – and my dad used to get up at five o'clock on a Monday morning and drive me back to school. I'd have good conversations with him. That was when we were living in Norfolk Road, when I was between twelve and thirteen years of age.

"Those drives were when I spent the most time with dad. He'd just tell me how to deal with life really. If there was bullying he'd tell me how *not* to stand for that. That really instilled me with confidence, so I could cope – and I knew I'd be alright. We'd talk about his success. The way that he and mum brought me up, has encouraged me to have ambition in life – to do well. His job and his hours of work were abnormal. You find that people in the entertainment industry have a different 'take' on life. Spending a lot of years in that false environment is not conducive to family life.

"Dad was always able to anticipate trends in the entertainment market, then change and re-market his clubs accordingly. You have to be able to do that in my business too, the stock-broking business. It's something that I've been interested in all my life, basically, from watching the film *Wall Street*. In America they've still got the traders on the floor, but nowadays, in the UK it's all computerised. So it can be done from home now; all you need is access to SETS – which stands for the Stock Exchange Trading Service, where all your trades are done and everything else. It's high pressure and I'm dealing with people's money, so it's a big responsibility. Luckily, I thrive on pressure.

"To be successful, you've got to be in a high-pressure environment, so I'm doing something that I'm really suited to. From the upbringing that I had, because my mum and dad were really successful, I like to study other people's successes and see what character traits such people have, and how they develop, to enable them to become successful," concludes Daniel. "Winston Churchill provided one of the best definitions: 'Success is the ability to go from one failure to another with no loss of enthusiasm.'"

Chapter Sixteen

MARLEEN

Eddie visits friends in Worcester – Carol, 'The Boots' and Anthony. He meets Marleen there, sister of Jeannet (pronounced Shenet) Anthony's Danish au pair, ten days before his final divorce. He's now living in Rodman Close, Edgbaston, but there are imminent tax problems.

So how did I meet Marleen, who became my second wife? Well, while I was in the Clinic, I met a guy who used to supply me with fish – crabs, lobsters and so forth. Also, the nicer one of the two Broadhurst sisters was in there. She wanted me to go home with her, to take care of me, because I was so thin, but I said no.

So I met Anthony, the Fishman, who supplied me with crab. He said: "Eddie, what are you doing in here?" He had a problem with drink, but was due to go home. He invited me to come and have dinner, when I came out. He lived in Worcester. This was about six weeks before my final divorce, which I described in the previous chapter.

Marleen recalls: "I met Eddie on 8 June seventeen years ago, on a blind date, arranged through Carol Walters. She phoned up and asked if I'd like to go out in a foursome, for dinner.

"Carol was actually a friend of Nina, Don's girlfriend. They lived in Worcester and my sister was their au pair. So I was invited to go out for a meal and I thought: 'Oh – yeah.' At first I said no, because I couldn't be bothered, but then I got bored and thought well, a meal would be okay. So I went to their house and she said that it would just be me and Edward. So I said: "Well in that case I'm not staying either; because I'm not going to be on my own, with someone I don't know." But then she said that she was only joking. Then Edward arrived, and she said you *are* going on your own. I was on my way out through the window, when Edward walked in through the kitchen door. I had to sit down for a while, then off we went. But he didn't take me out for a meal. He took me all the way up to Birmingham – to all the clubs.

Edward was a consultant for the Birmingham clubs at that time, when he sold out. He kept an eye on all the managers and stuff. I think he had a contract for three years. He had to do his round that night, so he dragged me along! So we were driving around to all the different night clubs. I'm not into night clubs at all. It's never been my scene – ever. It wasn't much fun. I wasn't impressed. Everybody got a bit drunk actually, because wherever he went people were saying: 'Oh, have a drink Eddie!' But no – the club scene is definitely not me. It's quite ironic really, because I'd go out to a pub for a quiet drink, but I wouldn't go out to a night club.

"So that was the first time I went out anywhere with him, although it wasn't a meal or a proper date. When I first met Eddie he frightened me to death! Because he walked through the door and said: 'Oh what big, beautiful eyes you've got!' It was like the Wolf and Little Red Riding Hood! He grabbed my face like that and said: 'And what kissable lips you have!' It was like: 'This is *not* good!' I felt a bit pushed. We ended up in the car and he said to me: 'What do you like? What do you want to do?' I said: 'Well, I thought we were coming over for a quiet meal.' He said: 'Right. Well I've got to meet some friends, but we'll go home to my place first.' I'm thinking: "I don't like the sound of this at all, because I don't know who you are." I was twenty when we met, because it was the 8 June 1990, and it was my twenty-first birthday on the 27 June. He sent me thirty-six red roses on my birthday, with a card. That was quite nice."

So now I was with Marleen. I invited her down to Rodman Close. Hazel lived in a big tower block nearby. You could see my house from her flat. Marleen stayed the night. The very next day, Hazel came sailing round in her Mercedes. Tammy Wynette's record, *D-I-V-O-R-C-E-* was blaring out on her car radio. She said: "How are you?" I said: "I'm alright. But listen, I've got to tell you," (because I'm like that). "You might want to go in a minute, because I've got a girl upstairs." She said she wanted to meet her. I called Marleen downstairs. Hazel said: "Do you love him? – because he broke my heart." Marleen said: "Yes, I do." I said: "There you are – you've heard that. You can go now." But she wouldn't leave for ages; she was telling her this and telling her that.

I'd got £900,000 left. Apparently, because I'd paid the cheques to Hazel out of the *company*, I was now going to be saddled with a million pound tax bill! If I paid that tax bill I'd be left with nothing. I explained the situation to Peter Langard, my accountant. I said: "What do you think? Can we get a 'stay' on this?" He said: "I've been trying for weeks. I've just had about ten letters."

You see, under Company Law, if you take money out of the company and give it to your wife, although it's your money, you have to pay tax on it. All of the money that she'd had, which the court had ordered me to pay, I owed them a further million pounds, in tax.

"We then started dating, I guess," recalls Marleen. "I used to go up there and he used to come down here. Edward was in Rodman Close. He'd always been there, from the time I first met him. I was down here living at Bodenham, in the big white house. I lodged with Jenny, the owner. I worked for myself. I used to go round cleaning houses. Jenny had problems with her husband, so did I – but that was way before I met Edward.

"We've been married two years, this 9 March; we were married in 2005; but we lived together for fifteen years before that. During that time, Edward would run back to Hazel and finish with me. This happened about three times. Every time he left he took a bit of my heart with him. You try to protect yourself, because you get so upset… if you love someone a lot and they just keep letting you down and leaving you.

"The third time, he said that he was actually going to re-marry her, because she wanted to get remarried – or something ridiculous. That was at Becky's wedding, in 2002. I think that killed a lot, when he told me that. I thought: 'Well, that's fine. Carry on – get on with life again', which I'd done all the other times when he'd phoned up and said: 'Well I know I shouldn't phone, but now I'm sat here on my own in the house again. Hazel knows I'm not seeing you any more, so she's not coming around. Nobody cares about me. I'm all on my own again.' I said: 'If you come back this time that's fine, but you must understand that my feelings are not the way that they used to be about you, because you keep hurting me. If you come back this time and you decide to leave again, then don't ever contact me again – because I won't ever want to see you again. If you're going to come back you either come and you stay and you tell her to go to hell – make her understand that it's finished between you… otherwise don't bother coming.' But then he came back and he's been with me ever since.

"There's a thirty-seven year age gap between Eddie and myself, but the worst thing wasn't the age gap between him and me; you don't feel it when you're in love, it's all the other people who're trying to ruin it for you, because that age gap is there. They said it was never going to work; it was always going to be like this – and so on. I think if you click with somebody and they're your best friend, then how can it not work? We never thought about the gap until other people started talking about it.

"I don't think that age matters, if you love someone. It's just the relationship of one person to another. I never thought about it. Edward goes on about it: 'I'm going to die before you.' I say: 'Well I might go before you,' because you can never tell. I could still go off on the road and get hit by a lorry, or one of the horses might kick me in the head!' I said: 'You've got to live life while you've got it, because tomorrow you might not be here. So why sit and be miserable?'"

Marleen has three sisters. "Elena has just become a teacher in Demark. She started this year. She teaches smaller children. She's living with another teacher who she met. I don't know why she wants to be a teacher, because it is a very hard and stressful job – but she is. A second sister, Sarah, works as a secretary for one of the biggest celebrity lawyers in Denmark. So she has a really nice job. They're twins and they're both twelve years younger than me, by a different father; he and my mum have been married for twenty-six years now.

"I didn't have any bridesmaids; I couldn't be bothered. I didn't have any pageboys either, because then there was no fighting, you see? Looking at the Wedding Album here, that's my mum and dad. There are the sisters. This is the twins and that's my other sister, Jeannet; we have the same dad. She's two years younger than me. Christian is Sarah's boyfriend and Lasse is Elena's boyfriend. Konrad is the twin's father. Jeannet (pronounced 'Shennet') and Lars are getting married this year. She's the sister, who was Carol's au pair.

"We got married first of all at Ross-on-Wye Registry Office, on Edward's birthday, 9 March 2005. Then on the 16 July 2005 we went and had the Church Blessing, in Norway. That was because my grandmother lives in Norway. She was ninety and I wanted her to come to the wedding. If it had been my father's request he would have chosen Denmark, as he's very ill with cancer. He made the trip over to Norway, which was very good of him. It would have been too much for my grandmother to travel to Denmark. She had a stroke the year after so she's wheelchair-bound now. But that was a really nice wedding."

Rita Radvanyi met Marleen at the surgery, initially: "Edward brought her down to see Nick, because he recommended Nick to lots of people. In retrospect she seemed rather quiet and reticent. I think that's because she felt conscious of the fact that I'd known Hazel for so many years and that I was Hazel's friend. I think that Marleen's been wonderful for Edward. He went through a period in his life when he just wasn't our normal Edward; he was very quiet and very serious. Now that he's re-married, I have to say that the old Edward has come back. She's obviously the reason that he's changed back to the person that he was – the 'larger-than-life' personality, and he seems to be extremely happy. I'm *amazed* that he's taken on yet another business. You'd have thought that he would have been only too happy to have retired completely. I think he loves a challenge. He's been fighting the planning application situation, in Much Marcle, for about ten years."

Chapter Seventeen

XL's TO MILLENNIUM

Eddie buys XL's in Broad Street, out of receivership, formerly 'Faces', plus two lap-dancing clubs: Xpose in Paradise Street and Zig-Zags, next door to XL's, in Auchinleck Square, Edgbaston. He then opens Club Millennium, in Merry Hill, which becomes the most successful of all his clubs – financially. His daughter, Becky, marries John Moon, in 2002. Eddie suffers a second breakdown, in 2003, keeping it a secret from all but a few. Tragically, Hazel dies from cancer, that same year.

It was 1991. Every single day I continued to receive letters about the outstanding debt, from the tax authorities. Finally I made a decision, which I'm quite good at doing, when I put my mind to it. I'd reached the stage when I thought; 'Sod everybody – I'll look after myself.' So I decided to use the million pounds, to buy *XL's*. It was up for sale by the Liquidators, for 1.2 million, I got on the phone and offered them £800,000, saying also that I couldn't see anybody catching me up on that offer, because it was a lot of money. Just before we closed the deal I said "I made a mistake – I should have offered you £700,000." So I nicked another hundred grand, knowing full well that all the paperwork had gone through, at that stage, so it would have been too expensive for them to find another buyer.

So I bought it for that, with the taxman's money, which meant that I now had £200,000 to spend on it. It's a law. It's quite easy really. They could have taken the house – but it would have been nasty. But they couldn't take the club, because I'd bought it through a new, Limited Company. Langard turned it into *XL's Nightclub Ltd*.

I'd used their money. All they could do was to have me for nicking their money, couldn't they? It's not stolen, because you've put it into the company, but they've got to get if off you. I'd just got the club going and I was doing quite well. The phone rang in the office and who was there, but the person from the Inland Revenue. I said: "I know who you are. You're driving me mad! Do you realise that I've just come out of Woodbourne? I'm recovering from a nervous breakdown, caused by all the stress I've been under. I've had a woman take me for everything that I've worked for, all of my life, seven days a week, since I was fourteen. I'm fifty-nine now; she's had the house and millions of pounds, and you, the Tax People, have had all the rest. I believe in paying my tax, I believe in being fair, but you have left me without a penny. I've written you several letters, explaining the situation, but over a period of forty years, you have had the lot.

"As far as I'm concerned, you are a very nasty person, and you're getting nothing more from me. I'll tell you what – I've just been into Woodbourne. I feel like blowing somebody away – and it's going to be you! You wait there. I'm coming round with a shotgun and I'm going to blow your head off!" I put the phone down and my daughter Rebecca said: "Dad!" Pete, my friend, who was an accountant in my office, said: "You'll have the police round in a minute." I said: "I don't care." I'd got to that stage, when I'd just had enough. Can you understand that?

I wasn't bothered – and I would have done it. Anyway, five minutes later, the phone rings and I thought: 'Oh God!' A voice on the other end said: "It's Inspector So-and-so here." I said: "Inspector *who*?" He said: "I'm the Chief Inspector of Taxes." I said: "You can do just exactly what I've told your bloody horrible woman to do! And if you like, you can be included too – I'll come and blow you away as well!" He said: "Mr. Fewtrell, please listen to me." I banged the phone down. So he phoned again: "Mr. Fewtrell, *please* listen to me." I said: "Alright – go ahead." He said, very tactfully: "I quite understand how you feel. I've looked at all the papers, and added up all the figures. I know what the situation is and you're perfectly right – there's only so much money in the pot; you've paid all the bills and you have got no money left.

"Listen, I believe you've bought *XL's*?" I said: "I have. I've got to get some money back. After all – it is my money!" So he said: "How long would you like to pay?" I said: "Two years." He said; "Right, if that's enough time, you've got two years. Your house is safe. If I can help you any more, please give me a ring."

I put the phone down and told Pete. He said: "I can't believe it!" I said: "It just shows you. Sometimes it pays to be a bit bloody-minded!" So consequently, they gave me two years to pay. Do you know – I swear-to-God,

I paid that bill off, within three months. At the same time, I'd bought *Xpose* and I was building up a living. I'd already got the *Rock Club*, which was in *Edward's Eight*, that I'd sold – it was just down the road. As soon as I said the word, that I was coming up here, they all came up here – I emptied that place! So it just went one way after that. After that I built *Millennium*, which was taking £50,000 a week.

Dave Juste explains: "In 1991 for various reasons I fell out with Ansells, over some things that they were trying to get us to do that I felt was unacceptable. So I left to go freelance – to *XL's Night Club*, in Auchinleck Square, Five Ways. It was in receivership and had absolutely no customers whatsoever. We brokered the deal, for us to do Rock Nights at the venue and we opened there around April or May 1991. Steve Webb was still with me, at that time. Within about eight weeks we'd taken everyone out of *Edward's* and put them into *XL's*. *Edward's* had gone from doing about thirteen or fourteen hundred people, on a Saturday night, to about two hundred and fifty. So I was working with Eddie again between, 1992 and 2003. Eddie bought *XL's* in 1992 and kept me on.

"I was basically running the Saturday nights for him. We tried to get going a couple of other nights in *XL's*, but it wasn't a success, because of the layout of the venue. *Zig-Zags* was underneath *XL's*, but I can't remember exactly when that opened. I'm guessing that it could have been 2001. It wasn't there all of the time; it got developed. At one point in time we used to use the room that was *Zig-Zags*, as part of the club."

Rita recalls: "I had left the fruit machine company that I was a junior partner in. Edward said: 'How about helping me to promote my clubs? We'll do fashion shows and all sorts of things – anything that you can think of. I'd like you to come in, just for a few weeks before Christmas.' Before that I'd only seen him in social situations, at parties and so on. But when I worked for him, for those eight-to-twelve weeks, it hit home just how many hours a week he *did* put in; how much administration there was to deal with. How he dealt with eight or nine clubs; staff problems, stocking levels and everything that goes with it, I just don't know. But he did.

Dave Juste recalls: "On my advice, he bought a club, by Birmingham Town Hall. It was formerly known as *Notes*, and was still trading. Eddie renamed it the *Xposure Rock Café*. We realised that there was nowhere for the Punks or Rockers to go: nobody wanted to know them, so he provided that new venue for them. He always seemed to be one step ahead and keeping up with the trends. Even though at that time he was probably in his late fifties, he was still always looking for a niche in the market, then he would provide. So his foresight was just amazing!" concludes Dave.

I bought three seventeen-seater mini coaches, to ferry people from *Xposure* to *XL's*.

Rita observes: "Something else that I always admired about Edward was that he always looked absolutely immaculate. Even when Nick was dying, he very much wanted to see Edward. He knew that the end was near. Edward was down in Ross-on-Wye. I phoned him and said: 'I know that this is tough, but Nick really wants to see you – he wants to say good-bye.' Edward came over and he looked as if he was going to a wedding – he looked so immaculate that day. So he drove up from Ross-on-Wye and he spent about an hour with Nick and was very tearful when he left.

"I went round to Edward's when they'd just returned from a World Cruise," continues Rita. "He went with Don and Don's girlfriend Nina. Eddie told me that he went 'cold turkey': he threw all of his tablets overboard and stayed in his cabin for about three days; shaking, sweating, being sick; feeling so ill, but he was determined that he was not going to continue taking medicine for the rest of his life... I don't know whether that was wise or not. But he came back off that cruise and spent time thinking what he was going to do with his life. I know that he felt dreadfully lonely, but he was always pleased to see me, and many times cooked me a sausage sandwich.

"He was with Marleen at the time. They lived together for a long time, before they got married. Edward lived at Rodman Close because he was near to all of his businesses. He sold the clubs, but then one day he said: 'Bab I'm going back to work.' I said: 'You never are! What's the point? You don't need the cash.' He said: 'No, but I need something to do with my mind, as well as my body. If you think that I worked not only during the day but at night as well, for probably forty years. Okay, I can go and play golf, or out to dinner, but after a time that gets dead boring. I've *got* to have something to occupy my mind.' *XL's* had gone bankrupt. Previously called *Faces*, it already had the *XL's* name, when Edward bought it. So he bought this empty club, which had been closed down for some time.

"I went into *XL's* once," continues Rita, "and there was a man on his knees, repairing one of the radiators in Reception. I suddenly realised that it wasn't a plumber, it was Eddie. I used to take my father, who's sadly now deceased, to the club and Edward would be in the kitchen, with his apron on, cooking! So I've got to say: 'Edward, you do a really good meal.' He's cooked for me on a few occasions.

"*Zig-Zags* was the restaurant part of *XL's*: he converted that into a busy little venue. He told me that he'd got his eye on a club at Merry Hill; he'd done a deal on that and he was putting forward his planning application to make it into a nightclub. Because he'd been over to Merry Hill and thought 'there's nothing on that side of town; they could do with a nightclub.'"

Dave Juste actually found the premises for that club too. We demolished the club side of it completely, but kept the pub side.

"Low and behold, because it had got a great big car park and he managed to get his planning applications, he opened *Club Millennium*, which was a vast club," continues Rita. "I went to the opening night. Again, it became very successful. He must have been in his sixties by then. So he also did a fantastic job in his later years – and it was only for something to do!"

Stephen Hands recalls: "Eddie opened a new group of clubs, from around 1992 onwards, after a three-year absence. I had a pub-restaurant in Wordsley, Stourbridge, and the guy I used employ, Greg, used to go to *Millennium*. By that stage I was into my thirties and not interested in that sort of lifestyle any more. So I can't really comment on any of his later clubs. By this time the Multinationals had captured the majority of the market; they owned most of Broad Street, there were very few independent players around. The Fewtrell name didn't have the same power that it had in those days. There was that much more choice."

Kenny Hatton returned to work for me again, when I had *XL's*. "I started there, just after he'd opened it, then I left *Old Royal* and went to work at the *Xposure Rock Café*. He had that and *XL's*," explains Ken. After that, he had the cigarette business, with the cigarette vending machines. I left *Xpose* and went to work on the cigarette vending machines, with Nobby Nobbs. I still run the cigarette business now. I'm the only one left with him now, with them closing all the clubs and everything.

"Going back to *XL's*, at Five Ways, Eddie had a little room downstairs there. I don't know… there was nothing there! There was a wall… and the next day he said 'I'm going to make a cloakroom out of that and an office.' You'd come in and the wall's gone; there's an office and a cloakroom in its place and you'd say: 'How the bloody hell has he done that?' He'd say: 'We'll knock that wall down there, take part away; make that section bigger' – and so on. I mean, you'd expect a top architect or someone like that to come and do all of this... which would take months. But no – he'd decide for himself how it would be done, and it would be done quickly. When he had the rock club – *XL's*, you probably had a few people coming in with drugs at that stage. This would be four or five years ago; but he would never stand anybody with drugs.

"You could always go to any one of Edward's clubs: you could have a good night and be safe, especially the girls – he wouldn't stand any nonsense – of fellas upsetting the girls, or taking liberties with them, because they would be out, straight away. And that's why his clubs were so popular. Everybody knew that they could go there, have a great time, enjoy themselves; spend their money, come home, and they'd be there again the following night."

Unfortunately, Richard Walker sacked Dave Juste, when I was ill, so that was the end of the Rock Club at *XL's*.

According to Phil Upton: "Another reason for Eddie's success was that he could put personal taste to one side, and just see what made business sense. So as long as we were taking money at the bar and had people on the dance floor, that worked. The same thing applied when he opened *Club Millennium* in 1996, when I went back to work for him. I was there for five years. We had a really good time when we launched that club in Dudley. Again, he was the only game in town. It was a super club – we had two thousand people in on the weekends. It was a totally DJ-driven nightclub, so we didn't have live acts there. He knew that that wouldn't have worked up there – and he was right; it wouldn't have done. We filled that club, at Merry Hill, on Friday and Saturday nights, for five years. That was a very brave move, because he was a Birmingham guy, and he was treading all over other peoples' territory there, in Dudley. There was a lot of hostility from the locals round there, when the club opened.

"He was providing a much-needed venue: the nearest club of that kind was *Goldsmith's*, which was in the middle of Dudley Town Centre. They closed that down. There was the *Robin*, the *Robin 2*; all of these were live music venues, but there wasn't an out-and-out nightclub. Bear in mind that it's 1996; the *Ministry of Sound* is huge, *Gatecrasher* is huge – all these big worldwide dance venues.

"The *Ministry of Sound* came out of the Elephant and Castle, and is now famous world-wide. The *Ministry of Sound* in London is a tourist attraction now – it's full of Japanese tourists! It's a nightclub, but it's also a fashion label too – all spawned out of a successful nightclub. The same for *Cream* – they even have their own Compilation CDs. These are all big businesses now.

"*Millennium* was, apparently, the most successful of Eddie's clubs – financially. It was absolutely packed out; it would be just a road block: queuing by half past ten. In that part of the world, when it opened, it was a revolution. Eddie had the foresight to use that property. Customers from that area no longer had to travel into the city centre. It was just across the road from the Merry Hill Shopping Centre. I only left there in 2001 because that's when I became a dad. My son was born in 2001 and I couldn't keep trekking over there and staying until three o'clock in the morning. So that's when I stopped working for him.

"A further reason for Eddie's success was that he built up a very loyal inner circle of people around him: Gianni Paladini, for example – look at what he'd doing now. There was an old guy who we always used to know as Luigi, aka 'Gigi', described in an earlier chapter. I can remember walking into Eddie's office and Luigi was still in there; it was like – you're not working, you're not drawing any money, but you're still here."

People knew that when they went into my clubs I would give them a very warm welcome; often using their Christian names and their wife or partner's, making them feel very much at home. In fact, my advisor would be standing next to me, whispering in my ear, reminding me who was who. Two minutes later, I'd probably forgotten the client's name, but the overall effect was to create the impression that I knew everyone in the club!

"Yes, so it was all part of the charm offensive. It's something that politicians have now," observes Phil. "People always said that as soon as you walked into the room, Bill Clinton would make you feel like you were the only person in the room. There might be forty thousand people around you, but when he spoke to you, it was just like 'you and me' – 'But we must move on – lovely to see you!'"

Becky and her husband John Moon, my son-in-law, attended a Cancer Charity Night, before they started dating. It was in 1998, and was organised by Chrissie; sadly, he died from the illness, the following year, in August 1999. John and Becky originally met through working with John's sister.

"I worked with Becky Moon," explains Rebecca. "She was first taken on to work at dad's club, *Club Millennium*. She worked there for a couple of years, but there wasn't much for her to do there, so dad brought her over to work with me at *XL's*. I needed more workers in the office there, as he was buying more and more clubs. Also, lots of other businesses – like block paving. He had a Security company too. So Becky came to work with me in the office. As we were both called Rebecca it could become very confusing. People used to phone up and we'd say: 'Well which one would you like to talk to?' So I met John through Becky. I used to go to her house and Becky became a very close friend; she's probably my closest friend now. So we were both Becky Moons, when I married John on 7 September 2002."

On a sad note, Rebecca remembers: "When my mum was really ill and was dying with cancer, Val Bevan went to see her in hospital and brought her some clothes. Even when she was really ill, you couldn't really tell, because she still looked really glamorous, although she had lost a lot of weight. She died on 5 August, 2003."

According to Dave Juste, "Steve and I eventually left *XL's* in 2003. We were offered the opportunity to do Saturday nights at the *Academy*. We decided, because of an article that we had seen in the Birmingham Evening Mail – that the Five Ways Shopping Centre, in Auchinleck Square, was all going to be knocked down and redeveloped. Also, the two people who were running the club for Eddie were negligent at best; taking advantage of the situation. Eddie was severely ill again, and in my opinion, they were taking advantage of the situation. There was a possibility that within a year, we were going to be out of work anyway. So we decided to jump, rather than be pushed and went to the *Academy*. *XL's* actually ceased trading on 2 May 2003. I went to Auchinleck Square the other week, for the first time in ages. A lot of the premises are shut. I can't see anybody opening shops in there – let's put it like that. It's only a matter of time before that goes, because it is very out-of-date."

Marleen explains: "Eddie became ill for a second time, in 2003, but only a couple of his friends phoned up. One of them had heard that he was ill and he was very sorry... and Gianni Paladini phoned up too."

There were other factors too, which contributed to this second nervous breakdown. I was in the clinic for a couple of months.

"I used to go off at three o'clock in the afternoon and come home at one o'clock in the morning, that second time," Marleen continues. "I did that every single day, for the two months that he was in the clinic. Nobody else knew that he was in there, except me, Bomber and Tommy and Paddy Lynch. Mum also came over to help me, because nobody would help me with Edward. He was at the same place, both times – the Woodbourne Clinic. When he became ill, *Club Millennium* got taken away."

According to my accountant's records, *Club Millennium* ceased trading on 2 May 2003, which corresponds with the time of my second breakdown. My two breakdowns were thirteen years apart. I have known Paddy and Tommy Lynch, who are brothers, since I opened the *Bermuda Club*.

"I phoned his brother, Bomber," continues Marleen. "I was really upset; I was in tears, because I couldn't cope. Bomber phoned Paddy Lynch up, who I'd never ever met. Paddy's the sweetest guy you could ever wish to meet. He came to the house, picked Edward up and managed to get him into the Clinic. He used to sit with him all day, until I arrived, then I would take over from there. I will be forever grateful to Paddy, and love him to bits, for helping me so much. Bomber was the only brother who came to see him, because he had to come over from Thailand; he saw Edward when he was being released. Edward didn't want anybody to know that he was in there. He didn't even tell the children," recalls Marleen. "They had no idea that he was in there."

Chapter Eighteen

AND THEN THERE
WERE FOUR

Sadly, of the original eight brothers, only four remain: Eddie, Johnny, Gordon and 'Bomber' – Roger Alan Fewtrell. Eddie remembers the four brothers whom the family have lost… Frank, Kenny, Chrissie and Don.

My brother, Frank, was in the army, out in Hong Kong, when he developed peritonitis – his appendix burst in his stomach. He actually *died* at the Royal Naval Hospital, in Hong Kong, which was right at the top of a mountain. They got him back to life again. The Red Cross were going to fly my mother over, but she was too ill to go, so they sent me – I was sixteen, so that was in 1948. I travelled all the way over there in a British Overseas Airways Argonaut. It was the first land plane that they put on, because they were all seaplanes at the time. The engine kept seizing up, so we kept getting grounded!

I came back on one ship and he came back as well. When he came back he was about four or five stone – a total wreck. We brought him back and nursed him. My mother died in October 1953, so there was just me, Frank and my father. My father was out, more or less all the time, but he would appear at ten or eleven o'clock at night, absolutely drunk out of his head; that's how he'd become. He was like that when my mother was alive, but after she died, he just became a total wreck.

As you know from earlier chapters, Frank and I used to go out together, working in the markets. I continued to look after him, because he was very frail. I'd take him to the casinos and all the rest of it. Then eventually, he got stronger, so we increased our work at the markets and with travelling shops and selling a range of goods. In time we changed to selling cars. We became partners in *F & E Motors*, and then opened our first nightclub together, in 1957, which was the *Bermuda Club*.

Frank was quite small; if anything he was smaller than me – like 'Bomber'. He had a fantastic personality. People used to like him. Although he was older than me, he was my friend. We used to go out together every night. In due course, we sold the *Bermuda* and I bought the *Cedar Club*, on Constitution Hill, on the site of an old factory. I had to sell the *Bermuda Club* because I couldn't go to court any more times; they said they'd lock me away for ever, so I had to get away from that!

Although he'd come out of the club business, Frankie used to come in the *Cedar Club* all the time. I'd put him in games as a croupier and so on. The night he died, he'd been playing for himself in a game of *Brag*, at the club, until about five o'clock in the morning. There was me, Frankie, Alan Wyant, Frankie Knight and Norman Robinson. We were the group who used to play all of the time, on our own; when everybody had gone home. My brother Frankie went what you call 'lights out': he lost everything and he said: "Well, that's the mortgage gone!" He had no money at all, so I gave him £100 and off he went. I said: "I'll see you tomorrow." That was about 4am.

Anyway, about an hour later I had a phone call at home saying to get over to Frank's place straight away, because he'd died in the bath. I drove over there, picking my own doctor up on the way, because I didn't know at that time that he was actually dead. I still thought that we might be able to help him, but apparently, he'd just collapsed in the bath and died. He didn't die of a heart attack; the veins in his arms had clogged up and the blood couldn't get through. But my doctor told me that if he'd have had more time, he might have been able to save him. He'd died in the bath, which had been in front of the fire. I don't think this other doctor of Frank's bothered. Had we got there in time, *my* doctor might have got him back. So that was that. He was only thirty-eight when he died.

But of all of my brothers, he was my best friend – I worked with him all of the time. He should have been a half-owner in the club, if he hadn't asked to withdraw from the business, at his wife's request, I did give him a very good job – more so than all the rest – and he was working at the *Cedar Club* up until he died.

My brother, Gordon, remembers: "The night Frank died he was also playing with me, at the Roulette Table. He asked me to get his leather coat. I made some remark about him rubbing his arm. Norman Robinson took him home. I went to bed. The next morning, I got a call from Eddie, around

9.30am, to say that Frank had died. Apparently, he'd been kneeling with his back to the fire. Vera and one of their sons had been rubbing his back, but Frank just dropped over and died."

Kenny was the oldest son, who we first mentioned in Chapters One; funnily enough, he didn't look anything like a Fewtrell! We'd have these gaps of three or four years between seeing him. I only just got to Vegas when I got a message from Hazel telling me that Kenny had died of pneumonia, in Sutton Coldfield hospital. He was sixty-odd at the time. The funeral was the next day, so Hazel and Daniel went, and represented me at the funeral, although I did pay for it.

Most our family has been cremated and their ashes have been interred at Perry Barr Crematorium. That includes both of my parents, and Chrissie and Donald. The only one who's been buried is Frankie, in a plot that I own in Handsworth Wood; all the rest have been cremated. So that was a few years ago that Kenny died. I came back from Vegas and found that my wife had been having an affair.

Moving on to Chrissie, he began to work for me as a young boy, from when he was fourteen. He first came to work for me in the *Cedar Club*: I had him on glass collection, because I couldn't have him behind the bar. As he got older, I put him on the door, because Chrissie was a very strong fighter; he was absolutely fearless. I mean I'm fearless, but he was *too* fearless, in some respects. But my main concern, with all of my brothers, was controlling them. The fact was, that having my brothers working for me, taught me to calm down and do a lot more talking, because had I got too wound up, they'd have done the same. I *had* to control them; otherwise things might have got out of hand.

Chrissie absolutely idolised me, so if he thought anybody was crossing me, he'd get very annoyed; so would Bomber. It's funny with brothers: you think you're doing all you can for them, but somehow or other, because they're your brothers, they tend to think that they should have everything that you've got too. They don't realise that you've risked your marriage and everything else, to build these things up; all they can see is what you've got now. In the early years, I was working all hours to make a living. We'd hardly any money, so my wife Hazel was keeping me, at one stage: working in an insurance office to make ends meet.

Pat Roach had known Chrissie since he was a young boy; they were good friends. The strangest part is that Chrissie, Roger and Gordon were all lovely kids, who idolised me, because I more or less brought them up, as children. They did everything that I told them, you know? I used to advise them about what to do and what not to do, and they'd listen to my advice. It's the same old story again. As they met their wives....

I explained in Chapter Nine how we introduced Chrissie to Paulette, who was Johnny Prescott's girlfriend. I used to go out to boxing matches with Paulette and Johnny and with his manager George Biddle. We'd go to all the fights. Johnny was up-and-coming and he worked for me on the door, at the *Bermuda Club*. Johnny was a regular customer at the *Bermuda Club* and my friend, as well. When he became famous poor old Paulette was somehow left out.

We were very friendly with her. She had mainly just worked in a shop, but in time we had her working behind the bar in the *Cedar Club* so that she could meet somebody else. The first one who got involved with her was our Chrissie. He really took to her and they both started going out together; he was falling in love with her. But Johnny kept away from the *Cedar Club* after that – for quite some time.

Eventually, Chrissie married Paulette; they divorced later and Lisa Delmain, a singer with the *Second City Sounds*, became his second wife. I didn't mess with any of the staff, because I'd already done that and I wasn't going there again – I had to confess to it in the end, because everybody was blackmailing me! That was a girl called Angela Morris, from Coventry.

However, Chrissie idolised Lisa and loved the fact that she was a singer. Unfortunately, she seemed to think she owned the club; she would undermine everything that I did. I was in the club one night and all of a sudden Hazel walked in, which was unusual. She'd been out with Paulette at *Barbarella's* – and Chrissie was there as well, you see?

Eventually the situation became so bad that I had to ban her from *Barbarella's*, so Chrissie said that he wouldn't be coming there either.

So I moved Chrissie down to *Boogie's*. Lisa wasn't working in any capacity whatsoever, but she was always in there. I realised that her band the *Second City Sound* was costing us something like £500 a week, although their particular sound wasn't suitable for a disco. It was more like cabaret music for a ship like the *QE2*. So I had to sack Lisa and the band. Lisa had a terrible row with me about it, so Chrissie moved to the *Cedar*, as a paid manager but it was becoming more and more impossible.

Chrissie finally got out of the clubs. He asked me if he could set up with Pat Cowdell and use my venues, which I supported, through boxing matches with Nobby. They put shows on at hotels and all that. They'd promote them in clubs, and you could sell the advertising space in a magazine. I had a magazine called *Night Scene*, so I could do my own advertising.

I fixed Chrissie him up in this promotional job and gave him plenty of backing. I'd sell all the tables for him at the events, because I'd got all my regular customers. Chrissie would do the organising of it, but he would then put boxing on, although he didn't link up with Ron Gray. I did a lot of things with Ron Gray and Nobby Nobbs, who worked on the door for me. We were doing all sorts of different things. Pat Cowdell came in, you see, and he was going to front the boxing side of things. Anyway, Chrissie started up and I contacted the people I'd got in my book, for selling tables to. I more or less used to sell all of the tables, take four or five tables myself and sponsor him, for a couple of grand, to pay for everything. That's the way it went on. Chrissie was doing that, and a bit later on, it turned out that he'd got cancer.

According to Pat Roach, even when Chrissie was very ill with cancer, if you spoke to him on the phone, you couldn't tell that there was anything wrong with him; he was still very sharp mentally. Then he started to suddenly go downhill. There are some really moving descriptions by Pat, about what happened to Chrissie, in Chapters One, Twelve and Seventeen of *Auf Wiedersehen Pat*.

Chrissie's regular doctor treated him for a bad chest and flu and then his friend, who was also a doctor, used to take him to all the boxing matches said: "Come up and see me." He found out straight away that Chrissie had got lung cancer, but this other doctor had been treating him for something else – an absolute and total waste of time. The next thing you know, Chrissie's doing all these things to raise money for cancer charities; everyone was helping him.

Then he died, on Wednesday 18 August, 1999, and I organised the funeral. He was in trouble with his house, so I gave his wife a substantial sum of money, to pay off the mortgage. I'd also paid to have his cancer treated privately. They promised me some new treatment from America, but all of a sudden, the cancer came back. All the expensive treatment did was to keep it at bay for an extra six weeks.

I caught most of the bill, although Bomber paid towards Chrissie's funeral: for the cars and the hearses. Bomber was the only one ever, who put anything to it. I was left with all the catering arrangements and everything, which cost an absolute fortune, because there were thousands there. They were serving food and free drinks, for twenty-four hours. It was at *XL's*. Chrissie had a fantastic turn-out. But even then, I had people having a go at me, about different things.

The strangest thing about it is that I've just been to my brother Don's funeral. Don Parsons' daughter did the Reception for me, at *Berrow Court*, in Harborne. Her father used to run the *Tow Rope* in Broad Street. He just died recently and left *Berrow Court* to her. Apparently, he got three years for bribing the police about speeding tickets and whatnot. He used to pay to have them 'straightened'. The sergeant and the police officer got three years – which they came to see me about. That's how it all started.

Don used to sit in with Chrissie when he was dying and he got talking to a lady there named Denise. Apparently her husband had just died. He'd been a friend of Chris's. Chris got to know here through that. Eventually, over those few weeks, Don got involved with her.

She's a nice lady and they used to go for holidays in Blackpool; weekends out. She used to look after him and phone him every day, but she wouldn't live with him. She didn't want to give up her house and she didn't want to live with Donald. He lived in a tiny bungalow, with only one bedroom. She'd got a son too.

So this went on for seven years and gradually Donald went blind. He'd got diabetes and he went to the doctor's because he couldn't see. He then told him that he'd got diabetes. I'd got Diabetes No. 2 myself, but because I found out much earlier I could do something about it. Anyway, Don was the next eldest to me – (I'm younger than him). I brought him out of where he worked in Coventry. He'd worked there since he was seventeen, got married to Ivy and went to live over in Coventry. He stayed there, away from the family, for years.

Then as I progressed, he came across and asked me for a job. I said: "Well, you can have a job if you want to, but you'll have to come and live over here." He said: "That's alright – I can talk the wife into it." I bought him a house in Handsworth Wood – just where I was. I bought him a Jaguar 38 car and he was like somebody who'd just won the Pools!

The only thing was that Donald was always a bit bombastic – it was his nature. He could be very pig-headed and the brothers didn't like him. He was very hard on them when they were little; whereas I'd looked after them all my life, because I'd promised my mother that I'd look after the kids.

I told Don: "The only reservation I've got about giving you the job is that you're older than me and you might tend to forget that I'm the boss. So whatever you do, don't try to take over." However, he came to work for me at the *Cedar Club*, which you'll have read about, in Chapter Five. Usually, we helped each other when there were problems. Unfortunately, Donald sometimes created problems that were fickle. My older brother, Frank, wouldn't be told what to do by Donald. They'd be fighting all the while – it was so ridiculous!

Eventually I opened *Rebecca's*, and I took all the brothers with me. So he was on his own at the *Cedar Club*, because nobody would stay with him. After a while I had a brother in each club, so that they couldn't fall out with each other! Then they all got married. Eventually, a club called *Pollyanna's* came up for sale. It was a restaurant owned by Johnny Hunt, but he'd gone skint. He phoned me up and I agreed to buy it. I named it *Gilly's*, after a bar in America, owned by Frank Sinatra. I'd had all the printing done and everything. People used to think that Donald had named it after his daughter, but it was my idea, as I've explained.

So all of a sudden Donald came to me and said: "You've bought a club restaurant haven't you? Why don't you give me a chance? I've got somebody who'll go into it with me. His name's 'Big Geoff'." I agreed, because I thought it would solve all the problems I'd been having, with the young kids who were working with him. I gave him a few quid and let him have a go with the place. I never charged him rent or anything.

But he ordered everything from the brewery using my name. So I had to actually have an article printed in the *Birmingham Mail*, saying that Edward George Fewtrell, owner of all the clubs et cetera, had nothing to do with Donald Fewtrell.' My accountants advised me that I had to issue a public statement like that; otherwise I would have been responsible for all his debts. It had to be done in the press, you see? I had to do it, under instructions from my solicitor and accountant.

Pollyanna's was in Newhall Street. Don ran it for a while. He got involved with Nina and went all over the place with her. She was Greek. All of a sudden Don decided to sell *Pollyanna's* and went to Spain. He eventually came back, potless, having sold his villa over there. Nina followed him back.

Don made a will, leaving several thousand pounds to Denise. He told me that no way were his son and daughter having anything. His daughter, allegedly, hadn't seen him for yonks; his son hadn't seen him for eighteen months. According to what he told me, they'd done nothing to help him at all, so he wanted Denise to have everything – he wanted me to arrange everything. But when the police found the body, they called his daughter. She immediately took possession of the house keys, which they then cleaned out. No will was found.

I had Don down here three or four times, and I used to speak to him every day on the phone. All the time he was saying: "I've had enough. I want to be out of here." All the time he was talking suicide. I asked our Phyllis to go and see him. I asked Gordon to take him to see Violet. Phyllis went to see him and cooked him meals. When I went over I took him some things.

The last twelve months of course, I've been in and out of hospital myself, so I couldn't go there so much. I could tell how stressed out he was; I'd be talking to him for hours, on the phone. Then eventually, every day was: "I've had enough. I've had enough." I kept telling Denise about it. The doctor, apparently, was giving him the wrong medicine. When I talked to Denise she'd say: "I'm fed up with him moaning."

I spoke to him the one day, then the next thing I know, I got a phone call from Bomber, in Bangkok, telling me that Don had taken his own life. I said: "Well how do you know, before me?" Apparently, Don's daughter hadn't even got my phone number. She phoned Bomber, thinking that it was Johnny's number, to get my number. Bomber then rang me. Denise found him at five o'clock. As she screamed, the next-door-neighbour then phoned the police.

The next thing was that we needed some kind of Wake. I asked the brothers to give me some support. I took it upon myself to print the cards. I invited two or three hundred people to *Berrow Court*, in Harborne, for the Reception afterwards, and they all came back. Gordon, John and I were bearers. So Don had a good funeral. I think it's what he wanted, in the end – to be out of it…when he realised that he would be totally blind.

Chapter Nineteen

THE SINGING STUD

Eddie and Marleen have been breeding thoroughbred and Trakehner horses for over twelve years. They currently have approximately 70 horses, with several foals on the way, at any given time. The September 2006 issue of Horse & Hound described how they have become the first UK breeders to produce an English Graded Trakehener stallion, in seven years. Marleen and Eddie talk about their Singing Stud business and their future plans.

I first got involved with horses some years ago, when I met a girl, just six weeks before my final divorce papers came through. As you'll know by now, her name was Marleen – and she was Danish. Her ambition was to have horses. I found her a little horse to ride and that's how she started. Funnily enough, the horse was going along one day and it just dropped dead of a heart attack. So I thought: 'Well that's nice!' So I bought her another one – with the insurance money from the first one. It was supposed to be really special, but funnily enough, it jumped over a fence and killed itself! So I wasn't having very much luck, with horses. That particular horse was 'mental'. You get crazy horses and good horses. So we'd begun with a heart attack horse and a crazy one!

Although I'm not professional, I've ridden a few horses, in my lifetime. I knew a gypsy guy called Johnny Cairo; he used to tie himself up, down the Bull Ring, with a chain, in a sack. Then he'd escape in no time at all. So we all went off to Torremolinos, in Spain, where I had a club. We went up into the mountains. There were six of us and we'd got these six horses out. I wanted the one with the big Spanish saddle, because it gave me more to hold on to. I jumped on that. I wasn't frightened of horses, although one or two of them had taken me back home to the stable, when I got on them.

So I'm sitting there. All of a sudden, Johnny Cairo takes the saddle off his. What we didn't realise was that he was on the Lead Horse. So he whips up his horse. Off it goes, straight across the field and... guess what? The other five horses followed it! So they're galloping down the mountain area and I'm holding onto this big bloody saddle... for my bloody life! I should have tied myself to the saddle – do you know what I mean? I thought I was definitely going to come off it – I couldn't keep on!

Anyway, we got to the bottom of the mountains and Cairo started going up the mountains, on these very narrow paths – all the way. The other horses were following him, and I'm about third. There was a great big drop – so I was petrified! I thought: 'This horse is going to fall off any minute,' but they don't – funnily enough. So I'm going up this mountain and all of a sudden I come to a little part where there was some ground, passing over, so I jumped off. They all carried on but then everybody else started jumping off. But Cairo still went up.

They all came down again, got back on their horses, although no way was I getting back on mine! But the horse scarpered back and left me on my own. They shouted: "We'll send somebody back for you!" So I walked back down the mountain then spent the next half hour trying to get back on my horse – but it wouldn't let me on.

The next thing I know, it's getting dark and this guy comes up on horseback with a bit of twig. He got off his horse, held my horse and said: "Get on. Now hold on tightly." I said: "I don't want to go fast." He said: "No, you won't." He showed my horse this twig. It reared up on its hind legs and galloped back at *three* hundred miles an hour! We reached the end, and as it took me into the stables I just happened to duck; otherwise it would have knocked me straight off.

I said: "I'll never get back on a horse, as long as I live!" So that was that, but then I got involved with horses. Bought Marleen these couple of horses – came unstuck. Then I found one, which was a nice horse, and she kept that. That's how she started off. Most of them were coloured, thoroughbred horses. We used to breed them and sell them – quite easily. Advertise them in the papers; no problem at all.

Then we went into the higher class horses – Trakehners. We still have Gypsy out in the field there. The Trakehener horses are German and amongst the finest horses that there are. Now we've been breeding them; we've bred some of the champions. We've just had a stallion graded – the first time in England for seven years. We bred it, Woodcroft trained it and it's passed all the grading. We were featured in *Horse & Hound*, because of that. We've won the championship, five years on the trot. The Germans say that we've now got one of the best herds in the world. At the moment, we're waiting for the children of Chabrol, the stallion that I bought in Germany. All those children: we're training another six now. They reckon that they'll be worth a fortune.

We've been doing this for over twelve years and now have the biggest stud in England. At the moment we have around seventy horses. Those are growing up and being trained. We've got something like twelve to fourteen mares in foal right now. They're in foal with some of the finest stallions there are. The next 'crop' of children of Arentino's... all the details are on our website: *www.singingtrakehner.co.uk*.

The Singing Stud Limited is the company that Marleen and I run together. She had a similar dream, when she was a little girl. Marleen continues the story...

"When I was a little girl I dreamed about having my own place. My original plan was to have a few Rescue Donkeys, a few Rescue Horses; a few dogs and a few cats that had been rescued. I imagined that it would be in Denmark. I had a job offer in Holland, to be a Private Secretary, for this guy who used to provide my dad with big machinery. My father used to sell on machines that had cameras attached to them, which were put down sewers, to find where blockages were; and big high pressure machines. They used to swill out systems. He bought them and sold them on to companies, who went out and did jobs like that.

My family home in Denmark was just a normal house – like anybody else might have. It wasn't a farm, where horses could be kept. No one in the family was into horses either. But, apparently my mum put me on a horse when I was four – and that was it! She had to take me for lessons all of the time, because I just wanted to ride. So I don't remember anything different to that.

I always wanted one or two horses, and I wanted thoroughbreds – Trakehners. I didn't read books or magazines about them; the knowledge just came to me as I grew up. As far as breeding goes I got the first thoroughbred mare and we put her out to foal, with a local stallion, but she died from a heart attack, as Edward has explained. So I lost the foal and mare, which was really sad.

I was living at the White House, in Bodenham, with Jenny. It was probably '92 or 93 actually – it goes back that far. I was sad at losing the mare, so the dealer where she was kept sold me his coloured mare, who I named *Gypsy* – that's how I got my first brood mare. Then it just went on from there. We went to an auction and bought a thoroughbred mare, which was in foal and that was our first to be foaled. I was living in a flat in Ross by this time. She jumped the gate and broke her neck, so I lost her and the foal. I quite missed her; she was a big chestnut mare. Then I got a Polish warm blood mare; she is still here, at the age of twenty. That's when we went out and got the first Trakehner really and it just escalated from there.

So we had Trakehners before we moved in here, at Hillington Barn. The stud really started in Ross-on-Wye. We've always kept our horses down the yard at Much Marcle. We were looking for a house, for some time, but when I found something that I thought was quite nice then Edward wouldn't like it, for some reason, and vice versa. Then we'd go out and look at something else. It carried on like that for a while. We often drove past this barn and thought: 'That would be nice – one day it might come up for sale', but other people were interested in it too. Then our friend Reg, who is a farmer down the road, phoned me up one day. We'd just come back from holiday. He said: "Marleen, that place up on top of the hill is for sale. That would be a really nice place for you and Edward, if you're interested." So I rang Edward up to see if he could arrange for us to see it.

He says that he did a good deal, but he was actually a bit optimistic. We never knew how much work was involved because Edward just bought it, there and then. I was waiting for him to arrange a weekend when we could go and have a look at it. You couldn't drive up here at the time, because of the state of the drive. We would have had to walk up here. Then he phoned me back three hours later and said: "I've bought it!"

I was so upset; I really was, because we've always gone to look at things together. If we didn't both like it, then we never bought it. We've always been like that. Even the things in the house: if one of us isn't keen on it, then it doesn't enter the door. Even clothes actually."

Of course, I was initially buying the 100 acres as an investment, because I believe that owning land is better than money in the bank. If Marleen hadn't liked it, I could have developed the property and sold it on at a profit.

"We've done really well with the Trakehners," continues Marleen. "We've had a Champion every single year that we've been showing them. And we have a First-graded stallion, which only 2-4% in the world are graded as, out of the colts born that year. So that's something like first out of four hundred.

Ours is definitely the biggest single Trakehner Stud in the UK. In my opinion, we have some of the best quality in the country. If the other breeders read that they'd probably get really upset, but we've been told by the Germans that our herd is of the highest quality. It's because of the quality of the mares that we bring in. On the stallion front, we've got some very good boys in bloodline too.

The reasons that we've been so successful are, firstly, I've got a husband who doesn't mind spending money to get the best, so I can get good quality mares. I've read an awful lot up on Bloodlines too. The other thing is taste as well. When we've been to auctions in Germany, I tick off the horses that I like, and I've found time and time again that it's the same bloodlines that I've been falling for. So there was a lot of reading up and learning. I think I've been able to therefore weed out what is not suitable for us, explains Marleen."

We should also add here that we have the best team in the country, working alongside of us. There is Kim, together with Susan and her daughter, Clare. Peter, from Hungary, is one of the best horse trainers in Europe. We also have our own special vet, who is brilliant!

"In the early days," continues Marleen, "we certainly made some mistakes, buying in horses that we shouldn't have bought. I can't really blame Edward, but he's like: 'Oh buy, buy, buy! I'm getting old. I'm going to die soon and you'll never get going.' It's not necessarily always what we actually need, but he buys it, because he feels we need to move on. But we've sold most of those off now, and we've just got a few more to wean. Success is 75-85% determined by the mares, so as long as you buy the right ones then you're okay. But you never know, unless she's had a foal, that the foal is going to be any good; you have to wait until you get her first foal, to see if it's going to be as good as the mum or dad, or hopefully, even better. But again, it doesn't mean that the second foal will be as good. If it isn't, I sell the mare – she doesn't stay. There's no point in me keeping something that is not breeding what I want.

Our website has been running for about three years, but it needs updating. We have a lot of people logging on to it. I have nearly fifteen hundred hits from America every week and Canada is coming on well now. It's the only way that I get business. Usually, what attracts them to the website is the stallion Arentino, because it is a rather nice picture of him and he is a 'scrummy' – a real gent. But now we're getting mares into stud, literally by word-of-mouth, so that's great – that's what we want. We've got a lot of new clients, just by people talking about us.

Eddie and I are members of the Trakehner Society – which is where people normally go in to look. We've three big stud farms, within the society, and there are probably another five smaller breeders, in Bedfordshire, Sussex – spread across the country. We've also got a new stud starting up, in Stratford-upon-Avon, with ten mares.

When I rented a flat in Ross-on-Wye it was called Brookfields. I didn't want to call the horses Brookfields something, because there's no point in using a name when you're going to move on. You use the name as a prefix, so when your foal is born you put a name, as a prefix, in front of every foal. As you sell the foal on, those people who buy it promise to keep the prefix, so people will recognise that it came from the Singing Stud. So it's like an advertisement really. I chose the word 'Singing' because although I sat thinking of other names like Goldrush, Wishing Well and whatever, most of them were taken and they didn't sound too good. Then I was up round the yard, working, and I was singing as I went along. I looked at all of the horses and thought how happy they looked. So I thought: 'When people are happy, they sing,' so that is how 'singing' came along.

My dream, like everyone else in the business, is to breed a horse that will be in an Olympic Team somewhere. At the moment we've got a really good one, so I'm going to try and send it to Denmark. It's a colt, which we're hoping to grade this year. I said to Edward: "We'll send them to Denmark and get the Danish riders on them." Then it would become a Danish National.

Edward is a hardworking person, and a gentleman. He always thinks about everybody else accept himself. He's kind and generous. That's how I know him, but I know that there's another side of him, because I heard about that, from people who used to work with him. But I know he's never hit a woman in his life – ever… because he hates people who do that. He really does. And whatever else has happened to Edward in his life, he has never forgotten his roots.

Although I think Edward has come to terms with living in the country, he is *definitely* a city person. When I met him it was all about being around thousands of people – towns, busy places. He likes smart things too – and nice clothes. Anything money can buy – Five Star Hotels. He won't admit it, but he does! Me – I like to stay with my family. I hate wearing my rings. None of my friends have them, so I feel really bad about that. If we've got to go out he likes me to wear them, but I don't like anything ostentatious. He'd like me to sell my Honda. He tried to give me a new car for my thirtieth birthday. He came down with a really smart Mercedes. But I told him I didn't like it and I wanted to keep my Honda. He got really upset! It was a £100,000 car, or more, and I wanted to keep my little Honda, which was also new at that time. I feel really comfortable with it; it's about twelve or thirteen years old now, and it's also very practical.

Sometimes I upset people a lot, because I tend to say what comes into my head. But I think you should. Why lie to people? When Eddie tells a story, for example about some huge fish he caught, I'm going: "Excuse me, but that wasn't how it happened!" He gets so upset because I ruin some of his stories, but I think that you should tell stories exactly how they happened. I used to lie to my mum, as a kid, and she always used to say to me: "You might as well stop telling lies, because it shows in your face." And I've never done it since – I don't bother – there's no point...except for maybe a fib or two. I like the countryside – I really do. I like being out here when there are no people; I could quite happily live on my own... I'm one of those people.

My twin sisters were only seven years old when I moved over here, so I haven't really had much to do with them really, but I do love to be with my family. We always used to be up in Norway as kids, where there's some beautiful nature. I always wanted to have a log cabin in Norway and live by a lake. We had no electricity or stuff like that. The loo was outside... I could even do that now, but there's no way that Edward could.

I miss my family a lot too. I don't know whether it's because I'm getting older. I'm missing out on all the birthdays and other events. They meet up once a fortnight for dinner – all the family: the boyfriends, husbands, children; they all go to mum's. So I'm not there – I'm missing every fortnight. But I visit them sometimes – I spent three weeks in Denmark just recently. Mum comes over here too – she's very good.

My family are very happy as they are. We're very close-knit and we've never felt that we have to pretend to be someone that we're not. You don't have to be with someone to be somebody; just to be us is enough. That's why

I'm so happy living here. I just go and do my own thing. But I think that Edward misses the showbiz life," observes Marleen.

I don't actually miss the showbiz *life*, but I *do* miss the live shows. Just mentioning the name of a group or a band brings it all back! The downside was the effect that it had on my family. It became like a roller-coaster. It was difficult to keep up with the lifestyle. I was highly successful in a professional sense, but then that has to be contrasted with my personal life, to get a realistic picture. I never wanted to go back to my original, poverty-stricken life, so I put tremendous effort into my work – becoming a workaholic, I suppose.

"He still is," acknowledges Marleen. "Edward can't settle down without doing anything. When we go away on holiday, we'll be relaxing on the sun-beds, nice and quiet. But by the third day he suddenly screams... it's quite a shock, when he does! 'I've got to go and phone Kenny!' And off he goes, with this new idea... of how to get more money into the club. If we have ten or maybe fourteen days, he goes: 'When is it we're leaving Marleen? When are we going home?' But he needs to get away, to come up with new ideas. When he was in his clubs, he couldn't distance himself from all the different problems that kept coming in and out. He didn't get the time to think." concludes Marleen.

Becky's husband, John Moon, is a great help. He drives down here quite often, to help me with various jobs. Yesterday, I've had my two cars out of the garage, the Brabus and the Jag, for the simple reason that I've built a gym in there. Yesterday, in all that rain, I moved everything out of the garage and put the cars back in. The Singing Stud is a full time occupation for us both – at the moment.

Chapter Twenty

NEW HORIZONS

A selection of our contributors summarise Eddie's life and possible reasons for his success. Although Eddie continues to be the main narrator, I've also added a few paragraphs of my own, about the show, Brum Rocks Live, and a summary at the end.
At seventy-five years of age, there's still no stopping Eddie!

Alan Wyant comments: "Eddie is a Natural... to make money. It must be something in the blood, because his old man, George, was in the buying and selling business. As Eddie made money, he would plough it back in – to make more. When he first opened the *Cedar* it was just a narrow part of a factory, but then he bought the building next door and knocked all the walls down."

According to Les Hemming: "Eddie Fewtrell was a catalyst, an innovator; a charismatic visionary who energised the entertainment industry. I'm sure that this is a common view, held by all of those who have been involved in the music industry in Birmingham, the Midlands, and beyond – all the 'Musos' – that where would we all have been, if it hadn't been for Eddie Fewtrell generating that platform, with his very glamorous places, and the work generated for Birmingham musicians?... who he always paid. That wasn't always true of the other nightclub owners and impresarios.

"It wasn't the prettiest of businesses to be in, but regardless of all the so-called 'Legendary Fewtrells', they ran right and proper places that were very upmarket and attracted good quality people to their door – both to work for them and to be entertained by them. There were some great quality bands around Brum, in those days," Les continues. "Some of them are still working. Bev Bevan's just got *The Move* title back again. with Trevor Burton, also from *The Move*. The *Rockin' Berries* are still going. The bottom line to all of this really, is that anybody who was involved in those exciting times was an absolute load of fun... and it beat doing a day's work. We were in the glamorous world of entertainment...driven by Eddie Fewtrell. Who could wish for more!"

My biographer, Shirley Thompson, comments: "Still on the subject of music, some of the major contributors to our book took part in the *Brum Rocks Live* show, both this year and last. We mentioned the show briefly, in the introduction to Chapter Six. I was in the audience, at *Solihull Library Theatre*, on Tuesday evening 29 May, 2007 – the second of two performances at the same theatre this year. It was a resounding success: one of the most outstanding live ensemble performances that I've ever seen on stage; certainly on a par with the top international musical *Mama Mia*. It's a stage adaptation, about the history of rock n' roll – in and around Birmingham, and features Laurie Hornsby as Narrator.

"The audience was ecstatic and kept shouting for encores, even after the encore itself! There were excellent and highly versatile performances from all the musicians involved, including Danny King, Steve Gibbons, Laurie Hornsby, *Bev Bevan's Move* and Trevor Burton. Trevor also referred to the *Cedar Club*, on stage. Brian Yeates, who staged the show, Laurie Hornsby, Bev Bevan and Steve Gibbons, can all be found here, in Eddie's book. My two favourite items were *Walking the Dog* and *Hey Baby*. The shows are due to be repeated next year, *possibly* on a national basis, and with a new title," Shirley adds. "If you get the chance to see it – don't hesitate!"

Another of our musicians, Froggie, says: "He's a very special human being, Eddie Fewtrell; one of God's special people. If people say detrimental things about him, they don't know him – it's as simple as that. Because every bone is his body is conditioned to being nice to people; that's his natural way. You refer earlier in your book, to his home life, and to looking after people; when you have to do that as a *child*, then looking after a business later isn't really that much to do, in comparison. As you told me, Eddie cleaned the house up and looked after his younger brothers. He would clean the club up and look after his customers, always, so it was just a natural thing for him.

"Apart from that, inwardly, God had given him a wonderful, warm personality. There's a wonderful kindness in Eddie, although he wouldn't have been the success that he's been if he was a fool – and he's not soft either. But you can't get kindness and care mixed up with softness, because that's not what it is. You don't have to be a bully to be kind; you have to be kind and thoughtful. If somebody's giving you grief, then give it to them – our business is like that. You have to fight back," continues Froggie.

"Eddie Fewtrell is one of the very few people that I know in our business, who is totally unaffected by show business... yet he *knows* everybody! Some of the greatest stars in the world Eddie won't even mention to you. But if he sees them, he'll say hello. There were certain times in my career when I had nowhere to live and he gave me a room in one of his homes, until I was called over to America. In that interim time, 'H' Cain had gone to Africa, touring with his family. I was pretty well lost, but Eddie took me under his wing and gave me a home, in one of three houses that he had in Gillott Road, Edgbaston; where he used to house various groups and musicians who were working for him, such as the *Pretty Things* et cetera. Ricky Rickaby lived there permanently, overseeing the whole thing.

"Whatever accolades Eddie ends up with," concludes Froggie, "he'll always have a place in my heart – always. Birmingham Clubland is totally due to Eddie Fewtrell... nobody else at all."

Kenny Lynch recalls: "I had a few nice late nights with Eddie and his brothers, and I knew that I was going to enjoy myself. Eddie was more like family – I can't really say that about anyone else on the nightclub scene. Although I was quite friendly with a few of the wrestlers up in Manchester, I would never phone them up to have a talk, like I would with Eddie – or go and see them.

"He's obviously got a lot of mystery about him. If you talk to him for more than about twenty minutes, you realise that there's a certain amount of skulduggery there – if you know what I mean? And you think: 'Worr – I wouldn't like to get on the wrong side of him!' He knows what he wants – he's one of *those* guys – and he knows how to get it. I used to describe him to Jimmy Tarbuck as the 'Bugsy Segal of Birmingham.' Bugsy was the guy who had the Mafia at the *Flamingo*, in Las Vegas – the first gambling club. He was actually a very evil man... but everybody liked him. He was a George Raft-type character...when Lucky Luciano was in charge. He reminded me of him. Not that Eddie would do things like that – Bugsy killed people!

"Bugsy was in Hollywood and he was a best friend of George Raft and Humphrey Bogart," Kenny Lynch continues. "He was just a big, congenial gangster; but apparently, he had the worst temper – he could snap in seconds.

But Eddie's not like that. Eddie will snap when he *thinks* about things. Eddie always speaks his mind – he tells it like it is – but he enjoys a laugh I've known him for forty years – and I've never had a cross word with him."

Kenny Hatton observes: "Edward walks in and you think: 'Oh God! Who's that?' You *would* be wary of him, if you didn't know him. You'd be careful what you said to him, in case you upset him, by saying the wrong thing. But in fact, you couldn't have found a nicer person than what Edward is. If you needed help, he would be there to help you.

"Edward was not frightened of *anybody*. It could be Pat Roach – it could be anybody. He has really been the only one in Birmingham to make the city what it is today, in terms of nightlife. Now that Broad Street has been taken over, it's entirely different. When he had all the clubs – *Edward's No.7*, *Edward's No.8*; as Broad Street is today, he had the equivalent of Broad Street, with all of his clubs.

"He was successful because he's got such a brain," Kenny Hatton explains. "He's far quicker than anybody else that I've known, for thinking things and doing things and getting things done. I think that he's mellowed now – he really has. I've admired him from the first time that I met him. What he's done and the way he's done things – he's a real entrepreneur... to have come up from the really rough upbringing that he had, when he started in Aston, to running the whole of Birmingham's nightlife – before Broad Street started."

Gianni Paladini comments: "I would say that Eddie' personality is quite complex. Although he's a very sociable person, he's also a shrewd businessman. He doesn't 'suffer fools' and you wouldn't want to cross him. If you do something wrong, he will tell you about it. But Eddie changed my life and for that I will always be grateful. If he gives you a job to do and you don't do it, he won't waste time with you – that's how he made his money. I learned from Eddie that if you have to make a decision, don't take too long ·to make it – and don't worry about it; once you've done it – just move on. And if you think that a person's not fit enough to do a job, then you *must* change them – but don't take too long to do it. All of the people with medals – they are dead. The good people get medals, but they die. You have to be ruthless, but you also have to be fair.

"I would say that Eddie was one of the most important people in my life," Gianni continues. "Obviously, my wife and kids are important to me, but outside of the family, Eddie has been the most influential person in my life. I had the most wonderful time with him. He taught me a lot about the good and bad things in life. He changed me – and made me a different man. When everybody else was earning between £10 and £15 a week, I was earning £100 a week. He changed my life and my lifestyle. I'll always be grateful to him."

My brother, John, makes the point: "Having the name Fewtrell, they thought we were all millionaires… they thought Carrie and I didn't need to run the *Red Lion*, in Shirley. But none of us were wealthy… it was Edward who was the millionaire."

Rita Radvanyi observes: "Edward is an *extremely* strong character. I'm not sure that people always realized that. He's also a very deep thinker. Most of us try to do positive things, but when difficulties come we do tend to throw the towel in. But difficult situations seem to make Edward stronger – and he's had many 'knock-backs'. If he *really* believes in something, he will achieve his goal, no matter what. I've seen it happen to him so many times.

"I worked for him once, for about three months. He would be at the office from about 10.00 or 10.30am and he virtually *ran* from club to club. The phone rang constantly. He used to carry his mobile phone with him. What he dealt with during the day, from 10am 'til 4pm was exhausting. He'd then go home, get washed and changed, have a meal. Then from about 10pm until 5am he'd be at the clubs. How he did it I do not know, because he was a great family man as well; he just *adored* his children. I think he was the most wonderful father – I really do.

"He's just got tremendous business acumen," continues Rita, "What's surprised me, over the years, is that he has changed the format of his clubs so much. We all know that it's the teenagers now who spend the money; they're the ones that have got the cash to go to these discotheques, so he's changed, with the times. So Edward was always one step ahead; I don't know how he ever managed to foresee what was going to be the next 'in thing'. Like when the Punks' came in. We were all shying away from them at the time, but Edward realised that this was the way things were going."

Phil Upton comments: "I still love, even all these years on, and I've progressed through BRMB and what-have-you, how Eddie claims that I would be nowhere without him. Every time I see him – and it might be years since I've seen him – when he introduces me to people, he says: 'This is Phil

Upton here. You know he started with me, don't you?' Every time he introduces me, my age gets younger: 'He was fourteen when he started with me...' 'He was nine when he started with me!' My neck must be red-raw from the number of times he's whacked me on the back of the neck, as he's introduced me to the latest Chief Constable, or whoever it might be, propped up at the end of his bar! But there's something very endearing and warm about Eddie," concludes Phil. "If you were straight with him he'd be straight with you... but woe betide you if you messed around!"

We began this book by explaining that Eddie's life is inextricably linked with the city of Birmingham itself, where he grew up. With regard to the city's future, Stacey Barnfield comments: "Around ten to fifteen years ago, looking at areas like Brindley Place and the Mailbox, it seemed that there were a lot more people spearheading and driving regeneration plans, which was the key to getting things moving. We had these fantastic places emerging, like Brindley Place, the Mailbox – and they cleaned up all the canals; created great social shopping areas. But we don't seem to have that leadership any longer. We seem to have caught something and pushed it forward, but now it's stalled again.

"Other cities have caught up, if not passed us. Liverpool has won the 'Capital of Culture' bid for 2008, next year. That's something that Birmingham pushed for, but didn't quite get. At the moment we just need these kinds of schemes to go ahead. In the newspaper industry, where I work, we hear a lot about them reaching planning level. There are these big schemes that need approval to get them moving. There's a helluva lot of residential development going on in the city. A lot of buildings are being cleaned up, in areas like the Jewellery Quarter. I also think you need the infrastructure of the retailer: the shops, the bars, beside that as well.

"There's an area around Millennium Point where there's going to be huge development. It is a huge swathe of land where they've knocked down a lot of factories. There was talk of moving the Central Library over there, it was going to be a stunning, architecturally-designed building, but the scheme was grounded for a variety of cost and planning issues," continues Stacey. "There are plans for another striking tower in the middle of Broad Street, which will certainly look spectacular but no doubt will contain the usual mix of apartments, a hotel and identikit bars and coffee houses that you would find in any city. What the city really needs is local independent input, which is the way the city was originally created. Places that are unique to Birmingham – *that's* what will bring in tourists."

Before his recent death, Ken Hardeman was the Managing Director of Regeneration and Planning, in Birmingham; one of a ten-man Executive. In March 2007 he described some of those plans to Shirley:

"There are no applications for new nightclubs or anything that is special, in terms of entertainment, but there *will* be development, in areas like the Jewellery Quarter and Digbeth .... Like the Irish Quarter – all around that – and I use the phrase: 'Get the grain right – get the mix right.' There are some fabulous buildings down there that lend themselves to special considerations.

"Birmingham is probably one of the most diverse cities, in its cultural groupings, in the UK. There are different art forms, and music forms... different everything. What I want to create therefore is the 'Incubator Space', where we can encourage those aspects which are less lucrative, in terms of gate money; because the success of the city has to service the diversity of the city. It's no good having a top cabaret club that will only cater for certain people. I can project, with confidence, that future generation in Birmingham will be around the city centre: what is now the Markets; the Digbeth area; the East Side area; right the way through; they are going to become the cultural quarters of Birmingham," Ken explained.

"Eddie's had a charisma about him. He'd got that 'cuddly' type of personality. I regard him as the pioneer of the 1950s, 60s and 70s, in Birmingham Nightlife... the Leader. There are major plans for that left-hand side of Broad Street – (as you're looking down it, with New Street behind you). It will be a Mixed Use Development. It's going to be part of the Calthorpe Estate; that applies to the other side of the road as well. There's going to be a major refurbishment. If I tell you that there are three hundred million pounds-worth for that area alone. Some of that new building might be in place, within the next five to eight years. It has to be judged – in planning terms; then the funding has to be put together.

"On Broad Street," continued Ken, "what used to be the old club, that's boarded, at the moment – Cordwell Richardson, that's going to be an Iconic Tower, with residential retail; again, outlined planning permission has been granted, but at the time of this interview, there's an issue around it. Down where the Registry Office is – next week I'm in Cannes, in the south of France, where a model will be unveiled, of *Arena Central*, which is a fifty-five story building. That's going to go where the Registry Office is – for *Central Television*. There's a five hundred million pound proposal for there.

"Across the other side of the road we've got Baskerville House, which is now office accommodation. The old library is going to be knocked down; the Music Conservatory there is going to be knocked down. There are *amazing* plans for regeneration, for that area. All of this is scheduled to happen within the next five-to-eight years, and so on. The Wholesale Market site around St Martin's Church will be moved eventually, in the not-too-distant-future. They're going to rebuild New Street Station, with a lot more development around that area; it's all going to happen. At the moment I've got, without exaggeration, fourteen billion pounds worth of economic activity going on around the city; eight billion of that is in the city centre.

Ken Hardeman concluded: "I am now a powerful person, in political terms, and Eddie was a powerful nightclub owner, in nightclub terms. We two... you wouldn't have thought there was a synergy between us... but there was."

According to Dave Juste, "Up until the redevelopment of Broad Street, there wasn't really any challenge. Until that point in time Eddie operated out of *XL's Night Club*, because he'd sold all of his other clubs to Ansells. By the time that he came back in, it had all changed. So I don't think that he had the challenges, when I was working for him, which he *did* have in the preceding twenty-five years. Given that Eddie had already achieved that level of success, he'd already become a very wealthy man. If money needed to be spent on the clubs, whether for promotion or developing and refurbishment, he'd already got it; he could spend what was necessary, to keep it that way."

Thanks Dave. I have *Healthstone PLC*, which is a cigarette machine vending company, and still does quite well. My friend, Kenny Hatton, is still doing that. I've still got the *Xpose* premises, in Birmingham, which was a Laptop Dancing Club, but has now closed down. History is repeating itself, because by the end of September 2007, Dave and I will have re-opened a venue for the Rock Club people, in those same premises, but under a new name – *Subside*. The premises belong to me – and 50% of the club. The company *Subside* belongs to Dave Juste, who is also running it. It's located in Fletcher's Walk, Birmingham City Centre, close to the Central Library. So all of you Rockers out there, come along and enjoy it!

As far as personal future's concerned, I have five grandchildren, who will live on, long after I'm 'pushing up the daisies'! Abigail and her husband, Irish musician, Dave Keogh, have two young sons, Connor and Finlay. My daughter, Becky, and her husband, John Moon, have a daughter named Isabella.

"She's three-and-a-half years old at the moment," explains Becky. "She was born 20 December 2003, not long after our wedding in September 2002. She's very forward for her age and she's got very long hair. She always reminds me of my sister when she was born, because she had loads of auburn hair. And the way she is too – they both have outgoing personalities.

"Dad came from such a poor background," Becky continues, "and he wanted to have the better things in life. He was driven by the feeling that he never wanted to go back to that situation. Although he's a workaholic, I think it does him good, because it keeps his mind active; keeps his body young. He was like that on our holidays; all the time he used to be phoning people."

My son Daniel met his wife, Leslie, through mutual friends. They married in 2003 and have two young children: George, born in 2002, named after Daniel's paternal grandfather and a young baby daughter, Florence, named after his maternal grandmother, Hazel's mother.

Daniel comments: "To be successful you've got to be in a high-pressure environment. I'm really interested in being successful. From the upbringing that I had, because my mum and dad were really successful, I like to study other people's successes and see what character traits such people have, and how they develop, to enable them to become successful. I suppose if it comes too quickly, if it's not planned, that's one of the things that *can* be a negative; you can be a victim of your own success.

"Life's all about keeping a sense of balance... and deciding how you want your life to be," continues Daniel. "In my dad's day you had to 'think on your feet'. I've seen how *his* life was affected by success; for me that's crucial. I don't want success to affect my family life."

And now, ladies and gentlemen, Norman 'Nobby' Nobbs brings our cabaret-style book to its close. We hope that you've enjoyed all fifty years of our club show...continuing into the future from September, with *Subside* – adjacent to Birmingham Town Hall. Even as we complete the book, dramatic changes are taking place: Eddie's personal and business life is undergoing a radical 'sea-change'. We hope to reveal more about this, in a sequel, in the near future. Furthermore, Eddie now has his own website on www.clubsking.com.

"I remember when Eddie and I used to catch a train from New Street Station and go to York Races together, with a bottle of champagne," recalls

Nobby. "Eddie has a great mind and can see all the angles and possibilities, in any given situation. He's always hated bullies and drugs, although drugs weren't so prevalent until the 80s & 90s.

"Martin Hone brought in world-class acts, on the jazz scene, at *The Opposite Lock*. They were different punters from what Eddie had, and again what Brendan Joyce had, at the *Gary Owen*; you were catering for three different sections of the community. Martin, Eddie and Brendan all did a great job. Eddie catered more for the working class. Don't forget, in those days, Longbridge and the Rover and places like that, in Perry Barr – that's where most of our punters came from. Longbridge must have employed thousands and thousands of people – and of a Saturday night, they wanted to go out. At the end of the day, I should say that his best clients were the working class of Birmingham.

"You don't tell people that you want their respect, because you won't get it then. With Eddie he didn't 'suffer fools'. He probably set me up a couple of times, to see if he could trust me; to test whether you were 'straight' or 'bent. He would sometimes give people enough rope – and see what they did with it! In his game, you had to have a Sixth Sense, or you wouldn't survive. He has a *great* Sixth Sense.

"Eddie was Mr. Nightclub. He happened to be around at the right time – and he was the right man for the right time. But working alongside him, you had to have your wits about you. My life's been a lot richer for having met him... and I wish him all the luck in the world."

SELECT BIBLIOGRAPHY

Auf Wiedersehen Pat – Pat Roach and Shirley Thompson, Brewin Books Ltd, September 2006.

Brum Rocked – Laurie Hornsby, Edited by Mike Lavender, TGM Ltd, 1999.

Brum Rocked On – Laurie Hornsby, Edited by Mike Lavender, TGM Ltd, 2003.

Chronology of the 20th Century – Philip Walker and John Rowett, Helicon Publishing Ltd, 1995.

Flying High – Don Maclean, Hodder & Stoughton 2003.

If – The Pat Roach Story, Pat Roach, with Shirley Thompson, Brewin Books Ltd, March 2002.

Inside the Firm – Tony Lambrianou, BCA, by arrangement with Smith Gryphon Ltd, 1992.

Pat Roach's Birmingham, Pat Roach and Shirley Thompson, Brewin Books Ltd, June 2004 .

Raymond Who? Autobiography – Raymond Froggatt, Scala Music Ltd, 1992.

Newspaper articles, Birmingham Mail & the Daily Telegraph: a wide range, relating to the fire at Edward's No.8; Eddie's forthcoming book; the death of Don Fewtrell; the death of Bernard Manning et cetera.

Websites: many and varied, relating to our various celebrity contributors.

Also, www.singingtrakehner.co.uk

OTHER BOOKS
BY SHIRLEY THOMPSON

There's More Out Than In, Brewin Books, 1999
If, The Pat Roach Story, Brewin Books, 2002
The Original Alton Douglas, Brewin Books, 2003
Pat Roach's Birmingham, Brewin Books, 2004
Auf Wiedersehen Pat, Brewin Books, 2006
Finally Meeting Princess Maud, Brewin Books, 2006